WRITING PALESTINE
1933-1950
DOROTHY KAHN BAR-ADON

WRITING PALESTINE 1933-1950

DOROTHY KAHN BAR-ADON

Edited by
ESTHER CARMEL HAKIM
NANCY ROSENFELD

Boston
2017

Library of Congress Cataloging-in-Publication Data:
A catalog record for this book is available from
the Library of Congress.

ISBN 978-1-61811-495-2 (hardback)
ISBN 978-1-61811-636-9 (paperback)
ISBN 978-1-61811-496-9 (electronic)

Book design by Kryon Publishing,
www.kryonpublishing.com

Academic Studies Press
28 Montfern Avenue
Brighton, MA 02135, USA
press@academicstudiespress.com
www.academicstudiespress.com

Table of Contents

Acknowledgements

First and foremost, we would like to thank Dorothy Bar-Adon's son, Doron Bar-Adon, for his generosity in making his mother's personal archive available to us, as well as for his help with funding.

Special thanks to Prof. Linda Steiner for all her help in obtaining material from the United States and for writing the foreword of this book. We should also like to thank *The Jerusalem Post* and its editor Steve Linde for allowing us to use published material from *The Palestine Post*.

We owe the idea for this book to Prof. Deborah Hertz. Thanks to Prof. Patricia Woods for all her help and support along the way; she encouraged us not to give up. We also wish to thank Claire Asarnow for her help.

We are also very grateful to the following foundations and institutions for the financial support that made the publication of this book possible:

Prof. Shulamit Reinharz, Prof. Sylvia Barak Fishman, and the Hadassah-Brandeis Institute at Brandeis University.

The Havatzelet Foundation for Cultural and Educational Institutions.

Foundation of History and Activities of the Jewish National Fund at Bar Ilan University.

Esther Carmel Hakim, Kibbutz Ramat Hashofet
Nancy Rosenfeld, Kibbutz Ein Hashofet
November 2015

Editors' Preface

This book is a collection of articles written by the journalist Dorothy Kahn Bar-Adon (1907–1950). From among hundreds of articles, three unpublished book-length manuscripts, and personal letters found in her archive, we have chosen materials representing a variety of burning issues of the time.

Dorothy Ruth Bar-Adon (née Kahn) was raised in a Reform Jewish milieu in Philadelphia, Pennsylvania and Atlantic City, New Jersey. After completing high school, she was employed as a journalist by the *Atlantic City Press*. Simultaneously she became interested in Zionism—although she did not belong to a specific Zionist organization—and in 1933 immigrated to Palestine, where she was employed as a staff journalist by *The Palestine Post* (later *The Jerusalem Post*) until her death in 1950. The opening chapter contains biographical material that provides context for Bar-Adon's writings.

Bar-Adon succeeded in sharing with her readers the sights, sounds, and smells of Palestine/Israel as she experienced them. Although Bar-Adon spoke and understood Hebrew, she wrote in English; indeed, most of her published material appeared in *The Palestine Post*, the only local English-language daily newspaper. Materials from the *Post* are available online in the paper's archives. However, most of the materials in this collection were never published, although—as noted in the bibliographical information accompanying the various articles—versions of some did appear in the *Post*.

In comparison to the majority of journalists living and working in Palestine in the period of 1933–1950, Bar-Adon was unusual in two ways. Firstly, she was not committed to any of the highly partisan Jewish-Zionist organizations of the time. Her writing was thus free of the partisan commitment that characterized almost all of the Hebrew-language daily press: indeed, most of Israel's earliest daily Hebrew-language newspapers were unabashedly sponsored by political parties. Her writing thus provides documentation generally unmediated by political, ideological considerations.

Secondly, most of the documentation of the period of the British Mandate that dealt with the Yishuv as a whole, with the new Jewish settlements, and with the developing conflicts between Jews, Arabs, and the Mandatory authorities was written by men. Although Bar-Adon herself does not appear to have what would later be called a feminist agenda, she often brought to her observations and writing different emphases from those of her male colleagues.

Indeed, Bar-Adon was received into circles that would have been closed to others: as a woman she was able to speak with Arab women; as one who wrote in English she gained entry to offices of British government authorities. Her interlocutors spoke to her with openness; Bar-Adon was thus enabled to write about daily life and culture in the Jewish and Arab towns and villages, the status of women in a variety of communities, Jewish immigration to Palestine, and the Jewish-Arab conflict as it was being played out under British rule. Years before practitioners of academic disciplines developed theories of high and low politics, political sociology, and social and cultural history, Bar-Adon produced writings that constitute valuable raw materials for these areas of study.

It is our belief that these articles will be of use to students and scholars of the period during which they were written.

EDITORS' NOTE: BAR-ADON'S USAGE

Dorothy Kahn Bar-Adon worked as a journalist for approximately twenty years: from the late 1920s to the early 1930s until her death in 1950. In other words, her career began some eighty years ago and came to an end well over half a century ago. It is therefore only to be expected that some twenty-first century readers will feel uncomfortable with Bar-Adon's use of certain words and expressions that were common usage at the time but have since become unacceptable in the context in which she used them. One example is *primitive*, in reference to *people hailing from pre-technological societies*. Another example is *colonials*, in reference to *people residing in a country or territory governed by a foreign power*.

The articles written by Bar-Adon contained in this collection were chosen for their historical interest. They should, in other words, be read as products of a particular situation, time, and place: a journalist writing in English about Mandatory Palestine/ Israel in the 1930s to 1940s. The editors therefore did not see fit to make changes in the author's lexical choices. Rather, we appeal to the reader to understand the occasional discomfiting usage as a sign that Bar-Adon—as is the case with most, or even all, working journalists—was indeed a woman of her time.

SOURCES

The materials in this collection are from Dorothy Kahn Bar-Adon's personal archive and generally were not previously published (although versions of some of the articles were published during her lifetime). Much of these materials come from two unpublished manuscripts: *Zif Zif* and *Inhabitants of the Rock*.

Bar-Adon's final illness was sudden, and her only son and executor was a child at the time of her death. Thus there are occasional texts for which dating is problematic. When the date of composition could not be determined, the material is undated. (In some cases, events mentioned in the text enabled us to provide tentative dates).

The editors are deeply grateful to Doron Bar-Adon for making his mother's archive available.

Foreword

This is the first, and most prominent account of the work of journalist Dorothy Kahn Bar-Adon. Kahn was born in 1907 to an assimilated Jewish Reformed family in Philadelphia. The Kahns later moved to Atlantic City, already then a lively and thriving beach resort. In her early and continuing concern for social justice, Dorothy Kahn was much like other children of immigrant Jewish parents. That said, she was met with "mixed" responses from gentile classmates when they realized she was Jewish; she herself joined a Christian (one might even say anti-Jewish) high school sorority. Meanwhile, her own family, or at least her sister, did not particularly like Jews. In a 1937 letter describing a working trip to Poland, Kahn admitted her own discomfort with some Orthodox religious practices.

But in 1933, after a few years working for the *Atlantic City Press*, the increasingly Jewish-identified Kahn moved to Palestine. With letters of introduction to some powerful Israeli pioneers, including the founder of *The Palestine Post*, Kahn had managed to secure a visa to Palestine. She described being the only woman writing for the English-language *Palestine Post* (later called *The Jerusalem Post*). Except for her self-effacing modesty, Kahn was not like most mid-twentieth century women and was drawn to journalism. She became a pioneer not by facing down sexism in journalism, or in the newsroom specifically, but by negotiating the major challenges as well as the minor frustrations confronting the settlers of Palestine—especially the "N.C.," the New Comers' community, as it was known. She immediately embraced the multitude of tasks: people had essentially created a new language for conversation (Kahn learned Hebrew once she got there) and were still creating new ways of finding self-esteem (especially in agriculture and other physical labor) and new ways of organizing social and religious life. Kahn proceeded to dig into her new life, literally. She described that grand experiment with grace and a sense of humor in her staff-written and freelance articles, publicity materials, letters, and her autobiography. She adamantly denied that she and the others were idealists, however. Instead, they were realists, building a real home for a people who really needed it.

Two years after her arrival, Kahn renounced her United States citizenship and became a citizen of Palestine. As Kahn put it, Palestine was less a country than a weak, unstable ward of the League of Nations. Nonetheless, her theory was that the only answer to anti-Semitism is Semitism—albeit a Semitism recognizing that Arabs and Jews were Semitic cousins. Indeed, Kahn was less offended by Arabs who openly hated Jews than by Americans or Europeans who disliked Jews for the size of their noses or who alleged that Jews are dirty or wily or were the power behind the financial crisis in America. Arabs had a more straightforward, and even more plausible, reason for disliking Jews: they regarded Jews as invading their country.

With forty years or so of feminist scholarship and women's history now available, including the history of women journalists, researchers have begun to turn away from biographies of individuals. The suggestion is that "bringing up women from the footnotes" is no longer important or necessary. Yet, this book on, about, and of Kahn shows why the processes of recovering women's histories—and the plural forms are intentional and significant—from around the world remain relevant. Now we understand: social history is more than men's history; men's history often ignores women's history; and also, just as men's histories are multiple and complex, so women's histories cannot be made homogenous. Scholars often become irritated by journalists' preference for the individual and anecdotal and their resistance to seeking out patterns. In this case, however, Kahn's refusal to buy into a sentimental, universalizing notion of women as a sex turned out to be a good instinct. Kahn was interested in Muslim women, interested enough to don a Muslim woman's voluminous black dress and veil and to try to walk with a water jug balanced on her head. Her main point, however, was that Muslim and Jewish women made claims to the same land, not that they shared a set of distinctly womanly values.

Most likely, no single story can be called typical. No single trajectory for women pursuing journalism careers can be identified as representative. That said, few women—or men, for that matter—seemed to have made the move Kahn did. Many of her early stories for the *Atlantic City Press* concerned Jewish-oriented local events as well as visiting celebrities— including major political figures. I must add that it was also a thrill to page through the *Atlantic City Press* and come across Kahn's front-page crime stories. Apparently, Atlantic City was rife with juicy crimes, including more than a few committed by women.

Meanwhile, after 1933 Kahn also witnessed the rise of the Nazis to power, the Arab revolts against the increasing dominance and status of Jews and Zionists and later against the State, the World War II and the Holocaust, the detainment by British Mandatory authorities of Jewish refugees, the establishment of the State of Israel in 1948, and the War of Independence and its aftermath in 1948–49. Meanwhile, there were all the quotidian challenges for diasporic Jews coming to Palestine, bringing along their different cultures, perceptions, skills, expectations, advantages, and handicaps.

Of course, in Israel, most journalists are Jewish. It is worth highlighting in particular how, over the larger course of history, few Jewish women have gone into journalism. Among the few exceptions that essentially prove the historical rule was Frances Davis Cohen. Writing under the name Frances Davis, she lived 1908–1983. Her parents were Russian immigrants who worked in the garment industry and were involved in the garment work-ers' union. While she was in high school, Davis was already a proofreader and writer of "fillers" for a weekly paper in one of the Boston suburbs. After graduation and a short, unsatisfying stab at journalism education, she wrote feature stories for papers in Boston and New York. In 1936, having convinced a few small New England and mid-Atlantic papers to buy the columns she promised to send from Europe, she went to Paris and then Spain to cover the fighting. Finally, the London *Daily Mail* hired her to report on the Spanish Civil War. While reporting from the bat-tlefront, Davis was slightly injured by a piece of shrapnel; by 1939, she became dangerously ill with septicemia and was forced to return home. The much more famous Flora Lewis, who lived 1922–2002, was a foreign affairs correspondent and columnist, as well as an author of books about international affairs and diplomacy. Lewis began her 60-year-long career in 1942 with the Associated Press and later wrote for *The Washington Post* and *Newsday*. Her greatest acclaim came at *The New York Times*. Her husband was a correspondent for *The New York Times*, which barred spouses from working for the paper. Once she was separated (and later divorced), the *Times* hired her as its Paris bureau chief and later its European diplomatic correspondent. Lewis covered the Communist takeover of Eastern Europe in 1946, the Polish and Hungarian uprisings against Communism in 1956, as well as the fall of Communism in Eastern Europe, the Vietnam War, and the 1948 and 1967 Arab-Israeli wars. Her peripatetic life is seen in the fact that her children were born in three different countries: Ireland, Israel, and Mexico.

Edith Lederer, born in 1943, has worked for the Associated Press since 1966, covering wars, famines, nuclear issues, and political upheavals. Although the AP foreign editor was unhappy about women covering wars and disasters, in 1971 Lederer became the AP's first woman to work full time covering the war in Vietnam. After nine months in Vietnam, she went to Israel to cover the 1973 Yom Kippur War. Lederer also covered wars in the Middle East, Afghanistan, Bosnia, and Somalia, as well as the troubles in Northern Ireland, the Soviet invasion of Afghanistan, the breakup of the Soviet Union, and the Romanian revolution. The AP's first woman to head an overseas bureau (in Peru), in 1998 she became the AP's chief correspondent at the United Nations, reporting on the diplomatic side of conflicts and major global issues. Lederer credited the feminist movement with inspiring women her age to believe they could do anything they wanted, including to compete in the "big leagues."

Given their shared commitment to helping the Jewish people and their more explicit identification with Judaism, Kahn is more like photojournalist Ruth Gruber. Indeed, Gruber lived long enough to report on some of the unfortunate consequences of some of the same anti-Jewish and anti-Zionist policies that Kahn and her fellow Zionists saw emerging. Born in 1911 (and still alive as of this writing), Gruber received her bachelor's degree at age sixteen and her PhD at twenty. She then began writing for *The New York Times* and the *New York Herald Tribune*, which assigned her to report on the status of women under Fascism and Communism. Known both for her writing and her photojournalism, Gruber went to the Soviet Arctic in the mid-1930s. In 1946, the *New York Post* assigned her to cover the Anglo-American Committee of Inquiry on Palestine, which was convened to decide the fate of about 100,000 European Jewish refugees then living in displaced persons' (DP) camps. She is most famous for covering the arrival of *Exodus 1947*; the ship, with its 4,500 Jewish refugees, was attacked by the Royal Navy as it approached Haifa. (Kahn also wrote about those unresisting refugees on the *Exodus*.) Gruber went along when the British sent the DPs to France; when refugees refused to disembark there, she accompanied them back to Germany. In the mid-1980s, Gruber reported on the rescue of Jews from Ethiopia.

Gruber also helped Jews outside her journalistic work. In 1944, the United States government secretly assigned her to help escort 1,000 Jewish refugees (as well as some wounded American soldiers) from Europe to the United States, where they were taken to Oswego, New York and locked behind a chain link fence. This was the government's only official attempt to shelter Jewish DPs during the war. Eventually, the refugees were allowed to apply for American residency. Gruber's *Haven: The Dramatic Story of 1,000 World War II Refugees and How They Came to America* was based on her interviews of the refugees. In 1978, Gruber spent a year in Israel writing a book about an Israeli nurse who worked in a British detention camp as well as in an Israeli hospital. Again, relatively few Jewish American women reporting for the general interest news media have explicitly identified as Jewish, much less practiced Judaism. Flora Lewis's family had observed Jewish holidays, but as an adult Lewis did not identify with Jewish life. Frances Cohen's family lived for eight years in a utopian community and, after they returned to the Boston area, they continued regular visits to "The Farm." Davis recuperated from her injuries at The Farm after returning from Spain but was apparently unable to convince friends there of the seriousness of the war's political consequences; she met her future husband there. So, it is from Kahn that we learn about secular Jews' life in American suburbs as well as, more importantly, about Jewish immigration to the new homeland and about Jewish (and Arab) life in villages and cities, both pre- and post-Statehood.

In this text are feature stories written with a generous heart and a light touch. Kahn does not describe her working life *per se*. She mentions that she undertook a trip to Poland to investigate the minority experience of Polish Jews because she needed the money. Yet, which stories she wanted to cover but were denied, or which stories she was assigned but that she regarded as gender stereotyped or beneath her we do not know. That said, Kahn avoids purple prose, hysteria, and false innocence while reporting and writing her stories. She remained consistent with her promise to be a journalist. As Esther Carmel Hakim and Nancy Rosenfeld note (and to whom we must be grateful for putting together this volume), Kahn gave the right answer when she was challenged by an editor who worried that Jews could not be simultaneously journalists and Zionists. Kahn was clear-eyed, correcting misconceptions and misrepresentations, large and small, and reporting the details of everyday life. That's no minor feat.

—*Linda Steiner, University of Maryland*

CHAPTER ONE

Biography of Dorothy Kahn Bar-Adon

1907–1950

As a journalist covering daily life and events in Palestine, much of Dorothy Kahn Bar-Adon's writing was autobiographical. This biography is therefore brief and is intended to supply a general overview of her short life, as well as severely limited central background information, which she assumed would have been familiar to her readers. More detailed background information is provided via notes and the glossary.

Many books have been, are, and will be written describing, analyzing, and arguing about the events to which Kahn responded in her writing: the rise of the Nazis to power in Europe; Jewish settlement of what became the State of Israel, World War II, the Holocaust, massive post-war immigration of Jewish refugees to Israel, detainment of these refugees in camps by the British Mandatory authorities, the establishment of the State of Israel in 1948, and the War of Independence and its aftermath in 1948–49. Clearly this collection, focusing as it does on the writings of one journalist, cannot hope to "cover" these events. We hope that readers who feel the need for wider background will make use of the Suggested Reading.

It might be thought strange to begin a biography with selections from an obituary of the subject; yet the obit published by *The Jerusalem Post* on August 7, 1950 not only reviews the major turning points of her life but also provides a summary of reasons for renewed interest in the life and work of Dorothy Kahn Bar-Adon, some sixty years after the day when her typewriter, lovingly preserved by her son Doron in his studio, began to collect dust:

DEATH OF DOROTHY KAHN BAR-ADON

We deeply regret to announce the death in Jerusalem of Mrs. Dorothy Kahn Bar-Adon, author, historian of the Emek [Jezreel Valley] and for many years a valued contributor to *The Jerusalem Post*.

Dorothy Bar-Adon was born in Philadelphia, United States in 1907 and was for some years a reporter on the *Atlantic City Press* until her migration to this country in 1933. She joined this newspaper [then called *The Palestine Post*] immediately, but later interrupted her career as a journalist for three years during which she joined the communal settlement of Givat Brenner as a working guest.

After her marriage, she went to live in the moshav, Merhavia, from where she regularly contributed to this paper a series of articles that provided an inimitable record on the life and progress of the Emek.

She is survived by her husband, Pessah Bar-Adon—shepherd, watchman, writer and archaeologist, and a young son.

The funeral service will take place at nine o'clock this morning at the Bikur Holim Hospital. The body will be taken from there to Merhavia for burial.

A TRIBUTE

The blurb on the dustcover of Dorothy Kahn's *Spring Up, O Well* refers to the author's "long journey back, from being an American of Jewish persuasion," to Jerusalem. This book was published in 1936. The last fourteen years of her life were a rounding-up completion. In these years of maturing she found the companionship of a mate of quality, and there is a son whose realm is the Emek and whose seat is Merhavia. She saw the birth of the State, and shared in the travail that preceded it. Her sharing was real and personal. She lived to taste every moment of Israel's great fight and to relish every morsel of the big victory.

But for all the fullness of the circle, from assimilated (not necessarily assimilationist) upbringing to consciousness of the Jewish need and its fulfillment on its own soil, Dorothy Kahn Bar-Adon should have been spared for many more years. She had much to give. Her gift of observation was unspent, her urge for expression, undiminished, her vision, undimmed, and her spring of friendship and neighborliness, unexhausted.

Her battered typewriter—"Dot" was not at home with one that was not battered—sang to her mild coaxing, sang with a twinkle. The twinkle was never absent. She could be devastatingly amusing—what reader of this paper will forget her "Alice in Wonderland" series—but never solemn and certainly never sinister. She knew man to be a tissue of foibles, and you might scold him for it, good-naturedly for choice, but never hatefully. If you could make your British Mandatory adversary feel foolish and act sheepish, you gained more for your side than by roundly denouncing him as a bounder. And anyway, hate begets hate, and that was not what Dot was after.

She was not out to amuse herself, or amuse her readers. But her sense of the grimness of life was modified by her sense of proportion. There was to her something fanciful in man's folly at the base of man's troubles—and the whole of the disordered cock-eyed world, wasn't it after all fey?

Fey Dorothy Kahn was herself, of course, but far, far from disordered. Solid position, solid comforts, even solid reputation—these did not matter half as much as the mild amusements she derived and inimitably passed on, from the antics of men and women, none of whom quite escaped appearing moderately grotesque.

She was a poet. "Jerusalem is a woman who sits among bleak hills combing her hair and smiling," she wrote. That suited her, doing something no matter what, with a twinkle and smiling. She smiled when she wrote paragraphs on Boardwalk society in Atlantic City; she smiled when she wrote news paragraphs for this paper; smiled when she expanded these paragraphs into causeries of lasting quality; smiled as ardent wife and doting mother, smiled knowing she was fey, when she knew she was about to die.

[*The Jerusalem Post*, August 7, 1950, p. 3]

Dorothy Ruth Kahn was born in Philadelphia, Pennsylvania on August 2, 1907. Her parents, George Kahn and Sarah Floss Kahn, had emigrated from Germany to the United States in the 1860s and raised their children—Dorothy and Beatrice—in an assimilated American-Jewish Reformed milieu.

In *Spring Up, O Well*[1] Kahn describes her journey to secular Judaism and Zionism. Her family did not maintain a kosher kitchen; Kahn and her parents traveled on Saturdays; the Kahn sisters were taught no Hebrew. Indeed, the family celebrated Christmas and Easter, although they saw the latter more as American national holidays than as religious festivals marking events in the life of Jesus Christ. Yet Dorothy was sent to a Reformed Sunday school to prepare for her confirmation (*bat mitzvah*). Kahn recalls the ceremony as a turning point in her identification with the Jewish people, "I still believe that it was the crimson and gold cover on the 'Torah' that made me shrivel into the whiteness of my dress, lost in a sudden realization of the glory and agony of Judaism" (35).

Kahn's awakening to the implications of her Jewishness gained strength in junior high school, when several gentile classmates stopped speaking to her on discovering she was Jewish, and the art teacher told her that "I didn't know you were a Jewess. You don't look like one. You're so different from the rest. Such a quiet child" (34). Offered the chance of pledging to a large Jewish sorority in high school or to "the most exclusive gentile sorority in the school," Kahn toyed with "outraging her parents and Christian friends" by joining the Jewish sorority, but she opted for Alpha Sigma, the gentile sorority.

Kahn describes the last sorority meeting before high school graduation, as plans are being made for the final dance:

> A lovely blonde, with the diplomacy of a Japanese statesman at a disarmament conference, reminding the girls that when they are inviting guests they must bear in mind that the Seaview Golf Club had "a Christian roster and we, as visitors, would hardly want to violate a tradition…"
>
> Remembering that I am the only Jew in the room.
>
> Feeling obliged to ask a feeble question.
>
> Being told that the Seaview Club doesn't mean me, of course. Haven't I always been invited there? Am I becoming supersensitive now? […]
>
> Wanting to stand up and shout defiance, but feeling that the world will topple if I am not dancing in my new sapphire chiffon frock at the Seaview Golf Club on the night before graduation. […]
>
> Then signing my name to the list of those who will be present (39).

---

[1]   New York: Henry Holt, 1936. Unless otherwise indicated, quotes from Bar Adon in this biography are from *Spring Up, O Well*.

During 1925 and 1926, years in which America "was spending money like a whore after the fleet has sailed" (41), Kahn had an unhappy love affair with a man whom she dubs Hilary, "an Irish Roman Catholic who flaunted a London accent, an ex-wife and a quiet passion for me with fetching grace when he was sober and equally fetching pathos when he was drunk" (43). Kahn's Jewishness seemed to matter neither to her nor to Hilary. Yet, on occasion, she was drawn to attend a play produced in Yiddish, or to a performance by the great cantor, Yossele Rosenblatt. Although Kahn did not believe that she would marry Hilary, she suffered great disappointment when he informed her of his sudden decision to marry a wealthy Roman Catholic widow, much older than Kahn:

> So I heard my voice, although I choose now to believe that it was only the wind, crying through the rain, "I can't go on alone. You never remembered that I was a Jew. I didn't either. Take me and I won't ever be a Jew again."
>
> And then Hilary suddenly stopped being subdued and fetching. I saw his nonchalant graces of two years roll into a hard pinpoint of reality. "I've never stopped remembering you were a Jew." His words were clipped shortly. "I wanted to. You wouldn't let me" (44–45).

On her twenty-first birthday Kahn attended services at what she describes as her family's "church-like Temple" (48). It was here that she met a young man whom she called David, the son of an orthodox rabbi, who took her under his wing and introduced her to his family, to the Sabbath, and to daily life of observant Jews, "During the five years that followed, David continued to wrap up bits of Jewish life in common-places and to hand them to me with the same careless gesture as he had handed me the Sabbath. Never was there drama. Never was he the Martin Luther disseminating light nor I a Joan d'Arc hearing heavenly voices" (54). Although Kahn was never religiously orthodox, her identity as a Jew grew steadily:

> True, an incident, a crisis, a Herr Hitler or a Hilary talking into the storm may jolt you into the realization that you must either live freely or honestly as a Jew or suffer complete spiritual disintegration. But you cannot be jolted into possessing the sources, the secret springs that make the living of such a life, in its richest sense, possible. You cannot be jolted. So you travel and search (55).

During her childhood, the family had moved to the seaside resort of Atlantic City, New Jersey, then, as now, known for its broad beaches and boardwalk, elegant hotels, and casinos. In 1924, when Kahn was seventeen years old, her father died suddenly; the family lost not only a beloved father and husband but also its main provider. On completing her high school education, Kahn went to work as a reporter for the *Atlantic City Press* while simultaneously developing her interest in her Jewish heritage and in the possibility of expressing this heritage by immigrating to Palestine. Writing under the bylines Dot Kahn, Dorothy Kahn, Dorothy R. Kahn, Member of the Press Staff, or Staff Correspondent, Kahn lived in Atlantic City and was employed by the newspaper until her immigration to Palestine in 1933.

Many late-nineteenth century newspapers, as Chambers et al. note, "aimed to attract more women readers by introducing what came to be labeled as 'women's journalism,' a style of news writing confined to society news, reports on changing fashions, and feature articles on domestic issues. These stories for women readers were written by women reporters" (17).[2] During World War I, according to Beasley and Gibbons, women journalists were hired to replace men; this phenomenon was to accelerate during World War II (53).[3]

By the early 1930s, it was thus not unusual for women to work as newspaper reporters. The best-known American reporter, Elizabeth Jane Cochrane (1864–1922), published under the pen name Nellie Bly. After a promising beginning on the *Pittsburgh Dispatch*, in 1887, Bly moved to New York. There she talked her way into the offices of Joseph Pulitzer's *New York World* and took on the assignment of investigating the treatment of women inmates confined in the Women's Lunatic Asylum on Blackwell Island. The subsequent expositive articles and book (*Ten Days in a Madhouse*) caused a sensation that resulted in government investigations of such institutions and led to improvements in the care of patients; they also brought Bly lasting fame and success as what is now called an investigative reporter.

The second project that Bly is best remembered for is her round-the-world voyage in 1889–90. Bly attempted to carry out in fact the journey described fictionally in Jules Verne's *Eighty Days Around the World*. *The World* kept up readers' interest in the feat by sponsoring a contest in which readers

---

2 Deborah Chambers, Linda Steiner, and Carole Fleming, *Women and Journalism* (London and New York: Routledge, 2004).

3 Maurine H. Beasley and Sheila J. Gibbons, *Taking Their Place: A Documentary History of Women and Journalism* (State College, PA: Strata, 2003), second edition.

were invited to estimate to the second Bly's arrival time. Bly completed the journey in some 72 days, thus setting a short-lived world record.

These two projects serve as useful examples of two trends in women's roles in journalism until the mid-twentieth century. On one hand, some women functioned as correspondents covering, or indeed revealing important news. On the other hand, women were seen as being especially suited to cover the arts, as well as what came to be known as "human interest" stories. Women's supposed humane, emotional side as expressed in their reporting often led to their being termed *"sob sisters."*[4]

During her years as a staff reporter at the *Atlantic City Press,* Kahn's writing seems to have found favor with her editors: many of her stories were placed on the paper's opening pages and bore her byline. While much of the paper's national and international news was provided by the Associated Press, Kahn often covered stories of international interest when assigned to interview visitors to Atlantic City who had a connection to the burning issues of the day. On June 10, 1930, for example, under the headline "Russian Prince Sees Rule of Soviets Nearing End Abroad," her byline appears on a page-two interview with Prince V. Koudacheff, "formerly of the Russian diplomatic service," who was staying at the Ambassador Hotel while recovering from a tonsil operation. Kahn's interview with the prince dealt mainly with matters of import:

> The death of the present leaders, or the outbreak of any war will mean
> the swan song of the present regime in Russia, is the prediction of the
> prince. He declared that all revolutions are short-lived because they
> terminate with the death of their instigators. He also pointed out that
> in the advent of another war, the soldiers would seize the government
> whether they returned crushed or victorious.

It is only in the last paragraph that the reader is treated to what might be called a bit of sob-sisterly trivia: Princess Koudacheff, the prince's American wife, describes their wedding, "We had the Greek orthodox service. Since it was my second marriage, only half of the service was required. However,

---

4   The Oxford English Dictionary lists the following definitions: "sob sister, a female journalist who writes sentimental reports or articles; a writer of sob stories; hence in various *transf.* uses, *esp.*: an actress who plays pathetic roles; a sentimental, impractical person, a do-gooder; a journalist who gives advice on readers' problems; sob story, a report or article designed to make a sentimental appeal to the emotions." It is thus not surprising that the image of the sob sister entered popular culture via films, novels, comics.

we and our guests had to stand through the entire ceremony, which lasted for forty-five minutes."

Following the 1929 Palestine Riots, 1930 saw an event initiated by the British Mandatory authorities in Palestine that threatened to limit Jewish immigration: the Hope-Simpson report recommended limiting Jewish immigration to Palestine according to the perceived ability of the territory to absorb immigrants. On October 21, 1930, Sidney James Webb, Lord Passfield, Secretary of State for the colonies, issued a White Paper restricting further land acquisition by Jews, thus slowing Jewish immigration. Page two of the *Press*'s November 6, 1930, edition features a bylined article by Kahn headlined "Resort Jews Resent British Palestine Edict: Pass Resolutions Condemning Act; Rabbi Neuman and Rev. Mellen Speak." The article describes an interfaith protest meeting attended by more than a thousand Jews gathered at a local community center the previous evening to protest the British government's recent issuing of the Second White Paper.[5] The article's lead sentence is based on a quotation from the rally's keynote speaker, Joseph Roschovsky, president of the local Zionist organization, "The calamity which has befallen the Jews in Palestine today may be compared to the calamity which befell our forefathers when Titus and his hordes destroyed the Temple." We may thus assume that at this point, some three years prior to her own immigration to Palestine, Kahn's growing identity with the Jewish people and its stateless plight was already well developed.

As the Great Depression went into its second and third years, Kahn's interest in the Jewish settlement of the land of Israel grew, as did her sense that she herself might take an active part in the Zionist enterprise by immigrating to Palestine. She and her friend David discussed the desperation that both felt on witnessing the extremes of poverty and wealth, so clear in a resort such as Atlantic City: sitting at a table in a restaurant she noted that obviously hungry people on the street outside were looking through the window and watching her and the other customers as they eat. Why didn't they smash the windows and grab the food? "Is patience such a virtue?" she asked. David's answer was that:

> This degradation was not peculiar to America. It was the history
> of the world. Degradation and then uprising. Perhaps that uprising

---

5   The First White Paper, June 3, 1922, limited the area covered by the Balfour Declaration to the west bank of the Jordan River, thus creating the Kingdom of Transjordan on the east bank. The Third White Paper, May 17, 1939, severely restricted both Jewish immigration to Palestine and severely limited the purchasing of land on the part of Jews.

would come to America too. Or perhaps prosperity would come first and then there would be a triumphant lull before the next period of degradation. And the solution? Perhaps it lay in [Soviet] Russia. Perhaps not. Perhaps there was no solution.

As for the Jew? If there was any solution at all, it was Palestine (66).

David's challenge clearly mingled with that posed by the gentile speaker at a public lecture, which Kahn attended, "How can any young Jew sit here and withstand the adventure of his people in Palestine?" he asked (68).

Having decided to immigrate to Palestine, Kahn spent two hectic weeks of preparation in New York. On the day before she sailed, Dorothy and her mother attended the City Hall wedding of Kahn's sister, Beatrice, to a gentile. Dorothy did not see her sister's marriage as a case of a Jew leaving the fold; rather "she had never come in." Dorothy recalled that Beatrice had refused to be "confirmed" (i.e. to have a *bat mitzvah*), claiming that she didn't feel like a Jew and found Jews to be nervous, noisy and sometimes dirty (77). Most of the busy fortnight in New York, however, was spent in the complicated process of obtaining a visa for Palestine from the British consulate; buying clothes and shoes; and especially collecting letters of recommendation from people who might be able to assist in smoothing her first steps in Palestine.

Rabbi Stephen S. Wise[6] provided Kahn with letters of introduction to, among others, Henrietta Szold,[7] David Yellin,[8] Irma Lindheim[9] and perhaps most important, Gershon Agronsky[10] of *The Palestine Post*. The

---

[6] Rabbi Stephen S. Wise (1874–1949) was a leader of American Reformed Judaism and a leading American Zionist.

[7] Henrietta Szold (1860–1945) was a leading American Zionist and the founder of the Hadassah Women's Organization. In 1933, she immigrated to Palestine and ran Youth Aliya, an organization which rescued some 22,000 children from Nazi-controlled Europe.

[8] David Yellin (1864–1941), in 1912, became deputy director of the Jerusalem Teachers' Seminary. When its administration insisted that the language of instruction be German rather than Hebrew, Yellin founded the Hebrew Teachers' Seminary; he continued to serve as its principal until his death.

[9] Irma Lindheim (1886–1978), an American Zionist activist, in 1926 succeeded Szold as president of Hadassah. She later immigrated to Palestine and joined Kibbutz Mishmar Ha'emek, where she lived for most of the rest of her life, with the exception of periods of international lobbying for Zionist causes.

[10] Gershon Agronsky (Agron) (1894–1959) was founder of *The Palestine Post*. Between 1949 and 1951, Agron headed Israel's government information service. Between 1955 and his death, he was the mayor of Jerusalem and played a major role in the development of the western sections of the city.

newspaper was to be Kahn's second home from her arrival in Tel Aviv in 1933 until her untimely death in 1950. She also visited two acquaintances who provided contrasting views of her approaching *aliyah* (immigration). Rebekah Kohut[11] had written on Palestine in *My Portion*. Kohut questions Kahn closely about her immediate plans but then speaks words of warm encouragement, "Nothing can happen to you. You are going to your own people…You won't have to worry about a home. Everyone's home will be yours" (70, 71). Dr. Maurice Hindus,[12] on the other hand, a supporter of Soviet Russia, who was preparing to sail for Russia within a fortnight, posed some difficult questions, "Isn't the day of the ghetto past? Can't Jews ever learn to be people? Isn't it enough that old Jews are bound up with sentimental, outworn tradition? How can a young, assimilated Jew choose voluntarily to return to segregation?" (72).

In June of 1933, at the end of a sea voyage of some two or three weeks, Kahn's boat docked in Jaffa port. After passing through customs she and her baggage were piled onto a horse-drawn carriage; they rode through Jaffa and into Tel Aviv, finally stopping at a *pension* that had been recommended by a companion on the boat. Tel Aviv was to be Kahn's home during her first years in Palestine; she wrote at length about the burgeoning, vibrant city, then undergoing an influx of Jews from Germany who had concluded that the rise of the Nazi Party to power was a threat to be taken seriously.

In his introduction to *Spring Up, O Well,* Henry W. Nevinson,[13] a British gentile supporter of Jewish settlement of Palestine, wrote:

> It was, I think, unfortunate that she landed at Jaffa and at once pro-
> ceeded to its great northern suburb, Tel Aviv, where, on the thickly
> pressed sands of the deserted coast, the Jews have founded their
> growing city. Here all is new and all is Jewish. Only Jews live there,
> and the only language spoken or written is Hebrew. There is nothing

---

[11] Rebekah Kohut (1864–1951) was active in Jewish women's organizations; she was an early leader of the National Council of Jewish Women.

[12] Maurice Gerschon Hindus (1891–1969) was a Jewish-Russian-American writer, foreign correspondent, lecturer, and authority on Soviet and Central European affairs.

[13] Henry W. Nevinson (1856–1941) was a British journalist known for his reporting on the Second Boer War and on slavery in Angola. In 1907, he helped found the Men's League for Women's Suffrage; as a correspondent in the Great War, he was wounded at Gallipoli.

to remind one of Palestine's ancient history. It is a "sudden town" that has sprung up like any sudden town in the United States, and to the gentile visitor it is little more. But to the Jew it is a realized dream, a holy work, the result of patriotic "mass emotion." Jews from all countries are crowding there, pushing, "ill-mannered," all in a desperate hurry to enjoy freedom (13–14).

Prior to her departure from New York, Kahn had met with an unnamed "Foreign Editor of a press service" who asked:

"Are you a journalist or a Zionist? We could use articles on Palestine but we can't get them. Jews seem to contract a sob in their throats whenever they begin writing about Palestine. That's all right for literature. But we need facts—not tears." I assured him that I was a journalist. And I believed that I was (70).

The above presents one view of the role of journalists "covering" events in which they have an emotional investment. Kahn was sensitive to the presence of this internal conflict; yet her years as a reporter for the *Atlantic City Press* had taught her that a correspondent is supposed to aim for an objective stance. A converse view of the role of the journalist was that which pertained to the Hebrew press at the time of Kahn's immigration to Palestine and for many years onward. Hebrew-language newspapers tended to be published under the aegis of political or religious groupings and owed loyalty to the views of their editorial boards. Kahn was not fluent in Hebrew during her first years in Palestine; she thus began to write for the English-language *The Palestine Post*, which became *The Jerusalem Post* in 1950.

The Palestine Post, edited by Gershon Agronsky (Agron), to whom Kahn had a letter of introduction, published its first issue on December 1, 1932. The intended readership included British military personnel and civil servants stationed in Palestine, many of whom opposed Jewish settlement; local members of the Arab community; businessmen; the growing tourist trade; and pilgrims and members of Christian religious institutions residing in Palestine. The paper's policy, to which the editor kept strictly, was based on fairness, objective reporting, and criticism founded on knowledge. Agronsky supported the maintenance of law and order and was not afraid

to take an editorial stand on important matters. In its first year, its distri-
bution was 4,000 copies; on June 6, 1944, it sold a record 49,000 copies.

From her arrival in Palestine in 1933 until 1936, Kahn lived in
Tel Aviv and Jerusalem while writing for the *Post* and composing her book
Spring Up, O Well, published in 1936. She travelled throughout the coun-
tryside, however, and wrote prolifically of the new and not-so-new villages,
communal settlements, and kibbutzim. She also met and wrote of members
of the Arab communities. Nevinson notes that:

> Like myself, Miss Dorothy Kahn turns with most pleasure to the
> Zionist settlements on the land. Our old Cobbett[14] asked with
> scorn, "Who ever saw a Jew with a spade in his hand?" But scattered
> throughout Palestine are the "colonies" of Jewish settlers who actually
> work the land themselves, and in many cases are forbidden to employ
> Arab labor. Most interesting to her, as to me, were the Kvutzah, or
> communal colonies, run on the principle that all should work alike
> and all share the produce of their work. It was in communal villages
> like Beit Alpha and Ein Harod, both at the foot of the mountains
> of Gilboa, that I found the hopes of Zionism even more truly real-
> ized than in the rushing industries of Tel Aviv and Haifa, or even in
> the great University on Mount Scopus [the Hebrew University of
> Jerusalem], from which Titus overlooked Jerusalem when he prepared
> the Holy City's destruction" (15–16).

From 1936 until 1938, Kahn lived in the kibbutz, Givat Brenner. She was
not a member of the collective but paid for her room and board by working in various agricultural branches (e.g., field crops and beekeeping), while
also spending time in Jerusalem. During these years, she continued to write
for *The Palestine Post*. In 1938, the paper sent her to Poland, where she
investigated and wrote about the place of the Jews as a minority. Prior to
her move to Givat Brenner, Kahn took a step that was as surprising then as
it would be even in the twenty-first century: she applied for, and received,
Palestinian citizenship, which necessitated renouncing her American citizenship. On September 13, 1935, the government of Palestine in Jerusalem

---

[14] William Cobbett (1763–1835) was a British farmer, journalist, pamphleteer, and Member of
Parliament. In his writing, he gave expression to an anti-Semitic bent.

issued her with *Certificate of Naturalization number 15770*. For Kahn, this was a statement of commitment and intention.

The years 1936–39 saw a series of events in Palestine and Europe that influenced both Kahn's daily life and her work as a journalist, even when the latter bore the nature of what is now called feature writing. 1936 saw the beginning of what came to be termed the Arab Revolt in Palestine. The revolt was aimed against Jewish immigration to Palestine as well as against the British Mandatory authority, which was seen as enabling the continuation of Jewish immigration. At first, the Revolt was led by the Higher Arab Committee and involved strikes and other political protests. From late 1937 on, the Revolt became increasingly violent; British forces and Jewish civilians were targeted. Simultaneously, the attention of Jews throughout the world was focused on events in Europe: although the scope of the genocide perpetrated on European Jewry could not have been imagined, it was clear that Jews in Germany and the rest of Europe were in danger. Thus, the middle years of the 1930s saw immigration of Jews from Germany to Palestine; this formed a central theme in Kahn's writings until the White Paper of 1939 severely limited Jewish immigration to Palestine.

In autumn of 1939, Dorothy Kahn met her future husband, Pessah Bar-Adon, in Jerusalem. The young people fell in love and began living together; Dorothy continued her work as a journalist, both for *The Palestine Post* and as a freelancer, while Pessah took part in archaeological digs. On August 17, 1940, their only son, Doron, was born.

Pessah Bar-Adon, né Panitsch (1907–85) was born in Kolno, Poland, to a religious Zionist family. On his immigration to Palestine in 1925, he worked in housing and road construction while majoring in Middle East studies at the recently opened Hebrew University of Jerusalem. He lived among the bedouin near Beit She'an and Kuneitra; he adopted bedouin garb and went by the name of Azziz Effendi ("Azziz" remained his wife's nickname for him). He was curious as to why many kings during the biblical period had been shepherds and hoped that familiarity with the customs of contemporary nomads would shed light on this quandary. In time, he become one of Israel's more prominent archaeologists, taking part in the excavations of Beit She'arim, Tel Bet Yerah, Tel Kasila, the Cave of the Treasure at Nahal Mishmar, among others. During the 1929 Arab riots and the 1936–39 Arab Revolt, he was active in the Haganah (the pre-State Jewish defense force), which became the Israel Defense Forces on the establishment of the State.

In 1943 the Bar-Adon family—Dorothy, Pessah and little Doron—left Jerusalem and moved to the village of Merhavia, where they lived until Dorothy's death. The family rented an apartment in the Blumenfeld House, which they called "the castle" because it had been the first stone building in the Jezreel Valley. To this day there are two adjacent settlements named Merhavia: one a kibbutz and the other a moshav (cooperative village). It was here that Dorothy and Pessah raised their son. The closeness of the two settlements, as well as her previous experience as a resident of the kibbutz, Givat Brenner, enabled Dorothy to contrast the two forms—kibbutz and moshav—from the standpoint of a mother. Her writing on the subject is nonpartisan, and this at a time when public debate about the various forms of cooperative settlement in Palestine tended to be partisan.

In his memoir of his parents, Doron Bar-Adon quotes Dolly Avidor, a neighbor from the village of Merhavia:

> Your mother was an unusual figure in the village. She fought hard in order to maintain and defend the "nest," at a time when the burden of supporting the family rested on her thin shoulders. She loved you; you were the center of the world for her. At the same time she fought hard to please your dad. She dressed for him and cooked for him; she searched cookbooks for special recipes, even though what he really wanted was chickpeas and rice […].
>
> Once I saw her observing you excitedly as you played with bottles filled with water—or maybe sand—to different heights, and then showed other kids how to play a tune on them; you knew how to organize other children in games. Mom was proud and happy as she watched you; she leaned on one foot and then on the other, chain-smoking.[15]

During the last decade of her life Dorothy was, indeed, the main support of the family, since Pessah's work as an archaeologist did not bring in a steady income. She wrote of daily life in the *Yishuv* [Jewish community in Palestine before 1948] during World War II, of the massive immigration of European Jewry to Palestine in the years immediately following the war's end, of the often successful attempts by the British Mandatory authorities

---

[15] Doron Bar Adon. *My Parents' Garments*. Published by the author. Israel: 2005, p. 250 (transl. N.R.)

to arrest and detain these immigrants in camps such as in Cyprus, of the events leading to the establishment of the State of Israel in 1948, of the War of Independence in which the young State was attacked from all sides by Arab armies, and of the war's end and the beginning of the building of a civil state. Dorothy continued to cover the central events of the day under the persona of a Jewish, Palestinian/ Israeli housewife residing in the agricultural heartland of the *Yishuv*. Simultaneously, from the same stance, she wrote of daily life in the villages and kibbutzim.

During her seventeen years in Palestine/Israel, Dorothy worked as a freelance writer in addition to her work as a staff reporter for *The Palestine Post*. She was a regular contributor to such foreign and Jewish journals as *The Jewish Advocate, The National Jewish Post, Palestine Review*, and *The Journal of Jewish Life and Letters*. She also composed publicity for a broad range of Jewish organizations in Palestine and abroad, among them Hadassah, Red Magen David, Youth Aliyah, and the Zionist Organization Youth Department.

In July 1950, Dorothy became ill; she was taken to Hadassah Hospital in Jerusalem and found to be suffering from kidney disease, characterized by uremia; at the time, such conditions were incurable.

Dorothy Kahn Bar-Adon is buried in the small cemetery adjoining the village of Merhavia, surrounded by the people she loved and the land whose story she told.

CHAPTER TWO

Zionism and Immigration to Palestine

INTRODUCTION

The wish to establish a Jewish national home has deep roots. During nearly two thousand years of forced exile from the land of Israel, Jews hoped and prayed to return to what they saw as their traditional homeland.

Zionism, viewed by many Jews as the national liberation movement of the Jewish people, arose in the mid- to late-nineteenth century in Central and Eastern Europe as a movement of national revival, having been influenced by the revolutionary wave of 1848, known as the Springtime of Nations. The latter began in France, but quickly spread to Austria, Hungary, the Ukraine, Poland, and other locales of large concentrations of Jews. Under the leadership of Theodore Herzl (1860–1904), a Jewish-Austrian journalist, the main goal of the Zionist movement became the establishment of a Jewish homeland in Palestine, then ruled by the Ottoman Empire. Starting in 1882, Jewish settlers trickled into Palestine from Eastern Europe until the outbreak of World War I, thus enlarging the extant Jewish population of the area, as well as setting up new Jewish towns and villages, known as the Yishuv.

In 1917 the British government issued the Balfour Declaration, which expressed support for the creation of a Jewish national home in Palestine. The 1922 post-World War I agreements among the victorious powers granted Great Britain a mandate (temporary control) over Palestine. The late 1920s and 1930s saw massive attacks by Arabs upon the local Jewish population. At the same time, Jewish immigrants from Europe flowed into Palestine, especially after the 1933 election to power of the Nazi Party in Germany. The British mandatory authorities, who controlled the issuing of immigration visas, limited Jewish immigration to Palestine during the mid- to late-1930s, culminating in the issuance of the White Paper of 1939, which severely limited immigration.

Massive Jewish immigration to North America at the turn of the twentieth century led to the establishment of Zionist organizations in various Jewish-American communities. The early 1920s saw the enactment of such laws as the Emergency Quota Act of 1921, which set strict limits on immigration to the United States from Eastern Europe, among other areas. Despite economic and cultural difficulties facing the immigrant generation, Jews already residing in the United States generally felt safe and "at home." However, many of those concerned about the families and communities that they had left in Europe did see the need for an active Zionist organization in the United States and Canada, even though they themselves had no interest in relocating to Palestine. Indeed, a popular joke once had it that "a Zionist is one who convinces another to contribute money to an organization which finances the immigration to Palestine of someone who couldn't succeed in America." Dorothy Kahn Bar-Adon's conviction of the necessity for a Jewish national home in Palestine led her to immigrate to Palestine and practice her profession as a journalist in her new country.

Much of what Bar-Adon wrote can, of course, be subsumed under the rubric of Zionism. The materials in this chapter have been chosen both for their historical interest and for their connection to burning issues of the early twenty-first century: attempts at delegitimizing the State of Israel as the Jewish homeland and objections on the part of some Jews (and non-Jews) to calls for diaspora Jews to immigrate to Israel.

PREFACE

Written in 1935, two years after Kahn's immigration to Palestine
Zif Zif,[1] pp. 1–4
Unpublished manuscript from Bar-Adon's personal archive

About a century ago it was the fashion for polite English ladies of title or high station to make the perilous crossing of the Mediterranean Sea to the Holy Land. These ladies kept detailed diaries of their wanderings and

---

[1]   *Zif zif is a generic term for sand on the beach.*

published them upon their return home, the royalties to benefit some girl's school or mission that was trying to spread the word of truth in Palestine.

These little books invariably contain a foreword explaining that this is Lady So-and-So's "personal" record. She never in the world would have been induced to submit it to the vulgar floodlight of publication were it not for the sake of such-and-such school whose pathetic and brave struggle for existence in the Holy Land has so touched the cockles of her heart.

These were worthy accounts by worthy ladies of the trivialities as well as the high spots of a leisurely journeys through Palestine [the term used for pre-State Israel]—for these journeys had to be leisurely, since traveling from Jaffa to Jerusalem required several days of hard riding.

The polite English ladies of title or high station disappeared. The need for "hard riding" disappeared. The Turks disappeared.

The British Mandate [commission granted by the League of Nations to a member nation for the establishment of a responsible government over a former German/Ottoman colony or other conquered territory] came. The Zionists came. A new Palestine came. Journalists and authors came.

They found a writer's paradise—a country replete with "problems" and "situations." For here was the fusing of the very old and the very new. Here was the fusing of the Occident and the Orient. Here was the fusing (or the failure to fuse) of the Jew and the Arab. What a welter!

Out of this welter come books and more books. Some defend the Jews. Some defend the Arabs. Some discuss the vast changes. But the polite English ladies of warm hearts and tender sentiment who, in the tents along the wayside, had nightly penned delicate trivialities by flickering candle-light are no more. So nobody discusses white calico umbrellas. More's the pity!

And had I set out deliberately to write a book about Palestine, I shouldn't have discussed white calico umbrellas either, but this book was not deliberate. So I do discuss umbrellas and such.

I am neither polite, nor English, nor titled, nor of high station. I am neither worthy, nor modest, or tender, nor sentimental. I have not the fluttering heart of a wren. I have no interest in endowing girls' schools or missions.

But I have been a member of *The Palestine Post* [English daily newspaper—changed its name to *The Jerusalem Post* in 1950], staff in Jerusalem for two years. If you look on our letterhead (which you probably won't) you will see that we are "the only English Daily Newspaper in Palestine,

Transjordan and Syria." Being the only woman writer on the staff of the "only English, etc." meant that I had to do a lot of scrawling.

Sometimes I scrawled about big things that mattered; most times I scrawled about little things that didn't matter at all—such as which calico umbrellas.

I scrawled in the rural settlements, imbibing communal ideology and swatting mosquitoes between the lines. I scrawled in a raging storm at the foot of Trumpeldor's monument [the first national monument in pre-State Israel, built in Tel Hai to commemorate the deaths of eight Jews, among them the one-armed Jewish hero, Joseph Trumpeldor, who died in an engagement on March 1, 1920, with bedouins who had been attacking settlements in the area]. I scrawled in the ruins of Old Tiberias after a cloudburst; and I scrawled when nothing more was happening than that the sun was shining or the rain was raining or the oranges were ripening or the olives were green or the Jews were mad or glad or sad or bad.

Then one day I reminded myself of the polite English ladies of title of high station (with whom I repeat I have nothing to do) and it seemed that there might be a remote affinity between their trivialities written with a quill pen by candlelight and mine, banged out on the typewriter day after day with no aforethought besides making an honest living. We had both had time to see the white calico umbrella.

All those not interested in umbrellas and such should close the book right here and lend it to the lady next door, who, if she's a respectable book borrower will never return it.

As for the name *Zif Zif* it's Arabic. It means sand and—mixed with other ingredients—it is building most of new Palestine. When you sit on the beach at Tel Aviv, life is just one long caravan of camels carrying "zif zif."

Already you are beginning to think that I chose "zif zif" because my admittedly trivial articles are sands from the upbuilding of Palestine. Or, you are thinking that I chose it because it has something to do with the sands of time and Palestine is timeless.

These would have been good enough reasons to have chosen the "zif zif" but they aren't my reasons because this book deals with umbrellas and not philosophy. I chose "zif zif" because it is one of the few words that is accepted by the three official languages.

"Zif zif" was accepted into Hebrew because they probably didn't know anything about it when Solomon built the Temple and the Jews needed a word for it. Recently it blossomed forth between the signified covers of the *Official Government Gazette*, which means that the English have given their blessing.

In a country where you are told in the three official languages to "Please close the door," "Do not smoke" and "No loitering here," it is refreshing to discover a universal word—especially when it is as delightfully silly as "zif zif."

So there ought to be a book written about "zif zif."

Here it is...

FIRST IMPRESSIONS OF TEL AVIV

Zif Zif, pp. 61–65
Unpublished manuscript from Bar-Adon's personal archive

This was probably the first article written by Kahn after her arrival in Tel Aviv in 1933. It presents a number of first impressions, including a visit to the editorial offices of Davar (a Hebrew-language newspaper published by the Histadrut—the Jewish Labor Federation).

Snatches of a Hebrew love song drift through my window from the street as I try to convince myself that this is actually Palestine—and Tel Aviv, the only all Jewish city in the world. Low modernistic houses of yellow, blue and pink; dusty roads, throngs of young people in the most heterogeneous attire, from the four corners of the world, teeming through the streets, Eskimo pies [chocolate-covered vanilla ice cream bar], Hebraic chatter, a flamingo tree, stars like grapes, scaffolding, and a great white synagogue.

Such are the chaotic impressions of Tel Aviv on the first night of arrival. The city bids fair to be the Atlantic City of Palestine and the growing pains through which it is now living would revive memories for many old time Atlantic Cityites.

Festivities on the SS *Esperia* began early last night and the drinking of wine, singing of vigorous Hebrew pioneer melodies, dancing of the *hora* [Jewish-Israeli circle folk dance] and story telling, continued until 4 a.m., when the rising sun drove us to an alcove in the prow of the boat. Here we huddled, eagerly awaiting the first glimpse of land, which did not appear until seven o'clock. More song and then the spell was broken in the hubbub of disembarking.

Immigration laws are rigid and one is put through the third degree before being allowed to load bag and baggage into the small boat that takes passengers to the port of Jaffa Baggage inspections, malaria injections and you are free and clattering through the Arab city of Jaffa, thinking that any moment the rickety buggy will collapse from the weight of your baggage.

The Montefiore, you have been told, is a commodious moderately priced hotel. You are expecting something like the average side avenue Atlantic City hotel.

You draw in front of a buff-color, brick, flower-covered building, comparable to a large Ventnor City [New Jersey] residence. You inquire for a room and bath and are told, "We have no baths but are building them." This is your first introduction to the pioneer spirit of Tel Aviv that you later learn is growing up in the midst of plaster, paint and constant hammering.

The man who spoke English has disappeared. You ask for a coat hanger and a towel, and six employees try courageously to understand you. You give up and begin to realize for the first time that you are actually in a Hebrew-speaking country. A few minutes later you start for Allenby Street [one of the main shopping streets of Tel Aviv] to purchase shoe-cleaning fluid. You point to your shoes and are shown shoes, shoe laces and shoe buckles. In despair you decide that your shoes aren't so dirty anyway. It is amazing even though you had known it before, that this Biblical tongue should be the key to everyday business life. By the time you make a few purchases and order a few meals in Tel Aviv, you are able to disassociate Hebrew from shepherds, kings and prophets and begin to think of it in terms of toothpaste and fried eggs.

In the center of the business district, across from the moving picture theater, I caught sight of a large store and through the window, an electric icebox. I had happened into Gruzenberg Street. Inside I found Max Greenberg and soon was being hustled to the Greenberg home on Rothschild Boulevard for dinner. The Greenberg family, including Carl, Sonny, Miriam and David, who have been away from Atlantic City for about a year, are fortunate in having entered Palestinian life while retaining a few of the American comforts. Their apartment is almost the only one in the city where hot water is on tap, and for the first time in several weeks I had a real American meal with spinach, good coffee and mashed potatoes. The rooms are tremendous—fashioned for comfort in hot weather and the balcony overlooks the tree-lined boulevard.

Questions flew at the dinner table, politics-beer-Hadassah-scripture.

Of course, the family can speak Hebrew—if they did not, they couldn't even communicate with the maid, who was formerly a *chalutza* [woman pioneer] in a colony. But lessons in the household are still in progress, as learning fluent Hebrew is a laborious task, even in Palestine.

During dinner, I learned more of the striking similarity between Tel Aviv and Atlantic City. It has about sixty thousand inhabitants. Located here on the Mediterranean Sea, much of the life centers about the beach and a street running parallel to the sea that serves as a boardwalk. Being about 40 miles from Jerusalem, it is a popular place for Jerusalemites to spend weekends during the summer.

Later in the evening, I discovered that novels and moving pictures, based on the hectic bustle of a newspaper office, won't be written soon in Palestine. Going into the editorial office of the "Davar" [Hebrew-language daily newspaper published by a workers' party] in search of mail, I found myself plunged into the "hysteria" of a Tel Aviv paper close to the deadline hour. The editorial room is on the third floor of a house and I listened for the familiar clatter of typewriters to guide me. All was silence. Poking my head into a doorway, I saw a group of men (one bearded and looking for all the world like a college professor) quietly scribbling with fountain pens.

Where are the reporters and where is the city desk, I inquired? This was the city desk, and these were the reporters preparing copy for the morning edition. When I mentioned typewriters they were aghast, and one of them explained that they could never concentrate amid the noise of typewriters. He exhibited neat pages of Hebrew letters that, he said, were prepared as quickly as typing. And were the stories concerning the recent Arlosoroff murder [left-wing Zionist leader whose murder in Tel Aviv was never solved] written this way, I inquired? They were. Indeed, the most sensational stories of the hour are prepared in this manner.

The city editor guided me down the steps (this building also was in the midst of being torn down or built up and we crept under scaffolds). As he stood in the debris bidding me "shalom," I felt the spirit that is building Palestine gripping me. He was speaking of Palestine, glowing and I said, "You have been here so long I should think you might take it for granted."

"You can't take life for granted here. Each day has its new joy, its new effort, its new sorrow. There are many Jews who come here merely to live and to work for themselves. We welcome them. But we who are the army cannot work only for ourselves and we cannot give up. We are the same as

Jews in other parts of the world and yet different; different because we have created here a new atmosphere."

I started down the dusty road. Groups of young people passed, singing. Here and there I caught sight of parties sipping drinks on secluded balconies and verandas. I sensed the peace and serenity of Biblical times, curiously charged with the vitality of surging life. Had a new atmosphere been created here? Perhaps, but you should not search too much the first night in Tel Aviv.

About seven years ago Mayor Meir Dizengoff of Tel Aviv [served as mayor from 1911 until his death in 1936] visited Atlantic City and was given the golden key of the resort by the late Mayor Edward L. Bade. He promised the latter that the first Atlantic City Mayor who visited Tel Aviv should receive the key of that city. He had discovered that Atlantic City mayors are too busy to travel to this portion of the world so decided to let me act as proxy. When I came to his office this morning, he took from his drawer the Atlantic City key carefully preserved. In Tel Aviv the "key to the city" is a figurative term, and so I was presented with an elaborate guidebook and map that will serve as a most practical "key."

The Mayor spoke enthusiastically of Atlantic City's boardwalk, which he hoped, when finances permit, to reproduce here.

The Mayor in Tel Aviv must be schooled in two arts that are spared an Atlantic City mayor. He must be a linguist—and he must be able to drink much Turkish coffee. Since Jews are flocking here from all parts of the world, the city is a Tower of Babel. The Mayor speaks German, English and a few other tongues to those who have not yet been initiated to Hebrew.

The kitchen seems an important part of the City Hall equipment. Despite the fact that about twenty people were waiting in the anteroom, trays containing tin cups of coffee disappeared several times into the Mayor's chamber, when the importance of the visitor required an extended chat.

I have been a Tel Avivian for a week—and what an adventure. To leave a land where the byword was "depression" and suddenly find myself in an atmosphere of "prosperity" is amazing in itself. But prosperity here seems of a different variety than we knew during the "boom days." One is inclined to believe that the prosperity is based on the fact that everyone has enough to supply his wants, and his wants are very simple. It is this extreme simplicity that seems to characterize life in Tel Aviv.

My first visit to the beach reminded me of home. Jostling, pleasure-bent crowds are reminiscent of the "big eight" weeks in Atlantic City.

Tel Aviv, however, seems to have captured one secret of the Orient and the continent that we have not. Life is lived completely in the open air and everyone parks on the doorstep of the sea. For a space of about four blocks, cafés are so close together that you cannot tell where one stops and the next begins. Here the people sit, in the open air, sipping tea or drinking beer and watching crowds which stream by in a....

SHORTAGE OF HANDS

Beginning of the 1930s
Zif Zif, pp. 162–166
Unpublished manuscript from Bar-Adon's personal archive

During the first few years of Kahn's residence in Palestine, there was an acute shortage of Jewish agricultural workers, and this at a time when many Zionists identified the Zionist endeavor with settlement of the land and establishment of Jewish agriculture. Kahn describes the process of being hired for work in the orange groves, in the Petah Tikva area, and her first day of work.

"Are you ready to work in the orange groves?"

This is the head of the Woman's Council of *Histadrut* (Jewish Labor Federation) speaking in the Workers' House of Petah Tikva (a large village near T.A.)

With this direct question she greets every newcomer who happens into the workers' quarters. Then a young man approaches and asks "Are you ready for work tomorrow?" He is the head of the skilled workers and searches every new face for a potential packer. The labor shortage in Palestine is so acute that even journalists answer the urgent call for hands. A number of young men and women are hurrying in and out of doorways, each seeming to silently question whether you "are ready for work tomorrow."

Your affirmative reply brings a cursory examination. Did you bring suitable clothing? Can you be at the Workers' Kitchen at 6:30 tomorrow morning? Your fingers are inspected and several heads shake in dire disapproval. Long nails might injure the skin of the oranges. Are you willing to have them chopped off? You steel yourself and answer, "Ein davar" (It is nothing). Now you are hired.

A terrific hubbub pervades in the Workers' House tonight. Oranges are at the core of it. So much work to be done and so few people to do it. Within five weeks the fruit must be off the trees. Now it seems like an impossible task. But the older pupils from the schools are starting to arrive and they will somewhat relieve conditions.

The man standing near the doorway, you are told, is a baker. At night he works in the bakery and during the day in the groves, managing to exist on a few hours sleep during these hectic labor-shortage days. Clerks, professional and business men and women from Petah Tikva and Tel Aviv are devoting one day a week to this urgent work. Building workers who can command 60 piasters a day in their own trade are picking for 20 piasters.

From the "mobilization" room you pass into the room known as "the battlefield." Growers are grouped about a desk making urgent requests for laborers. The room is crowded and the excited applicants bear down with their demands on the harassed shoulders of the Histadrut clerks.

"The battlefield has been like this for weeks." We are told, "They ask for twenty laborers and receive four."

It is six o'clock the next morning when you head toward the Workers' Kitchen.

You join the group of about thirty workers and envy them their confidence as they chatter among themselves. You are suffering grave misgivings. Will you be picking or wrapping and how do you pick an orange anyway! You only remember seeing them on the trees, looking very decorative, or in shops with the neat and finished appearance as though they grew there and not on trees.

You reach the grove and in the packinghouse you find great piles of golden fruit strewn on the floor. Squatting in Oriental fashion, the girls are wrapping them with flying fingers. Nearby sits a man in front of a box that rests upright on an easel. With apparently little effort he packs the fruit into place and calls for another box. You are told, however, that this is the most difficult of all work in the packinghouse. "It is always the packer who is the first to perspire," it is explained. It is necessary that the fruit be packed not only tightly enough to prevent moving during shipments, but also to allow for the shrinkage of the skin when the natural moisture evaporates.

The fruit flies from wrappers to sorters, to packers. The pile diminishes before your eyes. But, at best, it is a slow process. You can visualize that perhaps in a few years the workers will not be squatting in this fashion on the floor. Great belts and mysterious mechanical contrivances will be handling Palestine's orange treasure.

Time to start for the grove now. But first your fingernails must be shorn. You meditate that no newborn babe could be treated with more gentle care than the oranges.

You shut your eyes while one of the workers operates on you with a rusty clipper, the others gathering about to enjoy the impromptu beauty parlor rigged up in a shack.

You start down the narrow path, followed by a clatter of wooden conveyers bringing the baskets in your wake. As far as your eye can stretch the trees are like an artist's canvas running riot with rich green and orange. In the fresh morning breeze the perfume is intoxicating.

When you had viewed these groves from a passing bus, it had seemed a sabotage to shear these trees of their decorative fruits. But now, with those wooden boxes in the packinghouses and these baskets at your heels, yawning for the fruit, you feel an urge to clip every tree for miles around.

You are given a picking partner, a tree and a basket. Your partner shows you how to clip the fruit quickly without leaving any trace of the stem.

Standing under the branches you are bewildered for a moment. All around you, overhead, everywhere hangs the golden fruit, as plentiful as needles on a pine tree. Surely it will take an hour to denude this single tree.

Clip. Clip. Clip. It would be easy if you didn't have to trim the stem so closely. So you cut haltingly. But your partner is working rhythmically, almost as though she were dancing as her hands wave from branch to basket. And then, as if by magic, the baskets at your feet are filled, and the tree is bare except for the oranges in the top branches, which will be clipped later by the "ladder brigade" that is following.

The morning wears on. My partner and I have been assigned to a particular row of trees. But the branches are so heavily laden that they intertwine and form a canopy. It is difficult to distinguish your place. You find yourself, in some mysterious way, picking oranges several rows away and are only aware of your wanderings when your partner calls.

Almost the only spoken word is the constant call from the workers for a *sal* (a basket). The men are apparently having difficulty in trundling the baskets to the packinghouse and back to the grove quickly enough to supply the pickers. Whenever the pickers have to stop for a short interval to wait for baskets there are shouts of "scandal." But you do not have their energy and when you have the opportunity to stretch on the ground for a brief moment you do not feel that it is such a "scandal" and hope the basket carriers will tarry a bit on the way. But they do not. More baskets. More clipping.

And then lunch. You gather in a shack, sit on packing cases or stretch out on a straw mat. Loaves of bread, olives and cheese are heartily consumed. You, as a newcomer and an American, are deluged with questions. Do you know the Rosenfeld family in New York? You don't. That is strange because they are well known. Have you ever been to Providence? Is it a nice place? Someone has an uncle there. But all the questions do not concern America. Jerusalem holds much interest for some of the workers who came to Petah Tikva directly from the boat some time ago and have yet to visit Jerusalem.

Lunch hour is over and you trek back to the groves. Clipping. And then the sun sets on your first day as a picker in the orange groves.

RENUNCIATION

1935
Inhabitants of the Rock, pp. 92–97
Unpublished manuscript from Bar-Adon's personal archive

> *In 1935, some two years after her immigration to Palestine, Kahn decided to apply for Palestinian citizenship, via the Mandatory Immigration Department. This step involved, in effect, renouncing American citizenship (handing over her American passport to the Immigration Department was tantamount to renunciation), and becoming a citizen of an entity—Mandatory Palestine—whose status as a ward of the League of Nations was potentially unclear and certainly not permanent. Kahn justifies her decision, despite her sense of gratitude toward the United States and her understanding that citizenship of Mandatory Palestine was not identical to citizenship of a "Jewish national homeland."*

It was about nine o'clock in the morning. I was sitting on a bench in the office of the Immigration Department. I was waiting. Probably I would be waiting a long time. One always waits a long time for everything in Palestine.

But this morning I didn't mind waiting. For I knew that as soon as I was summoned to the little room on the left of the corridor, I would be required to hand over my American passport with its familiar maroon color cover. And I wasn't in a hurry to do it. Employees of the department busily darted to and fro. But none of them was interested in me. Good.

Ever since I applied for citizenship several months before, I knew of the necessity for handing over my American passport. And yet, this morning I was clinging to these few extra minutes when the passport was still in my handbag.

I few months after I arrived in Palestine, I began considering vaguely the necessity for becoming a citizen. Since I was to remain, I could not continue to accept the protection of the United States. Nor could I be a permanent guest of Palestine without offering my allegiance.

This reasoning was simple enough, everything was clear. I no longer felt vague. Sometimes I was impatient for the necessary two years of residency to elapse so that I could apply. I was jealous of the simplest Arab on the roadside. He was a Palestinian and I was not. And I could not consider him as my countryman or Palestine as my country until I had cut other ties.

On June 22, two years after my arrival, I went to the Immigration Department with no qualms. The clerk was nonchalant and cool. He could have been dispensing doughnuts or derby hats instead of citizenship papers. Together we filled out a questionnaire as bulky as a Sunday morning newspaper. When my citizenship was granted, I would be informed. Good day. I asked him to please rush it. He would try; but he feared it would take several months.

I didn't know why I had asked him to rush it. Perhaps I had a premonition about the doubts and fears that would fill those months of waiting. For from this moment, when nothing but formalities stood between me and the final papers, I was besieged by misgivings.

I could not remember having felt any particular patriotism toward America. Patriotism as such had always seemed rather foolish. In school you pledge allegiance to the stars and stripes and sing "America the Beautiful" and learn the story about George Washington crossing the Delaware on chunks of ice and Abraham Lincoln studying by candle light in a log cabin. But afterward you begin to realize that flags have caused more cruelty than anything else in the world at large. And patriotism is shelved except during Fourth of July parades or during the hysteria of wartimes.

But during those months of waiting for my final papers, a thousand and one sentiments cropped up that I hadn't expected. And they summed up to one thing. How dare one renounce the land of one's birth? It began to take on the aspect of a tremendous step. One went to bed thinking about it. Got up in the morning thinking about it. And sometimes dreamed about it. One consulted one's friends. One consulted oneself over and over again. How dare one renounce?

And, as some of my friends pointed out, one renounced for nothing at all. Few countries in the world have less national prestige than Palestine. It is hardly a country. It is only a Mandatory. And one cannot even be sure of British protection. Tomorrow it may be in the hands of Italy or Germany or the Turks. Who knows? And, besides, you are not becoming a citizen of the Jewish National Homeland. You are simply unnecessarily renouncing the powerful and stable protection of America. For what? For citizenship in a weak and unstable ward of the League of Nations.

And in time of disturbances? The American warships would come if necessary to protect her citizens. Then you would know the folly of having given up so much for so little. And disturbances in Palestine are inevitable. If you had been here during the savage outbreak in 1929 [1929 Palestinian Riots—attacks by Arabs on Jews accompanied by destruction of Jewish property], you would understand.

But in the meantime there were months of doubts and fear and misgivings. Never before had I considered so microscopically the Jewish position in Palestine.

No, I was not becoming a citizen of the Jewish National Homeland. On that score I could have no delusions. But I was becoming as much a citizen of the Homeland as anyone ever could. And I was giving physical expression to the theory that the only answer to anti-Semitism is Semitism; that the return of the Jew to Palestine must be an uncompromising return to the East; that the Semitic Arab is closer to me than any non-Semitic, even if we both happened to be born in Philadelphia.

This was harsh reasoning. One went to bed thinking about it. And got up thinking about it. One even waxed sentimental remembering the redness of the oak leaves in autumn in America. Leaves don't turn red in Palestine. And above all else, one remembered the kindness of America.

But the necessity for becoming a Palestinian transcended all this. It did not mean that one was less grateful for the kindness of America. It did not mean that one could ever get over nostalgia for the redness of the oak leaves and the overwhelming sadness of autumn in Pennsylvania. It meant only that one was a Semite. And as a Semite, one could best fulfill oneself by living among Semites. And one could not remain a permanent guest. Because one didn't want to be a guest. One wanted to be at home and being at home meant cutting all ties with another home.

And what of disturbances? Perhaps they would come again. Perhaps not. I had heard so much about 1929. But I couldn't picture it. A teacher had told me how she had been locked up in the Abyssinian [Ethiopian] consulate for days. The Abyssinians had been kind and had brought her food. She couldn't leave because Arabs were running through the streets with daggers dripping blood. I had visited Hebron and seen the quarters evacuated by the Jews. In this house four women and two children had been slaughtered. I had visited the graves of the students from the Talmudic School. Slaughtered. All slaughtered. So they told me.

But I couldn't picture it. I could picture the circle of barefoot Arabs dancing the debka on the road to Bethlehem. I could picture the old sheikh at the door of his tent watching the flanks of the camels tinted by the rising sun. I could picture the *muezzin* [person appointed at a mosque to lead and recite the call to prayer] chanting from his minaret at dawn. I could picture Nassim sitting cross-legged on the sand at Nabi Rubin [Arab village near Ramla with annual celebrations. There, Muslims from the area flocked throughout the month of August to celebrate the *mawsim*, a pilgrimage to Sheik Rubin's tomb to pay vows and celebrate festivals] with a magnificent repose. I could picture the hunchback patiently clambering up the path in Ramallah.

I could picture Arabs happy with a simple joy that I do not know. I could picture Arabs with a deep repose that I do not possess. I could picture Arabs with a charm that is not a part of me. I could picture Arabs as my friends. As my cousins. As my fellow citizens. But brandishing daggers dripping with blood I could not picture. I had visited the graves in Hebron. Thrown stones on them, as is the custom. And still I could not picture it.

But I knew it was true. Arabs do slaughter when they are roused. During those uneasy months I looked it as squarely in the face as I could. And yet all the time I knew that there was no other course open to me. I am a Semite.

And what of the position of Palestine? True, it is a ward of the League of Nations. Tomorrow Italy or Germany or Turkey might be wielding the authority now designated to Great Britain. It is a chance. Everything is a chance. It is a chance that we Jews take along with the Arabs.

All these doubts and fears of the last few months flooded back as I sat on the bench in the office of the Immigration Department. Employees of the department busily darted to and fro on this errand or that. Soon I would be summoned to hand over my American passport. So I tried to reduce everything to its least common denominator, in these last moments.

Renunciation is difficult. And renouncing one's American citizenship is particularly difficult because America had been kind. But more important than being an American is being a Semite. For you can stop being an American. But you can never stop being a Semite. It is in your blood. It was in your blood generations before being an American was in your blood. And being a Semite must mean coming as close as you can to Palestine and to the citizens of Palestine.

Employees of the department darted to and fro. Now one of them stopped by my bench. My papers were ready. Step this way. I was shown into an office. I fished in my handbag. Produced the American passport with its familiar maroon cover. Tried to appear as nonchalant and cool as the clerk who might have been dispensing doughnuts or derby hats. Handed over the passport.

So this was renunciation.

I was shown into another office. I took an oath. Signed my name. The officer was jovial. He congratulated me. He wished me happiness. Would I have a party to celebrate the occasion? Yes, perhaps I would have a party. I hadn't thought about it.

So this was allegiance.

PRIVATE LETTER FROM 1937

Ruth Kahn
Givat Brenner
A letter from Bar-Adon's personal archive

Much of this letter is devoted to a 10-day trip to Poland made in 1937. Kahn apparently spent most, or all, of her visit in Warsaw and met with Jews and gentiles. Her main interests were the social, cultural, and political situation of Jews in Poland; a definition of anti-Semitism as practiced in Poland; and understanding anti-Semitism's influence on Polish Jews. Kahn writes from the stance of a Zionist Jewish-Palestinian, as well as one who has an American cultural and political background.

Dear Elene:

Above address correct—they can't pronounce Dorothy. It was swell getting two letters from you yesterday. Yes we are six hundred people so have a post office.

I will start with Poland. It would take pages, even a book to tell you my reactions of those ten days. But it is so personal, and perhaps so cock-eyed, that I didn't write one work for publication, although Gershon [Agron—editor of *The Palestine Post*) plagued me for a series and I needed the money. I left there with the impressions I had on the boat unchanged and in some respects intensified. You must begin by remembering that one of my faults, or virtues, is being able to see the other fellow's point of view, which is annoying because it prevents me from coming out strongly for one side. In Warsaw I divided my time equally between Jews and goyim. While I could not talk to the Jews on the street, my Hebrew made it possible to talk to journalists, and the intelligentsia in general. I make no apology for having been so interested in the goyim—I know that most Jews who visit Warsaw are not—but I do not possibly see how we can get anywhere by only looking at ourselves, and not seeing ourselves in relation to the larger and general problem. Also you must take into account my Palestinian background, which I think makes us view Jews and their problems differ-ently. I find more anti-Semitism (but of a constructive kind) here than anywhere else. It is because we see so clearly our faults that we are dedi-cated to the job of doing away with them. We are intent upon having this country because we believe that much of what the anti-Semites say is true: that Jews love money inordinately, have little sense of beauty and order and more often than is necessary are "dirty Jews." We realize that they have become this way through no fault of their own, but we are not interested in the causes so much as remedies. We are wise rather than doting parents, as is the rest of Jewry. I would say that we are more alarmed by what kind of a person the Jew is today and more hopeful for what he can be, than the rest of Jewry, who either hate each other or think they are a race of messi-ahs. All this affected my approach to Poland. In other words, because I have seen healthy Jews in Palestine, I am able to recognize Jews who are decayed and crippled mentally and morally. Another important thing in approaching Poland is to know the history of Poland—not only the Jewish history; I read a great deal on the boat and afterward—you may not know it, as I didn't till I made the trip. Read of the periods when Poland flourished culturally—was the Paris of that part of the world (I saw relics of that period in the museum). Read also about the period when Russia came in like a beast, destroyed precious pictures, etc., and threw Poles into the Vistula river as though they were rats. Only against this background can you begin to understand what the freedom today means to Poland—how precious is the revival of their crushed language, etc. One of my books (perhaps I write as I please) on Europe, refers to the "persecution" complex from which Poland is suffering today—which was exactly my reaction—everything Polish means much more to them than to a normal country, which is understandable after you go through the museum and see rare china, etc., glued together—the pieces were recently returned to them through a treaty with Russia. The Polish theater today is excellent. All this I think I could understand more than you because it is so akin to Jewish national-ism in Palestine today. You have no idea what pride in the revived language means. A Polish goy mentioned to me the fact that most Jews speak Polish badly or Yiddish. What could I answer to his complaint that they mutilate a language when, in Palestine, I have heard people booed off a stage for speaking English. Also I am annoyed when people don't know that Hebrew is not Yiddish. Yet I have met many people who think Polish is a perverted Russian. In other words there are a multitude of things going on in Poland that Jews in America know nothing about—in our usual self-centered way we judge the problem only from our side. One other thing that must be remembered is Poland's ever present fear of Germany and Russia that drives her on to strengthen herself against possible attack—and her frantic fear in view of her oppressed history is also understandable. Now, consider the Jews against this background. They are ten percent of the population—a tremendously large percentage—they are more obvious because they are herded into the cities and not spread out. They monopolize some indus-tries—by the way, have you read *Brother Ashkenazi*—if not do so if you want to see how some Jews have behaved in Poland. You will see in that book that the Poles invited the Jewish spinners to come at a time when they were needed. But the Poles are people—and people are rather beastly—it would be saintly for them to remember now why the Jews came—people in general know little gratitude. The Jews in Poland are unassimilated in a way that you can't imagine. Great numbers of them cling to the *payot* and *streimel* [sidecurls and fur hat] (which turns the stomachs of many Jews—why should we expect the Poles to be more kindly?) They have remained a state within a state—which from the point of maintaining

Judaism is good. But it has kept out of the pale of the people, and in times like this when bread is literally at a premium, how can we expect the masses not to consider them as strangers, eating bread that is due to them (and I literally mean bread—you can't conceive of the poverty in Poland, not limited to Hebrews). In other words, I don't see how we can have our cake and eat it—I don't see how we can remain out of the family and in it at the same time. Some of our most pathetic Jewish literature is built up around Jewish soldiers trying to escape serving—and a Jewish soldier is pathetic because it isn't natural to us. But when you talk to the Poles, the Jews were simply slackers, cowards, or if forced at best bad soldiers. They see us less sentimentally than we see ourselves. And actually, in Palestine where we are fighting for our own, you don't see men who don't want to fight—which may prove that we are not such one-hundred-percenters in our adopted land as we think we are. Also, the charge that we are always in the front row of agitators is true—this is probably a virtue coming from our over-developed mentalities and love of justice—but what right have we to thrust this upon countries where we are guests and, as long as we insist on main-taining our statehood as Jews, must remain guests. I know that in Palestine, Jews deal firmly with Jewish communists—we don't want them because they are against the spirit of the country. In Poland a Jewish journalist told me proudly that most of the agitating communists were Jews. At the same time I read government proclamation stating clearly that Poland does not feel that Communism is to the best interest of the country. We always think that we are being oppressed—and yet in times of quiet we rise in profes-sions and industry (again, read *Brothers Ashkenazi*) until we overstep the bounds and are crushed again. It is a terrible cycle that you yet may see in America. I do not underestimate the difficulty of living like guests—but when the gates of Palestine were open (and they still are to capitalists) I didn't see Jews clamoring to come. Now, of course, they are clamoring to come and can't get in, or can't get their money out. But a few decades ago (when they had already had more than their share of suffering) they wouldn't risk the financial…uncertainty in Palestine in preference to their stinking factories in Lod, and those who came here were considered mad. Should a similar time come in America, I could hardly feel heartbroken for those Jews who all these years have gone blithely on, living on an incon-ceivably high scale and feeling virtuous when they give five dollars a year to the Zionist organization. If American Jewry had given anything in pro-portion of their wealth, we wouldn't have half our troubles here. The only time we'll see their money is if they're packed off here, bag and baggage like beggars (yes I am somewhat of an anti-Semite) But to get back to Poland. Here are three and a half million people, forming a separate state. Whether they chose it or it was forced on them is like asking which comes first, the chicken or the egg. Anyhow, it is not important—what make the Jew what he is does not matter. The only important thing is to remedy it—and of course, for me it boils down to Palestine where our over-bright boys can be farmers and carpenters and bricklayers instead of shyster lawyers or shopkeepers. This of course, is no solution for Poland. I left there feeling (there is an untranslatable German word for it)—the troubles of the world's sorrow—in some respects the Poles have been driven into this through terrific poverty and an ever-present fear of barbarous nations. The tragedy of the Jews is too terrible to put into words and anything you have read is mild. The worse the world treats them the worse they become, and the worse they become the worse the world treats them. At the present moment we are not the ideal people that we think we are. I see no solution except packing as many as possible into Palestine to grow orange trees for awhile until we get straightened out enough to write another Bible—and keep the rest in the desert for forty years like Moses, in his extreme wisdom, did.

But enough of this—now for little me. I am extremely happy now but, of course, don't make any prediction as to how long it will last.

Darn and your letter—I started at two o'clock and had a Hebrew lesson at three—when I looked at the clock it was a quarter to four, so I missed it. Meantime I had tea and heard something amusing—and tragic—which bears out my above contention that we are not all saints and sages. There are 450 people working here, and 50 old parents who have been brought over from Poland, Germany, etc. The parents have the best rooms and houses, they have a small synagogue and a special kosher dining room and kitchen, they can work or not as they please. They have nothing to do but live in peace in Palestine with their children and grandchildren. But being Jews, they are all smart. They fight so much among themselves that it is a scandal (I hear it is also true in all *kvutzoth* [communal and cooperative farms or settlements that are usually smaller than kibbutzim]). A member of the *kvutzah* [singular] was appointed to try to make peace and told me of the meeting last night. There are nineteen Jews who pray and they have two *minyonim* [*minyan*— the ten adult Jewish men needed for public, communal prayer]—they can't sit together even for prayer because of arguments. They have much better food than we do, eggs, butter, chicken, etc., and they fight over scraps of food like beasts. The comedy comes in because the men without wives are jealous of those with and say that their wives see that they get better food, etc. One man made a speech in which he said, "Let the kibbutz provide us with wives." The fact that twenty Jews can't pray together in Palestine is the sort of thing that makes us difficult people wherever we are. The twenty women fight so much in the kitchen that they have to have two girls from the kvutzah to help in their special kitchen.

Now back to me. I am devouring every minute because I have a feeling it won't last—something, probably my own restlessness, would take me away from this seclusion. Meantime I am satisfying two long-suppressed desires— one to get close to nature and the other to live the simplest possible life stripped of all superficialities such as shopping, beauty parlors, (even if I only spent half an hour a week there), people, etc. My adjustment was much easier than I expected—I feel very well physically and don't mind the coarse food: mostly tomatoes, cereals, rice and potatoes. The work was tiring, but only the first two weeks. My lift [a wood container used by immigrants from Germany to send their belonging to Palestine; became a dwelling cabin in the *kibbutzim*] is fixed up very nicely. The days are not long enough for all I am trying to do—I work till noon then study Hebrew and write. Before I know it, it is seven o'clock, time for dinner. The evening doesn't amount to much as I am in bed by nine. Altogether it is a very rich experience in every way, I always have to be kicked into the things that are best for me.

THE IDEALIST

Dorothy Kahn
Probably written in 1937
Givat Brenner
An article from Bar-Adon's personal archive

Among Jews residing in Europe and the Americas, the Zionist settlers of Palestine were often viewed as "idealists" who devoted their lives to a vision of establishing a Jewish homeland that would be a perfect society. Kahn rejected this approach to the Zionist endeavor, which she saw as being based squarely in reality: the creation of a national home in which Jews would be safe from anti-Semitic persecution and could achieve political, economic, and cultural sovereignty.

This week I received a letter from an American friend containing the following sentence: "The difference between you Jews in Palestine and us Jews in America is that you are idealists—you live for an ideal—we are just plain human beings, selfish and concerned only with the little spot on which we stand."

My friend is not an outstanding person. If she were, the passage would not be worth quoting. There are a goodly number of outstanding people talking about Palestine today. My friend is obscure. Therefore if I were corresponding with any one of the four million Jews in America instead of with Mrs. M., I might have received the same letter. Hence the passage is worth quoting. Most American Jews, whether they are Zionists, anti-Zionists or non-Zionists, believe that everyone who is living in Palestine by choice is an idealist.

The sentence annoyed me. I know that all honest people living in Palestine resent being called "idealists." It is untrue and it makes an unhealthy implication, inconsistent with the country and its people. It would be a great boon to Palestine if the words "idealists," "idealism," and "ideal," which have been attached to the country like an umbilical cord, could be severed for once and all.

"Answering to one's highest conception; existing only in idea; visionary; perfect type."

Has this definition ever applied to the modern settlement of Palestine? Has the settlement here ever existed only in idea? Did the Jews migrate here like dreamy-eyed Galahads in quest of the "perfect type"; or did they come as realists in quest of the one thing dearer than ideality—namely, reality.

Consider the earliest pioneers. It was following the bloody wholesale slaughter of the Jews in Russia in 1881 [the murder of the Russian tsar resulted in riots against the Jews] that groups of Choveve Zion (Lovers of Zion) grew up spontaneously. It was then, after the Russian minister of the interior announced that the Western frontier lay "open to the Jews" that the publicist Levanda who had aided assimilations efforts for twenty years cried out, "I know well where I am, who I am, and with whom I am." And it was then that Yehuda Leb Gordon, poet and champion of assimilation asked in despair and disillusionment, "Of what shall I speak and give warning, whereof shall I sing? All my dreams are void; all my ideals have proven vain and misleading."

It was then—when the assimilation movement Haskalah (Enlightenment) had dissolved and disintegrated—that the first Zionist pioneer group, the BILU, arose, taking its name from the characters of [Book of Isaiah, 2:5]"*Beit Ya'akov Lekhu Venelkha*" (House of Jacob, Come! Let us go!). Nothing more real can be imagined than this little group of BILU members arriving in the port of Jaffa and going to till the soil at the agricultural school of Mikveh Israel. There were realists in the same way that Leona, an Italian Jewess who arrived a fortnight ago from Padua and works with me in the orange groves, is a realist.

A few, like the Germans who settled here twenty yeas ago, came to Palestine because of foresight. Others have come because of hindsight. Others (Americans and English) have come because their longing for a spiritual as well as a physical home is satisfied here. But none have come because of that vague impetus known as "idealism," which suggests a saccharine altruism obnoxious to anyone engaged in the real task of building a real country for himself to inhabit. The caveman who hewed himself a home out of the rocks was not an "idealist." Since that time, no man who built himself a house was an "idealist"—except in Palestine.

Millions upon millions of words have been written about Palestine for dissemination in America. Is it the fault of those who write, or those who read, that any Jew who plows a field or drains a swamp or digs a well in Palestine, because he wants a country that he can call his own, must be dammed with the title of "idealist."

Granted that a few decades ago there was some excuse—although little foundation—for the affinity between "Palestine" and "idealism." The need for a physical as well as a spiritual home had not impressed itself on many Jewish minds. Therefore, a Jew who said, "I want to plant my own cabbage patch in my own country and live there or die there" was a strange creature who for want of a better name was known by some as an "idealist" and by others as a "madman." In the last analysis the words were synonymous indicating a subnormal or abnormal type of being.

However, it seems incredible that today—simply because the nightmares of Europe have not touched America—the Jews in America can still think of Palestine as an ideality rather than a reality. But such is the case, for I repeat that my friend, Mrs. M. is obscure and therefore characteristic. The average Jew (unless he is completely apathetic) would shed a few sentimental tears over the young Americans who are building Ein-Hashofet [the first kibbutz established by youth movement immigrants from the United States and Poland in 1937], an isolated settlement hemmed in by mountains. The last time I was there, the members told me how much they were paid for their sheep's wool a month ago, and how valuable their dove dung is for crop fertilizer. They don't call themselves "idealists." Neither do I. Call them wise. Call them courageous. But above all else, call them realists. For there is nothing more real on the face of the earth than the fruit trees of Ein-Hashofet, which they have wrung from the rocks.

In the same way that the Jews who are building this country are not "idealists," the country is not an "ideal." It is intensely real and so are its problems. Some worry about the sewage system in Tel Aviv—it leaks during the rainy season. Others operate chemical works where they make physiques to relieve constipation. Others make sausage links. And the proprietors of the factory for manufacturing contraceptives have to consider the high price of rubber importation. These are all very real problems that have little in common with Galahadian "idealism."

And what has become of all this reality? A reality. A country that—despite the precariousness of its political fortunes—contains more happy and dignified and stable Jews than almost any other country in the world. Despite the recent curbage of immigration, the population of Palestine is now 30% Jewish, which is a higher proportion than any other country, comparing with 9.8% in Poland, 4% in Romania, and 3.5% in the United States.

Also, Jewish manual workers in Palestine represent 78% of the wage earners (69,500 out of 88,500) comparing with 44% in the United States. This fact is also impressive at a time when the body and soul of the Jewish nation has become enervated and distorted by its abnormal attachment to the professions.

But more real than anything is our right to protest against injustice. Only a few months ago American Jewry protested against the threatened partition of Palestine [the report by the Peel Royal Commission from July 1937 that recommended partition of Palestine between Arabs and Jews]. There was no need to plead for mercy or pity or toleration. The plea was based on the fact that we had been promised a portion of this land to which we have a historic attachment and that we had fulfilled our obligation in developing it. This right to protest is precious. It is dignified. It is unique to Palestinian Jewry. It is reality.

This week I heard of a Jew from Palestine who, when traveling in Europe, was offered eight hundred pounds for his passport. There are pathetically few countries left now where a Jew would not sell his shirt for a certificate to Palestine. At one time, pious Jews kissed the soil of Palestine when they arrived. It is doubtful if any Jews were ever shaken by a deeper emotion than those wretched, broken creatures who are stepping onto the soil of Tel Aviv today.

All this has nothing to do with ideals and idealism and idealists. It is reality reduced to its simplest denominator. The cataclysm that has engulfed the Jewish nation elucidates, but does not alter, the original intention of the BILU settlers—to build a real home for a people who have a real need for a real home.

There never was a nation of more red-blooded realists than the Jews who inhabited Palestine two thousand years ago. They tilled their soil, tended their flocks, defended themselves against invasion, and lusted after women. All realistic literature is insipid compared to the realities of the Bible. Idealism with all of its accompanying illnesses was inflicted on the Jews as a result of their exile. Therefore, if idealists exist, surely it is those Jews in the Diaspora who have failed to grasp in any adequate manner the real need for a home, and not those who have returned to tend their flocks.

Mrs. M., although your intentions may be the best, I challenge your right to call us in Palestine "idealists." And I object to your reference to yourselves as "plain human beings, selfish"—for you imply that we in Palestine are not plain, selfish human beings. We are selfish. We want a home. We are plain human beings because wanting a home is the fundamental instinct of any plain human being. And we are as concerned with the little spot on which we stand as you are. For we believe that this little spot will solve actual problems for as many homeless Jews as we can get into it. And we believe that it will solve spiritual problems for those Jews who—while not in need of a home—are in need of the dignity that nothing short of a national home can give.

We believe this not as idealists but as the hardest-headed realists that Jewry has produced since those glorious days when Laban deceived Jacob [see biblical story of Laban who gave his daughter Leah in marriage to Jacob, after the latter had worked seven years for Rachel—Genesis 29] in a scandalous manner; Delilah snipped Samson's hair and Bar Kochba defended Bethar.

PRIVATE LETTER TO ELENE

Re: Visit from Jay and the Peel Commission's Recommendation

Summer of 1937
Givat Brenner
A letter from Bar-Adon's personal archive

After a two-week visit of her former boyfriend, the Rabbi Joel Karlin (Jay), Kahn wrote to her friend Elene. When Jay leaves, she realizes that he will not come to live in Palestine. When she rationally examines the challenges of immigration from his eyes, how difficult it is for an American rabbi to move to Palestine, she is upset but determined to stay. Kahn gives her own reaction to the Peel Commission's recommendation on the partition of Palestine to Jewish and Arab states.

Dear Elene:

It is Saturday and I should be doing some of the writing that I promised myself all week to do today. But I can't get down to it, so meantime I am writing to you. Jay left last week and I returned home after a two-week absence, so my work has piled up. I have been so depressed all week and unable to write. So, during my half free day I made a garden around my lift, which I had wanted to do for some time. No matter how you feel, you can dig the ground, carry manure, etc. I guess I will get back to normal soon, but Jay's being here has upset me very much. Like everything else, being alone becomes a habit. But after being with him for two weeks, it is hard to be alone again. In a few days it will be nine years since we met and I wonder if there has ever been such a mess. When I was in America I asked him to come here, if only for a week. I felt somehow that if I had him here alone in peace and away from his family, he would see it as I do and want to stay. He is talking about returning, but I have little hope that he will. The time went very quickly and it was simply impossible to have him see all the things I wanted to. We went flying around from place to place, seeing things and people, and I am afraid that in the end it must have been a jumble in his mind. Besides, the summer is a bad time for traveling and he is much more influenced by externals than I am. He suffered from the sun all the time and was usually tired. If we were delayed by buses or trains and he missed a meal, he had a headache. I never realize the difficulties of this country until I have an American visitor. Then it is more trying for me than for them because I feel responsible for everything, including the sun. Personally, I can't see where it's any hotter here than in Phila[delphia], but I guess I must be wrong. All in all, I feel discouraged. I think he is too old to start in here of his own free will as it would mean several years of getting adjusted, learning modern Hebrew, etc. and I'm afraid he hasn't the patience. If he were like the Germans he would do it. But otherwise, I don't think he is interested enough to face the readjustment. Also, I hesitated to persuade him too strongly as conditions here are such that to influence anyone to come is a responsibility. We wait daily for disturbances and there is no way of telling when, if ever, we can expect peace. Also, the economic future, under the new system with us paying tribute to the Arabs, is uncertain. None of us know what we are facing, which is all right for us—but you don't feel like dragging someone else into it. Also, I don't believe that anyone can face the worry and irritations of living here until they wholeheartedly believe in it—which is why I always feel so sorry for the Germans, even when I dislike them, as I usually do. I suppose the sensible thing for me to do would be to have returned with him. In a way I was tempted, and yet I never seriously considered it. I can't see where life in America would hold anything for either of us. I have never been interested in business. His main work is funerals and weddings, business of the lowest order. If he came here there might be hope of his doing some of the things I used to think he was capable of doing. In America, he won't. So I think it's best for me not to compromise; either to have him the way I want or not at all. Anyhow, it was a hectic two weeks and I feel like I'd been run over with a lawn mower…meanwhile, about six articles are long overdue and I can't seem to get down to anything. Before he came I was quite happy here but now it is very difficult. I am waiting anxiously now to hear the fate of my play. The next thing I will do is a children's story, which is all worked out in my mind and shouldn't take long. Then I hope to start a novel. I am still very happy about having given up the *Post*. Harry Davidowitz [writer and translator], who is the only one who has read my play, says that it is a much better and more mature piece of work than my book, and I feel too that it shows the effect of having been done in peace and quiet. As for politics, things are still so unsettled that no one knows what the end will be and you can read as much in the papers as I know. Some are very depressed and discouraged because we have so little, and not even Jerusalem. Others feel that we will be better off to have the thing settled once and for all, even if it is a small portion, and that later we may have the hope of buying land from the Arabs, as they are always glad to make money and not as antagonistic to us as the British like to believe. The other evening, Davidowitz said, and I think rightly, how little reason we have to be depressed. About thirty years ago, we had absolutely nothing, and people came here to settle under the Turkish rule with no protection whatever. Now, we are being offered a state, even though a small one. It is really the first time since biblical times we have had the opportunity to hold part of the country. So the work here has not been in vain. All in all, the people here are not as opposed to the plan as Dr. Wise [American Zionist leader, Reform rabbi] and others in America. I think that if the boundaries were a bit more generous and included Jerusalem, the majority of the population would favor the idea. But we have a lot of fun planning our Jewish State—it will mean foreign ambassadors, coins, add everything else that goes with a nation—and it will be half the width of the city of Cleveland. And no doubt we will be in a constant state of civil war just as they were in the Bible because the Jews haven't changed a bit. The most interesting feature will be that labor will be the ruling class—the only country outside of Russia—and things are so messy there that you don't know what's what. Well, now I've gotten started, maybe I'll do some writing after all.

Do let me hear from you.

Love Dot

WESTERN JEWRY AND PALESTINE

February 4, 1938
An article from Bar-Adon's personal archive

Kahn discusses the connection between the Jewish national home in Palestine and the Jewish communities of the Americas, the British Empire, and Western Europe, i.e., the wealthier, safer Jewish communities, whose support for Jewish settlement in Palestine tended to be financial and political. Kahn argues for greater involvement on the part of English-speaking Zionists via their advice and service to Zionist organizations

Signs have not been wanting lately of a deeper appreciation of the importance to Palestine of the Jewries of America, the British Empire and Western

Europe. Like many other truths, its realization has been quickened by world events. With startling rapidity, East European Jewry, since the World War, has suffered an increasing decline in wealth and political power. The once powerful Russian Jewry, the spiritual and material reservoir of the Jewish people before the War, is entirely absent from the theater of Jewish activity and hence, too, has no part in the work for Palestine. Polish Jewry, though three and a half million strong, is being cruelly and deliberately deprived of its strength, and for the most part must wrestle with the problem of self-preservation. With the rise to power of anti-Semitic elements, the mass of Romanian Jewry is now being threatened by a similar fate. In Yugoslavia, too, there are indications of the effect of the anti-Jewish persecution stimulated by Nazi Germany. It has become commonplace that the center of gravity of the Jewish world is inevitably moving westward, and that the fate of the Jewish people will increasingly lie with the Jews of those enlightened and democratic lands where they are able to serve their race in complete loyalty to their respective countries. The full implications of this profound change of emphasis—we might say, change of axis—of the Jewish world, need not be recited here. But in respect to Palestine, we would ask whether the far-reaching significance of this change has been adequately pondered and whether the measures that it logically and urgently demands, adopted? The assumption of office this week by Mrs. Rose Jacobs, who was President of American Hadassah, as the sole English-speaking member of the Jewish Agency Executive, draws attention to the very sparse representation of Western Jewry in the direction of the leading institutions of the Zionist organization [in those days, the Jewish Agency for Palestine] and the Yishuv, especially in Palestine. The wide discrepancy between the share of American and British Jewry in providing the revenue for maintaining and upbuilding the Jewish national home is on the one hand, and the share that they personally bear in the management of the organizational system, which automatically determines such representation, is on the other hand. The Zionist of the United States and such countries as Great Britain, South Africa and Canada have not emphasized their party affiliations, being far too occupied with the actual burden of fundraising, organization and propaganda activities. Hence other groups not more important or influential or useful, by concentrating on the use of the party machine, have obtained due and perhaps overdue representation in the administrative bodies. It is easy to assert that English-speaking Zionists must adapt themselves to party politics and that when they bring their influence to bear through the party channels, they will be able to pull their full weight. But such a bureaucratic defense of the present situation, while convenient, will only prolong existing conditions to the detriment of the movement as a whole.

The English-speaking Zionist does not press his claim to office or authority. He does not hammer at the gates of our institutions for a seat on their directorate. He is content to work loyally and modestly and anonymously. He will not pursue any party advantage to secure a position. His respect for those who have borne the burden of authority for so many years is too deep and his loyalty so unquestioned, that he will not seek to push himself in their place. When approached for service, he will respond, and make no demands. The point we are making is that we cannot afford to permit party *shibboleths* [catchwords] to withhold from Palestine the cooperation of these increasingly important sections of Jewry. It is their pride, and not to their discredit, that they have neglected party strategy for positive effort. If we desire to obtain the full advantage of the power and potentialities of the great Jewries of the West, overtures must be made to their leading personalities—they must be invited and encouraged, indeed we would say mobilized, to fill positions of influence and authority in the Yishuv and in the Zionist organizations. The board of directors of one of the two principal funds of the movement includes no Zionist from the countries we have mentioned; that of the other has two out of thirteen, both residents abroad. Yet half of the receipts of these funds come precisely from those lands. This is not due to the attitude of the management of those funds, but solely to the all-powerful party soulless machinery. If a loan were to be raised in certain circles, the lenders would doubtless insist upon representation in its disbursement, and equally doubtlessly obtain it, because that would not be a party transaction.

It is true that on their part, the Zionists of the English-speaking world owe a duty personally to identify themselves more fully with our work in Palestine, but in this respect there has been a considerable improvement in recent years. Americans and British Jews have, in many directions of public activity in Palestine, proved their ability and devotion and success. Miss Henrietta Szold [founded Hadassah in 1912, immigrated to Palestine in 1918, and was the first woman on the Zionist executive committee] is a shining example in more than one sphere. The Hebrew University owes a tremendous debt to another American Jew, Dr. J. L. Magnes [prominent Reform rabbi who immigrated to Palestine and served as the first chancellor of the Hebrew University (1925) and later as its president (1935–48)]. The Acting Chairman of the Zionist Bank, Mr. L. Braudo, was formerly the President of the South African Zionist Federation, and among the founders of one of the leading mortgage banks. Mr. J. Janower, formerly Chairman of the Jewish National Fund in South Africa. The campaign for middle-class Jewry in Palestine is being directed by an American Jew, Mr. E. Neumann, formerly a member of the Zionist Executive and Chairman of the J.N.F. in the United States and the founder of a number of economic enterprises in Palestine. The Palestine Economic Corporation of New York and the Palestine Corporation of London have assumed increasing importance in the economy of the country and have sent to the country Jews who have shown their capacity. In the artistic sphere, the Palestine Symphony Orchestra owes much to an English Jew in Palestine, while the social, charitable, as well as national activities of the Yishuv have benefited considerably from the advice and service of English-speaking Jews. But such activity has largely been rendered in a personal rather than a representative capacity and is by no means a scale in consonance with the weight and latent power of the Jewries from which these Zionists hail, and with which in most cases, they retain the closest ties.

Lest it be thought that we overlook the greater need of Palestine on the part of Eastern European Jewry, which naturally must provide for many years the bulk of immigration, we would emphasize that the strengthening of American and British influence in our movement will inevitably, by evoking a still great contribution from such Jewries, redound to the greater…

A CALL FOR THE YOUTH OF THE UNITED STATES TO IMMIGRATE TO ISRAEL

Without a date, probably the end of the 1930s
An article from Bar-Adon's personal archive

Kahn responds to Emil Bernhard Cohn's article in the December 22 [no year written] issue of New Palestine, a journal published by the Zionist Organization of America, in which Cohn argues that a Zionist who chooses not to immigrate to Palestine does not forfeit his moral integrity. Kahn understands that most older Americans would not subject themselves to the difficulties of beginning a new life in Palestine;

*in addition, the Zionist cause is in constant need of funds, which comes
mainly from American Zionists. Her call, however, is to young American
Zionists: they are desperately needed as pioneers.*

I read with interest "The Land vs. The People" by Emil Bernhard Cohn,
which appeared in the December 22 issue of *New Palestine* [journal published by the Zionist Organization of America]. He asked whether a
Zionist forfeits "his moral integrity unless he pursues his ideals to their
furthest conclusion—namely to Palestine?" And he answers "No."

I should like to dispute his answer, confining myself, however to the
American youth. Those who are acquainted with the present adjustment
struggles in Palestine of middle-aged European refugees could hardly
be fanatical enough to expect that many Americans would willfully and
unnecessarily subject themselves to similar trials. In addition, funds are,
and will continue to be for some time, one of the main lifestreams of the
country. The land of Israel must be redeemed with gold. Land purchase on
a comprehensible scale is just beginning. In view of present world catastro-
phes, this gold must come from America. Casting aside any other consideration, this reason alone would enable the American Zionist to retain his
moral integrity when he lends his support from afar.
As for the youth—

I believe that the Call to Arms of Yosef Vitkin [ardent Zionist who
expressed many of the ideals that led to the Second Aliyah. In 1905 he
wrote and distributed a pamphlet entitled "A Call to the Youth of Israel
whose Hearts are with their People and with Zion," in which he encouraged aliyah based on the principles of manual labor in the national home-
land], a Palestinian teacher to the youth of the Diaspora, is more meaningful
today than when it was uttered in 1904.

"Awake, O youth of Israel! Come to the aid of your people. Your
people lie in agony. Rush to its side. Band together; discipline yourselves
for life or death; forget all precious bonds of childhood; leave them behind
forever without a shadow of regret, and answer to the call of your people."

"We must fight with the courage of those for whom there is no possible retreat; with a fury equal to that of animals robbed of their young."

"You are not unneeded—though they told you so. You are as indis-
pensable to the people and the land as is air to every man. Arm yourselves
with love of land and people, with love of freedom, with great patience—
and come!"

For the young Zionist, wherever he is, Vitkin pointed the way in one word—"come." Anything less is compromise, which is incompatible with moral integrity. The land must be built with young hands. These hands are as necessary as in the days of the BILU. A decade ago, Palestine was primarily a land of youth. Such is not the case today. In recent years, refugee ships have been bringing us the old, the crushed, the disabled, the halt and the lame. To offset this, we need youth as never before. A literature has grown up around *chalutziut* [pioneering]. And still the waste places in Galilee and elsewhere cries out for hands. Our task has just begun.

There is the proverbial argument that Americans should not usurp the place of refugees. Surely this is rationalization to cover the woeful fact that until now the American Ha-Halutz movement has been practically nil, except theoretically. It is a movement of adherents who have not moved. American youth has a duty to fulfill in Palestine that is unique, and therefore he usurps the place of no one. The proportionately few instances where he has come, and has remained, give categorical testimony to the fact that the American comes bearing gifts. This is not because he is an American, but because every nation has its own gifts to bear.

The settlement of Ein-Hashofet in the mountains of Ephraim [established by youth movement immigrants from the United States and Poland in 1937] is the shining example of what Americans can do when they band together in sufficient numbers to make themselves felt. Although they speak only Hebrew—and although there is no Hebrew word for "efficiency"—they have introduced this valuable asset into all aspect of their settlement. They are young yet and it is too early to arrive at snap judgments. But even in these first stages, it is possible to see that American training is important in the Palestinian melting pot.

I think I will not be accused of bias if I say that there is no better material than the American youth who comes clean, strong and healthy from a land of freedom to participate in the upbuilding of the new-old land of freedom for his own people.

However, aside from the groups at Ein-Hashofet, Affikim and Kfar Menahem, his weight is scarcely felt in the settlements. On the whole, he does not come. And when he comes, he frequently returns before he has even smelt the smoke of battle. Oh, the crying shame of these young "America-bound." The ease with which these American youth abandon the challenge when they meet the first adjustment difficulties may be owing to the fact that they too believe that they can retain their moral integrity without pursuing the ideals to their furthest conclusions.

Comment on Vitkin's call of 1904 is redundancy. Today, as never before, we must fight "with a fury equal to that of animals robbed of their young."

Today, as never before, "Your people lies in agony."

Today, as never before, the Jewish youth must "forget all precious bonds of childhood."

No amount of rationalization can exempt with honor the American youth. At this hour, the future of the Jewish people rests, chiefly, on the shoulders of American and Palestinian Jewry. The duties in America can be adequately fulfilled by the middle-aged and the Zionistically inclined youth who do not demand complete moral integrity.

However, the American youth who seeks a moral integrity that recognizes no rationalization and no compromise has a straight road before him: "You are not unneeded—though they told you so. Arm yourselves with love of land and people, with love of freedom, with great patience—and come!" "And come!"

WOMEN IN THE HISTADRUT [JEWISH LABOR FEDERATION]

1941
An article from Bar-Adon's personal archive

This article discusses the place of women as workers and full-fledged members of the Jewish Labor Federation. Bar-Adon points out the transition made by Zionist pioneering women from road construction and the heaviest of farm labor to work in teaching, child care, and raising of vegetables and poultry. This transition was accompanied by the establishment of women's cooperatives for laundresses, seamstresses, and others.

Women. We had been told that the women of Palestine have written a daring chapter in the annals of labor federations. As members of the Histadrut, they enjoy absolute equality and voting privileges with the men. Strangely enough, the wives of workers may automatically become full-fledged members, even if they do not belong to a trade union.

In Palestine the housewife comes into her own, for her domestic duties are considered as a profession or trade. Running her own home puts her on par with a wage earner. Therefore women comprise 47% of the Histadrut membership, totaling 52,694. Of this number, 27,709 are housewives; 12,698 are wage earners; 9,565 are in communal settlements; and 2,722 are in cooperative settlements.

There is no condescension on the part of the Histadrut toward its women. Everything, including the granting of reduced dues, is done to encourage their active participation. Why? We are reminded again that the Histadrut is not only a labor federation, but looks toward a labor commonwealth. It is aware that no socialistic movement is basically strong unless it is wholeheartedly supported by the women. Since the Histadrut wishes to inculcate its ideology into every worker's home, it is of supreme importance that the women form an integral part of the federation.

"Are the women nominal members, mere shadows of their husbands, or do they carry weight as individuals?" we ask.

We are advised to visit a farm school, typical of others in various parts of the country, where young women receive agricultural training. These farm schools are one of the many activities sponsored by the Council of Women Workers, the autonomous organization of the women.

The Farm School is only a quarter of an hour's ride from the heart of Jerusalem, the next-door neighbor of Government House. The school enjoys an exquisite view of the Holy City, being far enough away to make it appear like a fine etching and close enough to render all the details, church towers and mosque cupolas.

Seen from here, Jerusalem is an ancient, picturesque relic. But in direct contrast is this modern farm school, founded and supervised by a woman Rachel Ben Zvi and run entirely by young women. Not only are these young women taught agriculture, equipping them to fill posts as specialists in settlements, but also the Farm School practically supports itself from its own products.

We tour the farm—fields of vegetables, fowl runs, and tree and flower nurseries. We see tens of sturdy young farmerettes going about their tasks and are told that they came from more than twenty different countries. Large numbers arrived only recently from Nazi-persecuted countries. Hardly have they descended from the gangplank of the ship when they are sent to these schools and equipped to play constructive roles in the upbuilding of the country.

And now we hear something of the gigantic role that women have played in Palestine. Indeed, the fact that the doors of the Histadrut are open to them is no mere gesture—they have earned equal rights. In the early days of settlement, women accompanied the men to every outpost no matter how desolate, perilous, or disease ridden. In the hundreds of small cemeteries that dot the country are the names of women who fell as victims of disease or of marauders. Many of those simple tombstones bear only the first names, "Rachel"—"Sara"—"Deborah"—and each tombstone tells a story of stirring days and stirring deeds.

Just as in other pioneer countries, the brunt of the burden fell on the women who had to manage the household and raise the children under most primitive conditions. Our narrator tells as stores of women, who, while rocking the baby's cradle, kept a watchful eye on snakes swinging from the roof rafters.

Not only did the women undergo the physical dangers and privations involved in pioneering, they were staunch followers and fiery leaders of the labor ideology. As early as 1907, Manya Shohat, who is today a leader in a Galilean settlement, was the moving spirit in the first experiment in collective living in Segrea, which was founded after Manya had toured collective settlements in America.

In those days the women demanded a full share in work as well as privileges. They undertook the heaviest farm work and did their part of the road construction. They were fine horsewomen and excellent marksmen. These women, as individuals and as a group are material for thrilling adventure stories—in fact they have already been put between covers in a book called *The Ploughwomen*.

Of course, as the country became more built up, the pendulum swung back. Women abandoned the heavy farm work and road construction for more suitable jobs in the children's houses, the kitchens, vegetable gardens, poultry runs, etc. But when the occasion arises, the old tradition is not broken. In the new settlements that are going up even today in isolated places, the women fill important and sometimes hazardous jobs. And during the disturbances of 1936–1940 [also called the Arab Revolt in Palestine—a nationalist uprising by Palestinian Arabs under the British Mandate against British colonial rule and mass Jewish immigration], they demanded and won the right to be on guard in order to relieve the men. Most of the signal towers—the only connection between endangered settlements—were in the hands of the women. In fact, a woman in a watchtower became the symbol of those trying years.

In the early pioneering days, life was harder but less complicated. There were fewer people and therefore fewer social problems. Today, it is not enough for a woman to know how to handle a gun or to ride a horse. There are thousands upon thousands of women in towns and villages who are looking to their sisters for help and guidance.

And now we hear of the activities of the Council of Women Workers. This council trains women, helps them to get jobs and even creates jobs when there are none. Since this is an immigrant country, there are thousands of young women here on their own hook, with no means of earning a livelihood.

There are other farm schools, such as this one we are visiting, where hundreds of girls receive agricultural training. Another major project is the "House for Pioneers," which was established largely through funds sent by the Women's League for Palestine in America. There are two such institutions, one in Haifa and one in Tel Aviv. The purpose of the first institution, started in Haifa, was merely to provide cheap lodgings for the immigrant girl until she got her bearings. However, it was found that assistance during the readjustment period was imperative. Many girls, coming from well-to-do homes were unequipped to do any useful work. Therefore the scope has vastly widened and the two homes now serve as training centers. The girls are trained in domestic science, weaving, nursing, shoemaking and other trades and professions. In 1940–41, 1,500 girls were trained, placed in jobs, and absorbed into constructive life in the country. When visiting the Haifa institution, we were struck by the fact that it succeeds in not resembling an institution at all. Tucked away behind trees and bushes, it achieves a homey atmosphere.

As part of their endeavor to help women earn a livelihood, the Council of Women Workers has been instrumental in establishing cooperatives all over the country, run by women. Laundresses, seamstresses, and others are members of these cooperatives. The largest is the three Workers' Kitchens in which four hundred women are employed.

It must be borne in mind that the Oriental attitude toward women was deeply embedded in Palestine, where the Arab still rides in state on his donkey while his wife trots after, often balancing the kindling wood on her head. Therefore securing proper working conditions and wages for women meant a battle on many fronts. Today women are taking their places in all kinds of work. For instance, during the past two years, 1,500 girls have worked in military camps, totaling 150,000.

OPEN LETTER FROM THE EMEK TO…A CHILD WENT FORTH

July 22, 1947
Merhavia
An article from Bar-Adon's personal archive

This was an open letter to a child who had been transferred from the Exodus 1947 ship to a battleship of the British Royal Fleet when the British Mandatory authorities refused to allow the Exodus 1947 passengers—Holocaust survivors who did not have legal immigration certificates to Palestine—to disembark in Haifa.

Dear Child:

You may be anyone of the nine hundred who are bound for anywhere or nowhere. Now that you have been transferred from the *Exodus 1947* to the royal fleet, you have oh so much more room to stretch your legs. Perhaps you can even lie down. But you felt better on the *Exodus 1947* [a ship carrying Jewish emigrants from France to Palestine, July 1947. Most of the emigrants were Holocaust survivors who had no legal immigration certificates to Palestine; they were sent back to Europe by the British Royal Navy] when you thought you were going home. If you could express yourself, you would call the more commodious ship that has snatched you back to exile the true "hell ship." But you won't protest. Those who saw you in Haifa told us that you are quiet, well behaved. That's bad for a child. But then, you've never been a child, really. You've never been a child.

So you won't have heard of a great American called Walt Whitman who wrote a great deal about freedom and liberty and justice. This man, Walt Whitman said, "Remember the hospitality that belongs to nations and men!—(Cursed be nation, woman, man, without hospitality!)" [*sic*] You, child, didn't ask for hospitality. You asked for the promised right to come home. You were denied even the hospitality.

This man, Walt Whitman, wrote about a child. The child wasn't you. He never knew children like you. There never were children like you. But this is what he wrote:

> *There was a child went forth every day,*
> *And the first object he looked upon…that object he became.*

And that object became part of him for the day,
or a certain part of the day, or for many
years, or stretching cycles of years.

This child in Whitman's poem wasn't you, because he looked upon so many things that you've never seen or perhaps never heard of: "the early lilacs"—"apple trees covered with blossoms"—"the schoolmistress that passed on her way to school"—"the mother at home quietly placing the dishes on a supper table."

You Saw the Carmel

All these wonderful things, like a mother preparing supper, the child of Whitman looked upon. Let's not recall what you have looked upon except for one thing. You have looked upon Palestine and seen the lights of Carmel in the dead of night and the misty dawn. So you know that there really and truly is a Palestine. All this was part of you before you looked upon it. And now, how much more so. You, child, were a part of us before you came. And now, how much more so.

If I tell you that the Emek was black today in spite of the July sunshine, will you understand? But first you must understand how golden and green and glad the Emek is. Today all this gold and green was black and sullen and outraged, and hurt beyond the power for tears, because a ship had been sent to nowhere, and you, Child, went forth. Farmers went to their barns and somehow saw your face in the pails of good frothy milk. They came back from the fields with wagons of corn, and somehow the sound of the wagon wheels was like the sound of a ship going nowhere. True, the farmers had only read about you, and yet, Child, they know you, for you are part of them. They have room for you here. Before you were born, Child, they were reviving this valley for you. So that's why the gold and green and fertility of this Emek was black and sullen and hurt today.

The Carmel will wait and the valley will wait and you will come back. The lies they may tell you about being "welcomed" elsewhere to help build up other countries you will not believe. The recognition of that lie will be in your blood. You have looked upon your home and it will be part of you "for many years of stretching cycles of years."

"There was a child went forth."You too, Child, went forth.You went forth as no other child has gone forth.And your going forth became a part of all of us here "for many years of stretching cycles of years."

PRIVATE LETTER TO ELENE: AFTER THE UNITED NATIONS RESOLUTION ON NOVEMBER 29, 1947

December 1, 1947
Merhavia, Eretz, Israel
A letter from Bar-Adon's personal archive

Bar-Adon wrote this letter two days after the United Nations' decision to divide Mandatory Palestine into two countries: Jewish and Arab. The "partition plan" was accepted by the Jewish leadership but was turned down by the Arab leadership. Bar-Adon expresses her feeling about the United Nations' decision, providing a description of the events as she experienced them and the reaction to the decision both at Merhavia, the moshav where she lived, and in the country.

Dear Elene:

As the first letter I am writing in my capacity of a citizen of this new Jewish State under the sun—the letter should be inspired and inspiring. But it won't be, because we're all still dog-tired. I kept saying to Azziz [Pessah Bar-Adon's nickname] that it seems like a dream—a state arising after two thousand years of interruption—to which my husband replied that I wasn't original because that was how David expressed it in Psalm 126—"We were like them that dream"; and in fact, the whole Psalm I can describe for you better than I can the rejoicing here—and since you are looking at the Bible, read, too, Psalm 129.

These are great days and it is a privilege to be alive in them. All last night the whole country rang with the song "Am Israel Hai" (the people of Israel lives)—and we really do!You can imagine the tension of the last few days with everything depending on America and America's stand being anything but clear after Greece voted "no." Then came the Thanksgiving recess when you no doubt gorged on turkey...but for us the day seemed endless. Then came Friday night when we expected the vote to be taken. Azziz drank "L'haim" at supper and added "To the Jewish State." I gave him a filthy look because I was afraid there might be a disappointment for Doron afterwards, so Azziz made a little speech "To the Jewish State, my son, whenever it comes, for some day it will come," and with that provision I, too, drank.

Friday night, at 12 o'clock here, France proposed the 24-hour post-ponement. So that we dragged through Saturday—I was sure and so were many others—that this postponement might lead to the acceptance of Colombia's proposal for a postponement of several months. Anyway, by Saturday night we heard that "yes" and "no" from Lake Success [the locale of the UN debate]—and it was terrific! And then the entire country just went mad for two whole days—singing and dancing in the streets, bars wide open and free drinks—flags—an armistice celebration that had been awaited two thousand years. I started the celebration in our village on our rooftop because this was the first house to be built in this valley forty years ago. After the announcement we just pinned the flag together, my blue wedding veil and a white towel and lit it up electrically. Then all the farmers rushed in dressed or half-dressed and went wild. After an hour of that we were called to the synagogue—a huge bonfire was lit outside—watchmen fired in the air like madmen, up to eighty danced in front of the ark—Azziz danced the Arab debka with a huge knife—and Doron whom I had pulled out of a sound sleep didn't close his mouth for three hours.

The first question Doron asked me when I awakened him was "When we get up tomorrow morning will the English be gone?" and when he asked me just what a "state" means and I explained that we would be just like any other nation, he answered, "Then the first thing we should do is to send Jews to England to bother them like they have bothered us.

There was so much to laugh about and so much to cry about—and the main point is that we still can't believe it. While I was deciding whether to get a turkey or a duck for the festive dinner, my husband announced, "Nothing should be killed to celebrate the Jewish State—an amnesty even for fowl"—I was disappointed, but saw his point—so we feasted on sardines, bologna and other long-dead things.

I am sure the drinking would have gone on for days, but seven Jews were killed on the roads and a three-day Arab demonstration began today, so there was some sobering up, but there is a feeling of confidence and I for one feel sure there will be no serious outbreak in Palestine—it may not be too pleasant for Jews in neighboring countries. Anyway, it's grand—and now we get down to things like creating a flag—stamps—coins—in fact, creating a whole nation and it's a tremendous job.

Last week I had to do a rush order—writing the text for a pamphlet of photos on Galilee. Although it is a short pamphlet, only about ten pages, I had to wade through lots of books for suitable quotations, etc., that recalled all the history of Galilee and made our present fight with the English seem just a contemporary sequel of battles with the Romans 1,500 years ago—For instance, the prayer of Bar Kochba who led the last revolt—"Don't help our enemies. As for us, we can take care of ourselves." Strangely enough, this is what the Agency has said and how the people feel here today. If England doesn't help the Arabs, we can take care of ourselves.

Crowds burst into the home of the old parents of Moshe Shertok's [head of the political department of the Jewish Agency and later Israel's second prime minister] wife and carried them through the streets on their shoulders, beds and all. The old man is said to have said in Yiddish—"I don't mind this performance, but there should have been a rehearsal." Did I tell you that people went nuts? I just read in the papers here of an old woman who asked her grandchild to dance in her dress—since she couldn't dance herself, she wanted her dress to dance!

Well enough for today—your Eretz Israel soil in a respectable container will be coming along—in the meanwhile I'll just put a few drops in this letter together with a cyclamen, the first spring flower to be on hand for the celebration—
Love
Dot

EPILOGUE

1948
Draft of the epilogue for the book, *Twin Villages of Merhavia*
From Bar-Adon's personal archive

Bar-Adon describes how she, her family, and neighbors marked the Partition Plan of November 29, 1947, in which the United Nations General Assembly decided on the establishment of two independent countries—one Arab and the other Jewish—in what was Mandatory Palestine.

In the early morning hours of November 30, 1947, the House [the Bar-Adon family lived in the first Jewish stone house built in the Jezreel Valley in 1911 by the agronomist Eliyahu Blumenfield and designed by the architect Alexander Baerwald] passed a milestone in its checkered career. An improvised blue and white flag fluttered from a corner of the flat roof as the villagers streamed to the House to celebrate the newly born Jewish State. I don't know whether this was the first flag to be hoisted in the Emek after the UN decision—but I like to think so. The House deserved that honor. And I like to think too that the first hora to the tune of "Am Israel Hai" ["The People of Israel Live"] was danced on the roof, with its parapet of petrified sandbags, relics of a stormy past.

Most of the villagers had retired. Who knew when or if the decision would be made that night? Besides, it was sowing season and they must be in the fields at daybreak. As one farmer said, "We've waited two thousand years—we can wait until tomorrow morning." But after that breathless counting of votes and the historic, "thirty-three in favor of partition…" we dispatched our neighbor on his motorcycle to honk the villagers to their feet and to ring the dairy gong.

Meantime what to do? Superstition had prevented us from preparing a flag or from stocking in wine and cakes. Over there, at Lake Success, our fate was in the lap of the gods and we tried to wait philosophically in the spirit of "what will be will be." Preparing things for a favorable decision might tempt the gods too much. Still, we housewives had allowed ourselves to lay in a few extra bottles of wine "for the Sabbath" we said. These we hastily arranged on the roof after the decision. With a piece of blue crepe and a length of toweling we nailed up an improvised flag and managed to floodlight it with reading lamps. Then we hastily painted "Am Israel Hai" and "Medina Ivrit" [Hebrew State] on planks and attached them to the petrified sandbags.

By this time, neighbors were climbing up the winding stairs to the roof. Together with the ringing of the dairy gong in the moshav, we could hear the dining hall gong in the kibbutz ringing down "Lover's Lane" and across the wadi [valley or riverbed that is usually dry]. In the distance, we could see torchlights and bonfires as Emek settlements signaled "mazal tov" one to the other and strove to attract the attention of those whose radios mightn't receive America.

The Jewish State, awaited for two thousand years, had been born, and we of this generation were privileged to be its first citizens. Can you believe it? Can it be true? These were the questions on the faces of those who trooped up our winding stairs. They had dressed hurriedly, some throwing clothes over their pajamas. There had been anticipation for months and tense waiting for weeks. Still, now that it had come, there was bewilderment and disbelief. Can it be true? But soon, the floodgates of joy broke wide open. All of this valley that stretched out from the roof was really theirs! Tomorrow they would be sowing their wheat and barley in the good earth that had become Jewish earth after two thousand years of waiting. Tonight under the stars—tomorrow under the sun—next month under the rain—this Emek had been pronounced theirs—of right.

Women who had worked together; suffered together; buried their dead together in this village clasped hands; looked long and deep into each other's eyes while the tears coursed down their cheeks unheeded. Men exchanged a gruff, unsteady "Mazal tov." The children, who had been roused from their sleep for this historic night and bundled up warmly, were nibbling the "strudel" and other goodies that the women had brought, asking questions about the "Medina Ivrit" (Jewish State), and gazing wide-eyed at the grown-ups. Why were the grown-ups behaving like children—except that they were a bit weepy?

The hora circle began and gradually widened. Feet stamped joyfully. Two old shomrim (watchmen) danced a hora in the center of the circle. Someone feared that the whole house might cave in from the impact. But those acquainted with the House harbored no doubt. On this night it was taking a new lease on life.

Suddenly word came that we were to convene in the synagogue. As we trooped down our main street toward the new white building, we saw the beginning of a bonfire in the open circle between the synagogue and the dairy. Dry branches were plentiful, for the rains had not yet begun. Late stragglers joined the party in twos and threes. Suddenly we were startled by shots. The men made a move toward their defense posts. Then came relieved laughter. It was only the watchmen firing into the air as part of the revelry.

The hora circle that began around the bonfire moved into the synagogue. The cooperative store had been opened and wine fetched. The elders of the village sat around a long table. The others danced—children, youth, parents, and grandparents. The swirling circle in the little synagogue took on the ecstatic quality of a "Simchat Torah" dance [the celebration marking the conclusion of the annual cycle of public Bible reading in which the celebrants dance all night]. For two thousand years this night had been awaited. And for decades, these villagers had waited, plowing their lands. Now it had come. We were only a few hundred—but the circle seemed to spread out to the other settlements in the Emek where the Hora was being danced—to the delirious streets of Tel Aviv—to Rehavia in Jerusalem—to the refugee camps—and to Broadway.

Shlomo, son of Noah, is dancing the Arab debka, flourishing a knife in bedouin fashion. Noah! Yenta Lea! All the others who had paved the way for this night. Scarcely a family in this little village tonight is without memories of those who, in the words of Noah, had plowed a furrow for the prophet Eliahu to see—but who had not been privileged to share in this night. Scarcely a family is without memories of dear ones slaughtered in Europe because the gate of Palestine had been closed. For them, it had come just too late.

Suddenly, I was tapped on the shoulder and asked to leave the circle of dancers. The other women were leaving too. The reason? A pious old man of eighty-three years wished to dance, and orthodoxy forbade him joining the circle with women. While we women made ourselves inconspicuous in corners, the all-male circle danced, the white-bearded patriarch seeming to gain strength as the tempo increased.

And within a fortnight, we paid our first toll. A son of the village, a lad of eighteen, was murdered while guarding a water pipeline in the Negev. Once again we gathered in the grassy circle between the dairy and the synagogue. There was no body to bring home. We gathered around a burning torch, at the foot of the flag, lying at half-mast. The same villagers in the same grassy plot as a fortnight ago. But tonight the youth were not dancing. They were in military formation. And as the torch burned low, and the figures of the farmers in their working clothes became blurred, one felt the grim bitterness and the will to fight to the end if need be, in this grassy plot. For the "neutrality" of the Mandatory was beginning to be felt, and where was the UN to enforce its own decision? As the torch flickered out, and the farmers drifted off again to the evening milking, we knew that even with the UN behind us, the battle might be lonely.

Today—several months later—the Emek waits, prepared to defend itself if necessary. It is March and the fields are green and fresh. On Givat Hamoreh, the anemone and cyclamen are in bloom, but there is neither time nor heart to pick them. At night, there is a symphony of light as one village projector mingles with the next. For the Emek never sleeps.

And the House? I think it is standing straighter than ever, and some of the lopsided shingles seem to have pulled themselves into line. Once again there are sandbags preparations—fortifications—for defense, which have characterized the House since it was built. One no longer exclaims with simple joy over the fact that the mountains of Transjordan can be seen so clearly from the roof, and revels in their changing color. Now one compute strategically, how far can be seen from the roof.

Farmers go to their fields during the day. Projectors comb the Valley at night. And there is a confident waiting for this chapter of history to be played out to the inevitable end.

On Atlantic City boardwalk with parents and sister, 1921

In Atlantic City, 1931

In Atlantic City, 1932

At a photographer's studio, 1932

Certificate of Naturalization as a citizen of Mandatory Palestine, 1935

Dorothy's trusty typewriter, 1930

Pioneers in the vegetable garden of Kibbutz Givat Brener. Bar Adon is first on left, 1938

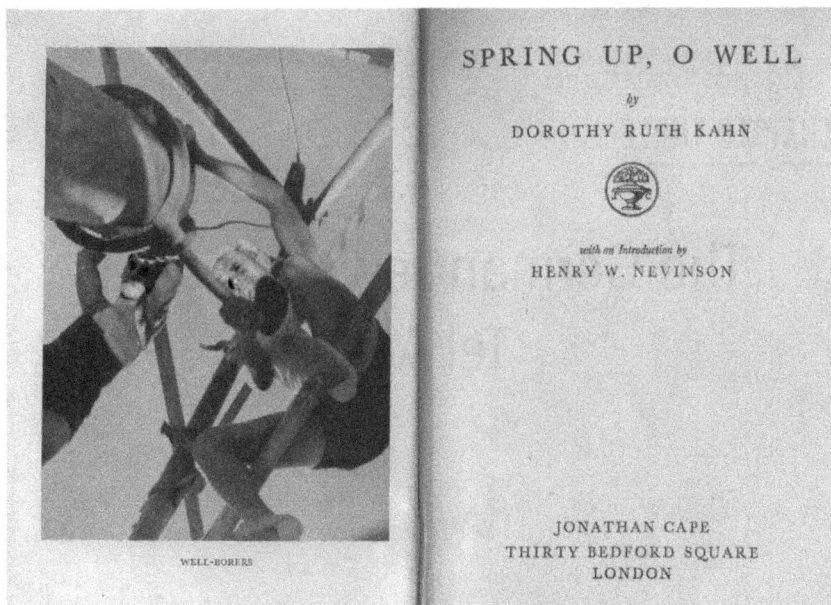

SPRING UP, O WELL

by

DOROTHY RUTH KAHN

with an Introduction by
HENRY W. NEVINSON

JONATHAN CAPE
THIRTY BEDFORD SQUARE
LONDON

WELL-BORERS

Frontispiece of Bar Adon's autobiography, 1936

CHAPTER THREE

The German Jews Conquer Tel Aviv

INTRODUCTION

From 1929 to 1939, the period of the fifth Aliya (the fifth "wave" of immigration of Jews to Palestine), some 220,000 Jews immigrated to Mandatory Palestine, thereby increasing the Jewish population from 175,000 to more than 400,000. Of those immigrants, 55,000–60,000 came from Germany, Austria, and Czechoslovakia. During the peak years of 1932 to 1935 some 30,000 immigrants (approximately one-fifth of the 150,000 immigrants during these years) came from Germany.

After the rise to power of the Nazi party in Germany in 1933, German Jews were forced out of the economic, cultural, scientific, political, and social life of the country in which their families had lived for centuries. Indeed, many Jews had seen themselves as Germans "of the Mosaic faith." The loss of businesses, possessions, and employment led many to emigrate. The refusal of a number of Western countries (the United States, Great Britain, France, and others) to accept Jewish-German emigrants led many to immigrate to Mandatory Palestine.

The immigrants from Central Europe came from countries that were culturally and economically modern and developed. Most of the immigrants had lived in big cities; many were business people, practitioners of the free professions, and well educated. As might be expected, on arriving in Palestine, they tended to settle in cities. The population of Tel Aviv thus grew from some 40,000 in 1931 to 135,000 in 1934. The economic, cultural, and human resources that they brought with them enabled the immigrants to greatly influence the growth of Tel Aviv, leading the city to become Mandatory Palestine's center of business, industry, trade (Tel Aviv Port was built), as well as culture and entertainment. The Israel Philharmonic Orchestra was founded in Tel Aviv, and the Habima and Ha'Matateh theaters were also active. A thriving nightlife, centered in restaurants and cafés, developed.

For Dorothy Bar-Adon, this economic blossoming, fueled as it was by a highly motivated, hardworking immigrant population, contrasted starkly with the America of the Great Depression that she had left. Bar-Adon wrote extensively about these immigrants and their struggles to build new lives for themselves, after leaving countries where they and their families had historic and cultural roots and leaving their immediate physical and cultural surroundings and sources of income.

Simultaneously Bar-Adon wrote about the contributions made by this immigrant population to the development of Tel Aviv in particular and the Yishuv as a whole. Today the headlines of some of her articles sound ironically surreal, even bordering on poor taste: "Hitler's Gift to Palestine," "The German Jews Conquer Tel Aviv," and "What Hitler Has Done to Tel Aviv." At the time, of course, nobody could have known the fate awaiting those millions of Jews who were unable or unwilling to leave Europe in the 1930s.

SAUSAGES AND BEER

Zif Zif, pp. 100–103
Unpublished manuscript from Bar-Adon's personal archive
Earlier version in *The Palestine Post*, "What Hitler Has Done to Tel Aviv," August 4, 1933

Kahn describes the transformation of Tel Aviv in August 1933 as a result of the influx of Jewish immigrants from Germany. Despite not speaking Hebrew, and often not able to work at the professions for which they had trained, the immigrants found work and began the process of integrating into the local Jewish communities. These immigrants brought with them high levels of medicine, culture, music, theater, dance, and architecture and left their marks on Tel Aviv.

The streets of Tel Aviv have been transformed by Herr Hitler. In fact they are no longer streets. They have become "Strassen." Tel Aviv can change her color as quickly as a chameleon, responding to the whims of a Russian czar, a brown shirt chancellor, or Wall Street quotations in America. Once Little Odessa, then Little Warsaw, now Little Berlin. The shops that display strings of fat and red sausages, varying in size and shape, are doing a rushing business, and schnitzel has leaped into the limelight. The wind, which carries the froth from beer steins, carries also the germs of new ideas—new enterprises—perhaps new culture.

In cafés and restaurants one is always conscious of the solidarity, which goes hand-in-hand with tweed caps and shorn heads, and of the substantiality, which distinguished the German frau from her more frilly sisters.

Word comes from America that Molly Picon [an American Jewish actress of stage, screen and television, as well as a lyricist and a star in the Yiddish theater], the comedienne, since her return from this country, is talking much of Palestine as the new "melting pot." Now while the German immigrants are still poised on the rim of the pot, we can witness the melting process. We see those who are preparing to leap in headfirst; those who are walking mincingly about the edge while eyeing the contents critically through thick glasses; those who are smacking their lips over the possibility of changing the flavor of the brew.

You cannot walk ten paces down any street in Tel Aviv without rubbing elbows with some German who arrived three months ago or three hours ago. How they will affect the Palestinian picture is a matter for speculation. However, today it is enough to sit back and watch them pouring into the city on every ship; milling about the streets; discarding tourist knickerbockers for linen shorts; surviving the consistently poor service in Tel Aviv restaurants; twisting good German into poor jargon, when necessary; attending night classes in Hebrew; and developing an appetite for Eskimo pies.

Numerous casual meetings with Germans in buses, restaurants and cafés, and sausage emporiums makes one believe that even while being melted the Deutsch are not to be caught off guard. While many are bewildered, the majority is processing with characteristic Teuton precision and exactitude.

This precision is apparently being shipped into Tel Aviv, along with the large packing crates that, these days, are making the port of Jaffa take on the aspect of a miniature New York harbor. It has even seeped into the bones of some of the more lackadaisical Tel Aviv merchants who are stocked up with a wide selection of German books.

A search during the past week for a Hebrew grammar in English was a complete failure. Book venders seemed amazed that an American could not learn Hebrew from a phrase book or an illustrated children's primer. Of course, if you would like a German-Hebrew grammar, you will be well accommodated. I wore out two pairs of sandals and a perfectly good temper while explaining in at least ten bookshops that if you couldn't read German, you couldn't find much light in a German grammar. Yes, the Germans are going about this business of learning Hebrew in a wholesale manner.

One newcomer was heard to remark, "We don't learn Hebrew as quickly as other people who come to Palestine but we will learn it more correctly."

Some of the immigrants seem to be exercising this same efficiency in locating themselves. Many of us require at least a fortnight to become what we term "adjusted" to physical Palestine. We remain in hotels fretting over the complications involved in searching for a room in a strange city where you don't know the language. Recently a young German girl shared a hotel room with me on the first night of her arrival. Late the following afternoon she returned to pack her luggage. Without speaking Hebrew, she had secured a clerical position and a room with a terrace and private entrance for one pound thirty piasters (although the rest of us are paying three and four pounds for a room because of the shortage said to be caused by the new immigration).

And so the melting continues—merrily for some, sadly for others. This week at a banquet I met a cinema photographer who wants to make pictures here à la Berlin, an orchestra conductor who is visiting symphonies in all cities and hamlets, and a woman dentist who would continue her specialty of straightening protruding teeth and also establish a branch of the Soroptimist (an international professional women's club).

There was the pretty blond girl who, over a glass of tea in an Allenby Street coffeehouse, confided in her limited English vocabulary that she has a position as a "propagandist" for a drug company. And in Germany, she had been studying medicine. Where is she living? In a room on Rothschild Boulevard "where the water runs always hot" for a few pounds a month. How long has she been in the country? Five days and a half.

There was the German boy who offered his assistance when I was haggling with an Arab over the purchase of a couple of red birds.

He completed the bargain and volunteered to carry the cage. What is he doing? Painting signs. And in Germany? He was an artist. He produces several interesting studies from the inside pocket of his dirty overalls, invites us to come to his studio-to-be for a sitting and departs with the most formal of continental bows ever achieved in a pair of overalls.

It is seven o'clock in the morning and a capable young person is solidly digging into cucumber salad. She tells us that she must hurry in order to be to her work in half an hour. She is working as a housemaid to augment the wages of her husband who was trying his hand as a plasterer. It is all rather an adventure. She is eighteen and he but a year older. The Hitler exodus brought about a hurried marriage and now they are honeymooning in Tel Aviv.

And so the pot is boiling—with much comedy as well as tragedy in the bubbles.

BY THE WATERS

Zif Zif, pp. 94–95
Unpublished manuscript from Bar-Adon's personal archive
Earlier version published in *The Palestine Post,* "By the Waters of Tel Aviv,"
August 15, 1933

Kahn shares a personal impression of the mixture of old and new, traditional and modern on the beach in Tel Aviv. Pioneers and tourists, children and caravans of camels, action, smells and moods, all are described vividly, enabling the reader to feel that he or she is experiencing the event.

"Rich man, poor man, beggar man, thief, doctor, lawyer, Arab chief." They're on the beach—all of them. The girl in the exaggerated suntan bathing suit who would be at home on the beaches of Miami or Lido is rubbing shoulders with two Muslim women who have daringly lifted their veils for a moment to glimpse the sea. A substantial looking real estate dealer from Brooklyn applies olive oil to a newly acquired sunburn while an Arab in the neighboring chair gathers his purple silk robe about his feet and settles down to enjoy "the big parade" for a few hours.

"This beach is just like Atlantic City," is the comment usually heard from newly arrived Americans. But one wonders if anywhere else in the world there is the conglomeration of yesterdays and tomorrows that is to be found on the Tel Aviv beach.

A bearded Jew who might have been walking along his seashore many, many centuries ago is almost sent sprawling by a bronzed *chalutz* [male pioneer] on a bicycle. An Arab girl whose face is partially hidden from view by jingling silver ornaments is surreptitiously eyed by a smart New Yorker garbed in mandarin pajamas. A party of about thirty scantily attired men and women who are sprinting down the beach in single file must break ranks to make way for a caravan of camels which is carrying sand from the Auja [Arabic for the Yarkon river]. A group of children, under the guidance of a teacher, are playing ball near the water's edge, completely nude, because science has proved the value of the sun's rays. Another group bathes nearby, completely nude, because they haven't any bathing suits.

No one need go hungry on the beach. One wonders what new product will be offered tomorrow, by some ingenious soul. "Eskimo Pies cold" and "Corn on the cob warm" are sung out in every key of the scale. Of course, there is enough soda in which to drown the entire population. Rolls are vended in a small way by boys carrying trays on their heads and on a big scale by those who "set up shop" in the middle of the sand. You have just begun to doze when some enterprising young tradesman begins calling out the virtues of his cakes. The next moment an Arab fisherman waves a string of small fish under your nose and lets you know that they can be purchased for a song. You politely tell him that, as far as you are concerned, he can take them back to the sea and drown them. He persists in exhibiting his catch which is now dangling on your knee.

Sophistication is slowly slipping into the Tel Aviv strand, you learn from one of the chair tenders, who tells you that all the smart bathing attire is a product of the last few years. He remembers when old shirts and petticoats comprised the average bathing costume.

And so the panorama is in action. There is a tourist being photographed atop a cardboard camel to give the folks at home a taste of the Orient. And a prime miss of three, nude except for a large string of blue crystal beads that is wetting her toes. A flat contraption, which is piloted by revolving oars, heads to the sea. A fat man in horn-rimmed spectacles is collecting shells in a cardboard box, and an Arab child follows in his tracks, picking up cigarette butts.

The Tel Aviv beach has many moods. The sun is setting now and the vendors have disbanded for dinner. In the distance is Jaffa and beyond, the outline of white vessels in the harbor. A handsome Arab in a flowing black robe rides into the last of the sunrays. The beach is bathed in a satisfying peace and quiet.

Unlike other beaches, the "Tel Aviv" beach does not have a "lockup" time. In a few hours it will be wide awake again with young people who will remain talking, singing and whispering until midnight and beyond.

A "POTATORIAN"

Zif Zif, pp. 81–83
Unpublished manuscript from Bar-Adon's personal archive
Earlier version in *The Palestine Post*, "On Tel Aviv Restaurants," August 17, 1933

> *During her first month in Tel Aviv, Kahn has to eat all her meals in restaurants; she witnesses the shortage of eating places for the hungry newcomers from all over the world. Her humoristic description and the advice she gives potential diners give a picture of the booming city.*

After a month of eating three meals a day in the restaurants of Tel Aviv one begins to wonder if a visit to Tel Aviv drove Gandhi [Mahatma Gandhi, preeminent leader of Indian independence movement] to his goat milk diet.

Anyone with a head for figures soon concludes that the most economically solid plan would be to rent a locker and a table in some restaurant, thereby dispensing with a room in which you can in any case spend very little time if you want three (or even two) square meals a day.

Much of life in Tel Aviv centers around the restaurants which have sprung up like mushrooms. However, with the continual influx of new arrivals, it is little wonder that the restaurateurs never seem to quite catch up with the hungry throng.

The newcomer who has normal curiosity happily seizes the opportunity to devote five and sometimes six hour of his day during his first fortnight to the process of being fed. In the dairy, vegetable, sausage and other miscellaneous eating places to be found in cellars, private parlors, roofs and every other conceivable spot, he is able to have a bird's eye view of life in Tel Aviv.

Youth from all parts of the world break bread (literally because usually during rush hours, the quarter loaves are not sliced). Everything from the depression in America to Bialik's poetry is discussed over beet salad or fruit soup. Newcomers sit down, utter with strangers, and before paying the bill, have decided to share a room. Girls come to dinner wondering how they will spend the evening and, after the second cup of tea, have accepted the invitation from someone at their table who was wondering the same thing. Camaraderie quickly replaces discretion and the following questions are often asked and answered over an order of cucumbers. "When did you come? Where are you from? Have you a job? How much is your salary? What do you pay for your room?"

Yes, living in restaurants for a fortnight is an education, making you feel that you have placed your finger on the pulse of bustling, laughing, pushing, growing, hungry Tel Aviv.

Then something happens. Like the *One-Hoss Shay* [a poem by Oliver Wendell Holmes], your curiosity, digestion (which is now indigestion) and your patience go to pieces at the same time. You seem to have left your sense of humor in some restaurant between the Yarkon and the sea.

The restaurant proprietors have no regard for the law of supply and demand. This correspondent counted on one occasion that fifty persons were being served (or harbored hopes of being served) by a solitary waiter. This waiter and his many confreres throughout the city are extremists. They either sublimely disregard the fact that you have been screaming *bassar* (meat) like a cannibal for the last hour, or they rush about in such a state of sustained haste that they bring *gefilte* fish instead. And you eat and give thinks for all small blessings. Due, perhaps, to the fact that the population is supposed to increase between the morning and evening hours, the most popular byword is, "There is no more." And the supply of everything on hand always seems to give out when the person at your table is demolishing a plate of everything for which you asked. This, however, has its advantages. You feel that you are at home and raiding the icebox when you say, "Well then, fry up a couple of eggs and bring me anything else that's handy."

During the fifth week, you are liable to develop peculiar symptoms. You will leave three of four restaurants in disgust, after waiting to be served a half hour in each place. At the fifth restaurant you realize that you would be better off to have waited the hour and a half in one place. Or you disdainfully order three portions of potatoes to prove to the proprietor that his poor service has reduced you to the state of not caring what becomes of you. Your gesture is in vain. The proprietor isn't impressed and decides that you are a potatorian. Ships are bringing stranger things that into Tel Aviv.

The most excruciating anguish suffered by the non-Hebrew speaking diner is that he can only express his chagrin in distorted facial expressions to which nobody pays attention. If only you could slam down your napkin and shout with gusto, "Don't bring my order at all. Do you think I've got all night to spend in this place?"

And so the process of feeding Tel Aviv goes on with the haphazardness and nonchalance that is sublime.

HEDER [ROOM]

Written in the first months in Tel Aviv, 1933
Zif Zif, pp. 66–68
Unpublished manuscript from Bar-Adon's personal archive

Renting a room in Tel Aviv in 1933 is a challenging and frustrating task that requires the ability to trek all over the city, and it demands complicated negotiation skills. Kahn is introduced to a variety of landlords and neighborhoods.

Tel Aviv is living through a boom, with a capital B, if room rents are to be taken as a criterion. Since the excessive demands of the landlords must be a sign of overwhelming progress, three cheers for Tel Aviv. But woe unto the newly arrived tourist in quest of a place to lay his head.

After wandering through the highways and byways of Tel Aviv for two days in search of the phantom room that it is said one can secure for three pounds a month, you have a speaking acquaintance with every apartment house owner in the city and have patted all their children on the head at least twice (once coming in and once going out).

When you are newly arrived in the country, you take the first room at hand, believing that high rents are "just an old Spanish custom" in Palestine. In a month or so, worse luck, you meet some old time Tel Avivians or Jerusalemites who completely demoralize you by relating yarns about the rooms, gardens, terraces and whatnots that their friends have procured for a couple of pounds. At first you don't pay much attention to their...but since rooms and room rents are a favorite and consuming topic of conversation in Tel Aviv, and the tales keep dripping into your ears like water on a rock, you must eventually succumb.

So then you start out on your room hunt which, as an outdoor and indoor sport, is highly recommended for those who, at eventide like to feel tired but invigorated. You don't admit it even to yourself, but as you are drinking your morning coffee, you are playing with the idea that you may happen across a little nook overlooking a garden. By the time you are drinking your evening tea, you would be happy to find a barn overlooking a junk pile.

You have trudged up and down streets, paved and unpaved. You have penetrated into "rural" sections that you never knew existed in Tel Aviv. You have followed the trail of "Heder" (room) signs until you could almost smell them before you saw them. You have related your needs to women in every state of dress and undress from satin gowns to Turkish towels. You have seen more pretty Yemenite servant girls than you thought existed in all Yemen.

You have tried with great trial and tribulation to carry on a conversation in Hebrew only to find, at your departure, that you were addressing an English woman. Another woman argues with you for fifteen minutes over the price of the room before she tells you that her husband would only rent the room to a man. As you are leaving, your prospective landlady tells you, incidentally, that it's really only half a room because two other people will be sleeping in it. You have seen a man look you straight in the face and ask you six pounds for a very average room.

In the meantime you have become acquainted with each and every neighborhood pharmacy and grocery store because it is here that the "to let" signs are to be seen.

It is evening and you try to believe that tomorrow you will find the evasive room. Meantime you ponder on two things: why people in Tel Aviv merely place a "Room to let" sign on the front of an apartment house making you climb three flights of stairs and ring nine doorbells until you find the vacancy, and, what is the price of a houseboat on the Yarkon River.

THIRD DEGREE

End of 1933
Zif Zif, pp. 69–70
Unpublished manuscript from Bar-Adon's personal archive

"Third degree" questioning of newcomers to Tel Aviv by veteran residents is a common phenomenon, and newcomers soon get into the spirit and readily "strip their souls bare."

There is a fraternity in Tel Aviv that is doubtless the most unique of its kind in the world. It is known as the N.C., has no officers, demands no dues, the maximum extent of membership is two months, and it is most democratic in its policy.

The moment you put foot on Palestine soil you automatically become a member of the "newcomers" fraternity. This means that you are the recipient of favors of various descriptions. It seems that nowhere else is there such an overwhelming interest in new arrivals, and one wonders how the native Tel Avivians retain their enthusiasm in the face of the constant stream of newcomers.

Of course it means also that you relinquish many personal liberties and find yourself with as little privacy as the proverbial goldfish. At first you may become a little flustered when policemen, soda water vendors, bus drivers and anyone else with whom you have any dealings ask you, "When did you come? Are you here alone? Have you a job? How much do you make? Do you like it here? Where is your family? What is their business?"

But after you have gone through this third degree questioning several times, you get into the spirit of the thing. You can strip your soul bare with little reticence. You begin to quote the answers to the questions as mechanically as you used to quote Shakespeare in the classroom. The only difficulty is that you say, "I've been here a month" so often that you find yourself still saying it after you've been here a month and a half. And your liable to forget that you earned a pound more this week than last, thereby giving the "market quotation" most incorrectly.

The innermost corners of the life of an N.C. are pried into even to the extent of discussing what hour you rise in the morning and why. On one occasion I returned an alarm clock that I had purchased the previous day. Despite having been "guaranteed" in several languages, it proved to have a typically Oriental idea of time. The shopkeeper, unable to understand the complaint, waylaid an English-speaking policeman who explained to him in Hebrew that the timepiece must be repaired immediately for use early in the next morning. This, it seems, was impossible. Thereupon I became mildly hysterical, which had no effect on the shopkeeper who phlegmatically continued to pore over a piece of jewelry. The policeman, however, took the matter to heart. After learning how long I had been here, why I needed to rise so early, and if I intended to remain in Palestine, he announced, "Give me your address and at six o'clock tomorrow morning I will knock on your window."

On another day I went in search of a carpenter shop to have a surf-board made. Finding four men engaged in construction of a house, I made known my need. Work on the house was postponed while a surfboard was constructed that would do honor to the Mediterranean. After asking how long I had been here, one of the men proclaimed, "We are from Vienna. I have been here a month and eight days. He has been here four days. Those two have each been here a month." Whereupon one of the men rushed out for beer and seated on woodpiles, we celebrated the fact that we were all member of the N.C.

SIMCHAT TORAH

1935
Zif Zif, pp. 91–93
Unpublished manuscript from Bar-Adon's personal archive

Kahn compares the celebration of Simchat Torah in 1933 (a few months after her arrival in Palestine) to the celebration in 1935. Whether due to the fears engendered by the rise of Fascist regimes in Europe, or because of the rising standard of living in Tel Aviv, the celebrations in 1935 are less spontaneous and more structured and "cultured."

Some said it was because there are so many British policemen stationed in Tel Aviv this year. Some say it was because the Italian-Ethiopian conflict [a war that started in October 1935 and ended in May 1936, resulting in the Italian military occupation of Ethiopia] had a depressing effect. Some newcomers to Palestine didn't even know the difference.

But there was a difference between the Simchat Torah of 1935 and the Simchat Torah of 1934; and a vast difference between the Simchat Torah of 1935 and of 1933.

In two short years a festival of a distinctly Jewish and distinctly Palestinian character has been transformed into a mere festival. A day of ecstatic joy and exultation has become, to many, merely a day when one is released from work and eats bigger meals.

If the change is due to policemen or foreign conflict, then we may hope for a spirited revival of Simchat Torah next year. I, for one, cannot believe that external circumstances had anything to do with the matter. I believe that the joy-intoxicated celebration of three years ago would have had the British policemen dancing hora and the polka with them; and if they could not have danced Friday night, they would have danced Saturday night.

I believe that the form of the celebration this year was a physical expression of the intangible spiritual changes that Tel Aviv has been undergoing; and that this year marked the end of an epoch in Palestine's urban life. Those who reveled in the spirit of former Simchat Torahs may look back upon them with nostalgia, for it is improbable that they will witness another. Men grow away from simplicity—they seldom return to it.

This year I dined on Simchat Torah night (celebrated on Saturday) in a German open-air restaurant on Allenby Road. A five-piece orchestra played concert music, unusual in Palestine where even the more ambitious restaurants boast no more than a gramophone or a radio. The music was excellent, one tuneful operetta following another. Passersby stopped on the street to listen. The steak was well served and tasty. The waiter was pleasant and efficient (another innovation in Palestine). The ice cream was tempting and showed evidences of having been made from milk rather than water (also an innovation). Well-dressed women brushed by one's table perfectly groomed from the patent leather tips of their shoes to the kid tips of their gloves.

The air was exceedingly warm for October. The street promenade, as always in Tel Aviv, was fascinating. Neon electric signs blinked down on the endless jostling crowds. Young people were pushing their way into the Opera Mograbi across the street. The line of traffic—buses and automobiles—was unbroken.

While sipping wine after a satisfying meal, one was inclined to lean back in one's chair and watch this little Jewish world passing by with an immense sense of gratification. Music—well-dressed women—thousands of people going somewhere. Ah—this was a city complete. One might be sitting in Berlin or New York. The Jew has nothing for which to apologize. He has concert music and ice cream and neon electric signs in his city. And he has people—less people of course than in New York but people going somewhere.

Then, perhaps merely from perverse sentimentality, my mind traveled back to 1933 when, on this night people were going nowhere. It was a madly joyous night and I remember it in chaotic patches. The old men danced in the synagogues, as they still do, with Torahs in their arms. But the young men—the young men danced in streets and coffeehouses with beer bottles in their arms—with chairs—with tables. And yet in their dancing was the same exultation of the more obviously pious. They had taken an ancient rite and fashioned it to suit their needs and none with eyes to see could say that it was not good.

Large circles of hora dancers stretched down Allenby Road to the sea. Blue-bloused youths swayed to the tune of their own singing—then others joined the circle—middle-aged women—old men—tourists. The circles broke up. New ones formed. Nearby a vast crowd was gathered around a young couple who where executing a lively hora. Hasidic melodies [music that originated in Jewish mystical sects] intermingled with pioneer songs. Joy of the evening seemed to infuse the dancers with a strength beyond themselves. No one was drunk but everyone was intoxicated. Midnight came. One o'clock. Two o'clock. Festivities went on.

At five o'clock, I remember, dawn was breaking over the Mediterranean. Groups of youths still sat at long tables singing. I was tired. I could no longer distinguish between the Hasidic and the new pioneer melodies. How did I want to? They were one.

This was not a festivity that could have been staged in Berlin, or New York, or Paris. It was a festival of Palestine.

It was these chaotic patches that come back to me this year. But I fought against giving myself over to nostalgia—I left the garden restaurant in pursuit of the "celebration."

The Tarshish Café near the sea now has a roof garden and an orchestra. It was jammed with people. The jazz music was peppy. More well-dressed women—more good ice cream. I moved on. The Sapphire Café was using four rooms for dancing as well as the terrace. The jazz music was peppy. More well-dressed women—more good ice cream. I tried to dance but it was as crowded as a New York nightclub. I was wearing sandals and people stepped on my toes. It was hot and stuffy. I moved on.

I met a friend of mine and asked, "Aren't there horas?" He answered, "There was one about an hour ago near the sea but a policeman stopped it."

It was midnight. Everyone was still going somewhere. After all, it was a holiday night. It might have been the Fourth of July in America or the Bank Holiday in England. People were gay and on the move. Everybody was going somewhere. I wanted badly to go nowhere. To dance in circles and go nowhere. In lieu of which I went home.

There is too much that is real and vital and honest in Tel Aviv today to allow ourselves to indulge in backward glances or sickly sentimentalities.

Changes come and we cannot stem the tide. It is too soon yet to know where we would stem it if we could.

So this is not commentary. It is merely a record that New Palestine's first interpretation of Simchat Torah seems to have passed.

HITLER'S GIFT TO PALESTINE

1935

Zif Zif, pp. 174–176

Unpublished manuscript from Bar-Adon's personal archive

Kahn asks herself what Palestine can give to Jewish refugees from Germany and what the German refugees can give to Palestine. Most impressive is the connection of the young refugees—immigrants from Germany—to the soil, as seen in the rural settlements (kibbutzim and moshavim); one example is the Ramot HaShavim moshav where doctors from Germany became farmers. Kahn sees the children from Germany as "Hitler's gift to Palestine" who will bridge the gap from past to future.

What will Palestine do for the German refugee? What will the German refugee do for Palestine? As far as the adult refugee is concerned, it is too soon to judge for we are still in the midst of the drama. Almost daily, new boatloads of these uprooted men and women land in Jaffa or Haifa. There are those who come strong in courage and hope; there are those who come leaden-eyed like mere bodies, their souls still lingering in the Germany that they and their fathers have known and loved.

What can Palestine give to these men past fifty who have neither the strength nor the desire to begin life anew? Perhaps the vitality of the Jewish National Homeland, which is still an unknown land to many of these Germans, will in time revive their strength and their desire. Perhaps Palestine will never be more to them than a haven where they may relive their past in safety and peace. They gamble with their future. So does Palestine.

But in the children of these refugees there is no element of chance, no gamble. We need not wait for time to deliver up the answer of what they will give to Palestine or of what Palestine will give to them. The answer streams from the lips of every German child whom one hears babbling Hebrew in the streets of the cities and the roads of the colonies.

The genius of all children is their capacity for living in the present so completely. Despite the harrowing experiences through which some of these young victims have passed, their memory is short. Soon after their arrival they are living with zest in the present and this present to them means Palestine.

Whether in city or in settlement, these children seem to pick up Hebrew from thin air. They have to pick it up or they can't play with the little boy next door. The guttural sounds that label their father's halting "German Hebrew" is not to be found in their easy flow.

But in the colonies one is conscious of a change more vital than the mere change of language. For here the victims of Hitler's spleen are being bound to the soil of Palestine as though they themselves were the young orange saplings that they are so skillfully grafting. Miss Henrietta Szold [an American who founded Hadassah in 1912, immigrated to Palestine in 1918, and was the first woman on the Zionist executive committee], who, two years ago, at the age of seventy-three assumed the gigantic task of settling these children and whom I recently heard referred to by a pioneer from Ein Harod [the first kibbutz established in the Jezreel Valley in 1921; it took in the first group of youth from Germany in 1934] as "the belle of the Emek" [the Jezreel Valley], believes that the number of these children who later will abandon the soil is negligible. For these children are not only becoming Palestinians—but more important still—Palestinian farmers.

I remember seeing these same youths, with others from Kibbutz Tel Joseph, Degania [the first kibbutz—founded in 1909] and neighboring colonies studying the ruins of the old synagogue in Capernaum. Tourists walked about gingerly, Baedekers [guidebooks] in hand, according the broken stones the awe and respect earned by antiquity. But these blue-bloused Germans did not behave as though they were in a museum. They had been brought here in wagons with their teachers for a history and geography lesson. Soberly they moved from one broken capitol to the next, listening intently to what the teacher had to say of the history and significance of these monuments. Now and again they took notes as though they were in a lecture hall. To these youths there is no demarcation where the new Palestine in which they are planting vineyards and the ancient Palestine of these ruins begins. Past and present are submerged. They are not surprised that Palestine should have had a past because all countries had a past. And that Palestine should have a present and a future is as normal and as simple to these earnest youths. For a long time I watched these blue-blouses against the white ruins, studying Jewish history at its fountainhead. Here was death and life again, just as there is always life again for the Jew.

In Ramot HaShavim [a collective village established in 1933 by immigrants from Germany] near Petah Tikva [one of the first colonies established by Jews from Jerusalem in 1878], which is called the "egg colony" [because its main source of income was eggs], I found thirty-six German families, of which eighteen of the men had been doctors in Germany, devoting themselves to poultry. Rural life is difficult, but they are making a noble attempt at readjustment. "We have brought over our own furniture. If we could not come home at night to that touch of the west, we could not bear the life here," said my guide. Then he told me that they had just celebrated the birth of the colony's first baby. This baby is Hitler's gift to Palestine, for unlike his father there will be nothing for him to bear. His eyes saw the plains of Judea before they saw anything else.

One night I sat in a room crowded with pioneers who were celebrating the finding of water. In speeches and with song they eulogized water. On a wooden bench in front of me sat a stout German hausfrau with ear cupped. Her little daughter was patiently translating for her, word by word, the Hebrew that was being spoken on the platform.

And so it is from one end of the land to another, these children, Hitler's gift to Palestine, are bridging the gap from the hopeless past to the hopeful future.

THERE IS NO GERMANY

1935
Zif Zif, pp. 172–173
Unpublished manuscript from Bar-Adon's personal archive
Earlier version published in *The Palestine Post*, "Mr. Arnold Zweig in Jerusalem,
Author To Become a Palestinian Citizen," June 21, 1935

In this article Kahn describes a meeting with Arnold Zweig, internationally known Jewish-German writer and antiwar activist who had decided to renounce his German citizenship and become a Palestinian, because as he said, "there is no Germany." Hitler's regime had not only forced Jewish writers into exile, it had also silenced gentile writers and stifled the close connections between the two groups.

The Palestine Post had a visitor yesterday morning in the person of Mr. Arnold Zwieg [internationally-known Jewish-German writer and antiwar activist], the well-known German author now living in Haifa. In deference to the hot morning he had doffed his coat, but it was plain to see from his profuse apology that the author of The Case of Sergeant Grischa is not yet a real Palestinian. However, coat or no coat, he will be a Palestinian after April of next year (1936) for he has made application for the return of his German passport to Herr Hitler and for Palestinian citizenship.

Mr. Zweig denies that he is undergoing any sentimental misgivings at his impending change in his national status. His explanation is that under the present regime, "there is no Germany."

Relinquishing one's citizenship in Germany, which "is not," is not painful, as it has nothing to do with one's feelings toward the real Germany.

Mr. Zweig told of the dispersal of Germany's literary and spiritual life. The fourteen years of the Republic, prior to Hitler, formed perhaps one of the richest epochs that Germany has ever known. Berlin was fairly seething with creative energy and expression. But the thunderclap of the Fuehrer has dispersed not only the Jews, but also the gentiles. The gentile writers, those still in Germany, have become dumb. He told of several instances of well-known writers who, overpowered by Hitler's blow to liberal thought, have taken refuge in complete seclusion. In sad disillusionment, they watch the changing scene but cannot write.

As for the Jewish writers, they are completely scattered. From his stronghold on the top of the Carmel, Mr. Zweig writes many letters. Some go to Switzerland, many to Paris, a few to America. In the pre-Hitler days, Mr. Zweig was close to Thomas Mann and others. "We had a rich spiritual intercourse," said Mr. Zweig in recounting that so-and-so lived but twenty minutes away from his home and so-and-so lived around the corner. The literary folk, who awakened after the political explosion to find themselves separated by thousands of miles, are trying to make their letters a substitute for the intimate flow of conversation they once enjoyed. Mr. Zweig does not always receive the letters. If the sender does not mark the route specifically on the envelope so as to exclude Germany, the letters are usually confiscated.

"Art Be Hanged"

The uprooting has not stifled Mr. Zweig's work. Indeed, he has found stim- ulation in Palestine. He mentioned, particularly, a play that he has written concerning Napoleon in Acre. He retains sufficient sense of humor to laugh at, rather than revolt against, the present reign of nationalism, which seems to be saying in no uncertain terms, "Art be hanged." Theatrical production in Germany is impossible, and he has learned from France that producers there would be afraid to let themselves be on speaking terms with anyone writing on Napoleon—because nowadays in France one dare not speak of war. So he is expecting to have his Napoleon produced in America—"I think they are far enough away to risk it," he says.

TEL AVIV: APRIL 22, 1936

Dorothy Kahn
Jerusalem
The Palestine Post
An article from Bar-Adon's personal archive

Kahn describes the atmosphere in Tel Aviv during the Arab Revolt against the British. Ten defenseless Jews were murdered over a period of three days. The people of Tel Aviv, dressed in their everyday work clothes, honored the funeral procession in almost complete silence as it passed through the streets. Amazingly, despite their grief and anger, the young refrained from taking revenge.

Tel Aviv, April 22: Tel Aviv is the youngest city of its size in the world. In times of peace and joy, this extreme youth is revealed in enthusiasm, exuberance, energy and periodic misbehavior. Should a police officer tell a Tel Avivian to desist from crossing the street on his head, he would probably be asked "why." Therefore, Tel Avivians have acquired the reputation of being noisy, pushy, argumentative, opinionated and sometimes incorrigible. Perhaps they are. It is a sign of youthful well-being and healthy, adolescent growing pains.

But in times of disturbance [a term used by Jews to refer to the Arab Revolt against the British, 1936–1939] and deep sorrow, such as we are experiencing now, a new Tel Aviv reveals itself. Lovers of Tel Aviv say, "I told you so," and are proud; harsh critics of the city are a bit shame-faced. For Tel Aviv is dignified with all the calm mellowness and understanding of an old man who has seen much and learned from seeing. At the same time, it retains the vital courage and hardihood of its youth. A strange combination. A strange city. An admirable city.

The facts of the happenings during the past few days were reported in news cables. On Friday, Israel Khazan, who was brutally murdered by Arab brigands, was buried in the Old Cemetery in Tel Aviv. On Saturday indignation still rankled in the breasts of the population and a few hot-headed youths prevented Arab bootblacks and carriage drivers of Jaffa from entering Tel Aviv. On Sunday morning Tel Aviv settled down to routine jobs. Between nine and ten o'clock the murderous onslaughts began in Jaffa. Before nightfall, nine defenseless Jews had been slaughtered and over forty injured.

These are the facts. But the spirit of the city cannot be expressed so concisely. Those who lived through this period feel that they had never before really known or understood the hidden resources of strength and self-control buried in the city under a guise of effervescent youth.

On Monday morning at about dawn, Tel Aviv's population rose to bury its dead. It was grey, damp, drizzly. The length of Allenby Road was a sea of packed humanity. Pallid faces were pressed against windowpanes. Little groups herded together on balconies. Solemn-eyed youngsters sat on rooftops or in tree branches.

The cortege passed slowly from Hadassah Hospital to the Municipality on Bialik Street. The bodies were carried in simple orthodox manner, on wooden stretchers. The white shrouds were tightly tied around the necks and ankles of the corpses. No one, not even the families, dare glimpse these bodies mutilated until the flesh hung in ribbons. One white shroud followed another down Allenby Road. Only nine in all. But the procession of sacrifices seemed endless. There might have been ninety or nine hundred, so long did it seem in passing.

Jews are reputed to be hysterical. And yet in the face of this starkly tragic procession, scarcely a sound was uttered in the entire mourning city. There was not a dry eye. But there was not a sound. The drama of this complete silence in the early morning grayness was not to be described. It was only to be felt and wondered at. Tens of thousands of Jews bereft (and in Tel Aviv such loss is a personal bereavement) and yet not a sound, only deep silence.

Eulogies were delivered from the balcony of the Municipality. Still silence, except for the sobs from bereaved mothers and fathers who came to Palestine too late in life to learn how new Palestine bears its losses.

The pathetic procession moved on to the cemetery. What an odd funeral procession. Young men and women wearing shorts and blouses.

No top hats. No gloves. No mourning suits. No black veils. No flowers. No trappings and trimmings of any kind.

Just working people in working clothes carrying their nine dead, tied up like white sacks, to the most honored section of the cemetery. Tears on the cheeks of the seventeen- and eighteen-year-old youths who formed the cordon separating the procession from the crowds. Tears on the cheeks of young working women who wore red bandannas on their heads. For Tel Aviv needed no trappings to emphasize or dignify its grief.

On Tuesday the procession was repeated. Six more laid in graves adjoining the graves dug yesterday. Again Tel Aviv rose early. Again there was this awing silence. Deepened since yesterday.

Those who know the dignity of death only when it is intensified by black coats and veils do not know the dignity of death at all. Here was death linked to life without cessation. Pallbearers in working clothes. Pallbearers who stopped work to bury their dead and went back to work.

But the story of Tel Aviv's dignity did not end with the funerals. Only those who know the strength and courage of Tel Aviv's youth can measure the self-control need to refrain from taking an eye for an eye.

Comrades had been butchered. Retaliation is the expected reply of normal, red-blooded youth. And Tel Aviv's youth is normal and red-blooded. But they had been told to hold themselves in check. They did. A British officer was overheard telling a group of young Jews, "The reason why there are no Arab casualties is because you haven't got the guts to fight back." Others thought the same thing. It wasn't true. Tel Aviv's youth swallowed it because the city was behaving like an old man who has seen much and learned from seeing. Nothing to be gained in the long run by slaughter. Better to be told you have no guts when you know you have.

The air in Tel Aviv was tense—still is. Disturbing traffic moving along Allenby Road. A lorry bringing in a load of Yemenite refugees from Jaffa. A fire engine. An ambulance rounding the Hadassah Hospital corner.

Hundreds of young people milling around the new Beit Brenner of the Histadrut [the location of the workers' center on Brenner street in Tel Aviv]. They exchange opinions. Read the latest edition of the Hebrew newspapers. At the least grinding of a brake on Allenby, the building is deserted. Then, having satisfied themselves that it is nothing, they pour back to the building.

Knots of people on every corner. Watching. Waiting. Restless. Resentful. Reading the late bulletins posted on hoardings. Seven thousand

Yemenite refugees distributed throughout the city, some in synagogues and others in clubs and empty flats. Still others on the streets with their belongings.

But there is no undue noise. No hysteria. Tel Aviv waits with dignity and does its best to go about its routine business.

At seven o'clock the chase for last-minute newspaper editions and the chatter in cafés is suddenly silenced. Curfew is enforced. There are few violators of the law. All are content to stay within their four walls or to sit in family groups on their doorsteps. Gone is the youthful bravado and misbehavior. And in its place is this strange mellowness and dignity—this magnificent dignity that so many people fail to associate with this new baby city of the Jewish nation.

"INNOCENT ABROAD"

An article from Bar-Adon's personal archive

Kahn travels abroad to Poland, Romania, and Turkey and is dismayed by the sentiments she hears from common people that reflect a transformation of positive feelings of patriotism to destructive feelings of nationalism that exclude and demonize the "other." In Poland, she is impressed by the ardor of the youth who are rebuilding the country after the destruction caused by Russia, but she is disturbed by the anti-Semitism they demonstrate. Bar-Adon returns to Palestine on March 7, 1937.

Toward the end of September, I sailed from Haifa. The port area was crowded with troops arriving from England. The imposition of martial law was imminent. The "disturbances" were almost six months old. The country was extremely weary. When viewed from a few miles out at sea, it seemed a pathetic little waif, crouching against the horizon. One watched the hills disappear from sight with the question, "To what will I return?" The possibility that one might return to an unchanged situation, except for heightened weariness, was not entertaining.

A fortnight ago, when the Polonia docked in Haifa, a British constable who boarded the ship told us that the North was terrorized and Jerusalem under curfew. In a sentence, he had answered the question, "To what will I return?" A disheartening answer. And yet, as the small launch neared the harbor, Palestine seemed less a waif and more a potential tower of strength than it had when departing.

A Jew, returning home, refreshed (?) by contacts with the outside world, sees Palestine in a new light. He may not feel anything new. But the things he felt day in and day out—such as the imperative need for opening the doors of Palestine to persecuted Jews—he feels more deeply. His perspective may be said to have deepened rather than broadened.

With this deepened perspective, he sees this waif of a land, torn and mauled though it may be, as one of the few—and perhaps the sole bulwark between the Jewish people and a nameless abyss.

We repeat that for a Palestinian, this is hardly a new sentiment. It is as much a formula as "life, liberty and the pursuit of happiness" is to the American. But the "innocent abroad" necessarily return in this spirit of rededication, realizing anew that the fate of Palestine can no longer rest on the outcome of a squabble between the Jews, Arabs and British and realizing that the passing of each day makes it more of an international concern that, sooner or later, must be recognized as such by the world at large.

This is because the world at large today is a distinctly unpleasant place and, as usual, the Jews are bearing the brunt of this unpleasantness. One need not, of course, leave the shores of Palestine to be aware of this unpleasantness that is brought to us from every direction in newspapers and periodicals.

Yet, it is by rubbing shoulders and exchanging pleasantries on ships and on trains with stray, unimportant and therefore representative members of the world's population, that one feels the more personal and hence more crushing impact of this unpleasantness.

Perhaps "unpleasant" is hardly the word. Perplexed, bewildered, or frightened might more justly describe the sentiments that have congealed into nationalisms, more terrifying and disheartening when you meet them in simple, fundamentally kind folk than when you meet them in newsprint. People are thoughtlessly braying, "My Country 'Tis of Thee" with an ardor that has nothing to do with harmless, sentimental patriotism and everything to do with harmful, destructive nationalism.

My first view of Poland was from the upper deck of the SS Batory as we neared the port of Gdynia. The ten-year-old wonder port of Poland stretched before us like a festoon of lights draped over a Christmas tree. A young Pole at my elbow became ecstatic. "Can you imagine that ten years ago there was nothing here but a few fishermen's huts?" he asked. Could I believe my ears, or was it an enthusiastic Palestinian speaking of Tel Aviv?

That night, traveling from Gdynia to Warsaw, there was much talk in the crowded compartment. One young Pole told us of the Chopin festivities to be staged that week. We were urged not to miss seeing, in Lazienski Park, the impressive monument of Chopin listening to the melodies of the wind. Someday, there will be another Chopin in Poland, we were assured.

Another youth told us of the Four Year Plan and implored us not to judge Warsaw by what we would see today. The National Museum was not yet completed. They were still repairing the ravages of the Russians. We must return in five years

Such brave young talk, this talk about Gdynia, Chopin and the National Museum. Few people, least of all a Palestinian Jew, could fail to understand this passion for rebuilding an old-new land. Yes, this might have been a Palestinian train, except for the endless stretches of snow through which we were passing.

But, there is talk in Poland that has nothing to do with Chopin, talk of "Poland for the Poles." And, of course, Jews are not Poles, they will tell you. When you press these young people further into intricacies of nationalism, they will talk of their fear of Germany and Russia, of over-population, of poverty, of their need to band together for strength. Sometimes what they say makes sense, sometimes nonsense.

The Polish picture is large and complex. One leaves with many impressions. But of one impression there can be no doubt. The family is drawing about the hearthside closely to reinforce themselves against outsiders. The Jew is not considered one of the family. You will be told—and have every reason to believe—that the Pole is as poor as the Jew. But as long as there is bread, the Pole may look forward to sharing it; the Jew may look forward to nothing.

There are rumblings in Romania.

And even when we were homeward bound and nearing Istanbul, a young Turk delivered himself as follows, "Turkey is for the Turks. In these troublous days, we have to be strong. If the Jew will assimilate and become a Turk, he can stay. Otherwise we will have to kick him out as Hitler did in Germany."

Was this a flea or a body of men whom my friend disposed of so lightly but categorically, over his glass of cognac? It would be useless to remind him that the Jews had been ousted from Germany because they had assimilated too well. It would be useless to reply to all because he spoke not as an individual but from the depth of the malignant fever of nationalism.

It is useless to rationalize with this fever, bred of fear, suspicion and hatred. One knows only that the symptoms are everywhere, in the most calm and lovely spots, be it the vigor of the North Sea or the languor of the Bosporus.

The "Innocent Abroad" may return to Haifa with a thousand and one jumbled impressions. But one impression stands out as clear as Mt. Carmel. The nations of the world are drawing to their own hearthside. The wrongness, rightness, stupidity, or insanity of this sweeping passion is beside the point. What is not beside the point is that place must be made at his own hearthside for the Jew who has no other.

NEW PORT OF TEL AVIV

1938
An article from Bar-Adon's personal archive

On her return trip to Palestine on the SS Polonia, the passengers are informed that they will dock in Tel Aviv, the world's youngest port. When land is finally sighted, the passengers crowd the deck, singing Hatikvah. Small launches ferry them to land, where they go through customs in this newest of ports.

It was about four o'clock on Sunday afternoon that the wireless operator of the *Polonia* received the instructions that the vessel was to dock in the port of Tel Aviv. By word of mouth the news spread like wildfire among the passengers. Returning Palestinians made individual excursions to the wireless cabin to see the telegram with their own eyes before they could believe the glad tidings. Then, convinced, they gathered in knots to chatter and sing the popular songs dedicated to the port.

On another corner of the deck, old men gathered for special sunset prayers. They and the rest of the passengers were conscious that the ship had already changed her direction and pointed her prow toward Tel Aviv.

But the majority of the passengers were bewildered. They were tourists from Poland and Romania, coming for an eight-day Passover excursion. Whether they landed in Tel Aviv or Haifa was of little import. And besides, they were a bit disconcerted at the thought of arriving in a "half-finished" port.

In the evening there were a few sporadic attempts to sing Palestinian songs. But the foxtrot and the rumba proved more popular with the tourists, and the Palestinian residents had to content themselves with sitting in corners and conjecturing on the preparations that were being made in Tel Aviv to receive passenger ships.

But by noontime next day, one was conscious of a tension spreading throughout the vessel. Textile manufacturers from Lodz and bankers from Romania were beginning to feel excited at the prospect of landing in the world's youngest port. At about two o'clock came the usual false cry of "land." The bow filled up with passengers. Then, for several hours, they remained standing and straining their eyes to the deep blue horizon which seemed to be deliberately withholding the white dot for which they waited. Telescopes were used, but no device could produce anything except a glass-like sea met by a cloudless sky.

Then someone noticed that three members of the crew were standing on the bridge, also peering intently through glasses. Again the cry of "land" went up. And this time it was true. Slowly white specks began to stand out on the horizon. But it was an hour or more before the specks began to take shape and another hour before one could discern clearly the minarets of Jaffa at one end of the shore and the Rutenberg works at the other.

Then came the cry, "The flag!" The blue and white flag slowly made its way up the mast. For a few seconds it was caught in the rope. Then, in the face of the breeze it unfurled. The passengers sang *Hatikva* [Israel's national anthem] and, by now, Tel Aviv was stretched before us, a white city [Tel Aviv's nickname because of its white houses], except for the "Red House" [a house stood on the beach used by the Tel Aviv workers' union and its youth movement; the name was taken from its color and political orientation; today the Sheraton Hotel stands on this spot] on the seafront.

Now came the whir of wings overhead. Since the cable arrived, we had had a longing to feel the pulse of Tel Aviv. These welcoming planes were the first signs. The passengers waved frantically and were overjoyed to be able to see clearly the answering wave of the pilot. Now there was little distinction between the passengers who came from Warsaw for a holiday and those who were returning home. It was as though drums were beating in the engines of the plane. Tel Aviv is not as imposing as the Haifa skyline. But one and all were intoxicated by the beauty of the white city, bordering the blue sea like a silken fringe. The planes circled again and dipped down. The pilots waved and the passengers answered.

The anchor was cast. We left the upper decks and hugged the rails on the lower decks. The inspectors were coming on board. The sea was rough and the distance between the ship and the shore was great. The small launches bobbed up and down like corks. Gradually they approached the side of the ship. On the canvas roof of the launch stood a young boatman poised like a dancer, despite the tossing of the sea, and holding a grappling hook. But before he used the hook for more practical purposes, he waved it in the air like a baton, and broke into Hebrew song. The other boatmen joined in and so did the passengers. There were few passengers now who did not understand all this ado about landing in Tel Aviv.

The boatmen came aboard, fourteen of them, husky Jewish youths from Germany, Yugoslavia, Poland, Yemen and other parts of the world. It had been a hard pull out to the *Polonia*, but they were exhilarated rather than weary. This was the first time that they had come to bring hundreds of passengers to Tel Aviv. They could have gone five times the distance.

It was too late to disembark. Everyone remained on board. But there was little serious sleeping. Although breakfast was to be served at five o'clock, bearded old men could be seen hovering near the rails long after midnight. With Tel Aviv almost at arm's distance, sleep was difficult.

As arranged, the first passengers embarked at six o'clock in the morning. The motor launch seemed like a small yacht, with its carpeted floor, comfortable seats, and brass-railing stairway. Everything shone, as new and bright as the morning into which we were pushing. Again the boatmen broke into song. Two smaller boats escorted the launch on either side. Other small boats bobbed up from nowhere. And two large cargo boats, ribboned with red bands, added to the impression of a real port. "Shaloms" were called across the water by porters seated atop loads of lumber. And already we could hear cheers from the waiting crowds.

The customs house was as crisp and fresh as a month-old baby should be. It seemed a shame to place one' baggage on the brand new counters for customs inspection. And how dare one sit on the new, white benches? Even the pads of the inspectors seemed too new to be used.

And the personnel in the customs house were as new as the benches and the counters. The young woman, who examined you for the control, had been a clerk in a pharmacist's shop until yesterday. She takes her new duties seriously. When you tell her that this section of your pocketbook contains only cosmetics, she demands that you open your powder case. She stares intently at the puff; satisfies herself that it is harmless; and prepares to mark your pocketbook with white chalk. But what is the "okay" mark in the Tel Aviv port? She is not sure. She dashes out, obtains the information, and efficiently gives you the chalk mark.

The porters are also new and enthusiastic. They have never handled baggage before. A group of them come from a communal settlement in Ra'anana. One of them, however, proudly admits to having received his training in the harbor of Hamburg.

So you make out a new customs slip, and a new porter helps you out the new door of the new port of Tel Aviv.

REMINISCENCE OF TEL AVIV

1938
An article from Bar-Adon's personal archive

Bar-Adon looks back on her first five years in the country. She recalls the informal meetings between Jews and Arabs, meetings so prevalent in 1933, that had all but disappeared. With delightful humor, she describes her first living arrangements, starting with a room let by a journalist and an English teacher, who introduced her to concerts in Dizengoff's house and a "furnished" room containing only two chairs and a picture. She fled an overly regimented German rental and finally settled with a Russian woman where she set the house on fire. How trivial and yet human all this seems to her compared to the fear and depression prevalent in 1938.

In slow moving countries, it requires half a century before one can reminisce. But in Palestine, half a decade suffices to reveal many changes. For one who lives like a bedouin, wandering from room to room, a review of the landlords and landladies during the past five years is a barometer of social, economic and political situations.

By a lucky quirk, the first "room to let" sign I happened across when I arrived in Tel Aviv in 1933 was in the apartment of a Hebrew journalist whose wife was an English schoolteacher. The rent was eighteen dollars a month without service, which I was told was exorbitant. But this was 1933—Palestine was boasted to be the only country in world not suffering from depression or unemployment. It was a privilege to have a room at all and one did not quibble over the price.

My landlord kindly inducted me into the chief recreation of that era—attending informal concerts at the home of Meir Dizengoff [first mayor of Tel Aviv] and visiting Nahim Bialik on Friday evenings. There was excellent conversation in many languages to be heard at both homes. But the two men and the peace of the "pre-disturbance" days, which fostered the conversation, have passed.

Among my outstanding memories of that summer are being awakened in the early morning by the shrill but oftentimes melodious cries of the Arab hucksters—now extinct in Tel Aviv. A favorite pastime was walking along the beach to Jaffa; stopping to chat with the Arab fishermen, boat menders, and cameleers who came to the sea to shave their animals; and ending up with a Turkish coffee in a Jaffa coffeehouse. And in those distant days the effendis [respected men] still strolled down to Tel Aviv for a glimpse of the Jewish girls in their low-cut bathing costumes, although from the dignified look on their faces one might have supposed that they were discussing the price of Damascus silk or the political situation in Iraq. But nowadays, one walks in the opposite direction from Jaffa and, if in quest of diversion, watches the Jewish boatmenders in the Tel Aviv port.

My next move was to a furnished room with a Polish family where two chairs and a picture on the wall comprised the furniture. The bed, table, closet and other accessories were to be supplied next day. For four nights I slept on a broken army cot in the dining room. No action seemed to be taken in the matter of my furniture. Early on the fifth morning I fled. My landlady made no protest. Prosperity and the room shortage had now reached a dizzy height and she would have no difficulty in finding someone who would be grateful for a furnished room without furniture. Since that time prices have fallen and rooms have been had for the asking. But within the past few months, owing to the influx of immigrants, rooms are again becoming scarce and agitations for "rent restrictions" are beginning.

In desperation, I tumbled into a tumbledown room in a tumbledown house along the seafront, the like of which no longer exists in this section of the city. Again, the furniture was sparse. My landlady—a Russian woman—agreed that I might have some shelves made. I started out in question of a carpenter. But in the merry days of 1933 there was no carpenter to be had for love or money. The idea of having a shelf put up in less than a fortnight was ludicrous.

I decided—like thousands of others in Tel Aviv—that I was lucky to have a bed, and my waking hours could be spent in the streets. Despite the fact that we had no common language (or maybe because of it) my Russian landlady developed an affection for me, and my last memory of her is standing on the balcony with streaming eyes when I left, bag and baggage in a horse and carriage. Carriages have also become extinct in Tel Aviv—Jews drive taxis and Arab carriage drivers may not enter.

And now the scene shifts to Himmelfarb's hotel in Jerusalem where so many newcomers passed a few weeks until they settled permanently. The pipes from Ras el Ein had not been laid and Jerusalemites budgeted their shower baths and watered their plants with dishwater. But Mr. Himmelfarb was obliging and ingenious. He would supply you with a bottle of soda water, to wash away the soapsuds when the water supply was turned off, before you had finished your shower.

While at Himmelfarb's, I was turning out copious copy about the bandit, Abu Jilda [a highway robber who killed a policeman and was sentenced to death in 1934]. The fact that he held up, robbed, and even murdered a few people was frontpage news for some time and numerous editorials were written against the laxity of government in failing to apprehend the criminal. How dim and distant and rosy seem those days when a single Arab bandit was news!

My next move was to the house of a German family. German immigrants were now arriving in large numbers, and importing their much-beloved "order." What a delightful contrast was this room to the unfurnished "furnished" room of the Polish family! I settled down to enjoy this thing called "German order." But I soon discovered that it is not as pleasant as American efficiency. It sometimes borders on Prussian regimentation. If breakfast is served at 8:00 you may not have it at 8:15. I have a blurred memory of bolting from the house of my German landlady in a few days, without even stopping to pack my belongings; handbags and skirts were haphazardly strewn along the garden path, as I made a record dash for freedom. A favorite purple handkerchief was never retrieved—my tribute to "German order." I was convinced that their order would be a boon to our inefficient country—but I would be content in future to watch it functioning from a distance.

And so I gratefully took refuge in a room in the bosom of a Russian family—and reveled in the disorder of the easy-going household where 8:00 breakfast is served punctually at 9:15. It was here that I contrived to set the house on fire by washing clothes in benzene near an open fire. In those distant days—four years ago—there was not a fire engine in all of Jerusalem. I called the police. A British constable arrived on a bicycle, saw the flames shooting from the windows and agreed that there was a fire. The only question was what to do about it. He stood, leaning on his cycle and looking quite dejected as the flames were obviously spreading. "It's moving to the next room," he reported. It was one o'clock in the morning. We roused some of the neighbors. They would be only too glad to help but there was no more than a few bucketsful of water to be obtained in the entire neighborhood. The fire was eventually extinguished by suffocation combined with a few cups of water.

Then came April 19, 1936 [the beginning of the Arab Revolt with the murder of two Jews who were on their way to Nablus]. Water shortages and Abu Jilda were no longer topics for conversation. The clip of machine guns were heard from Mt. Scopus every night. Ambulances passed our door on the way to Hadassah Hospital. There was curfew; my Russian landlord could no longer go to play chess in the café in the evening. A new period in Palestine's history had begun.

NEW PALESTINE

1938–1939
An article from Bar-Adon's personal archive

Kahn reflects soberly on the atmosphere in the urban centers of Palestine as live concerts, cafés, lectures, hairdressers, flirtations, a Jewish satirical theater, bridge games, and a new zoo (although, due to the high cost of feeding, the gift of an elephant was regretfully declined) goes on against the background of the ongoing shootings, bombings, and violence.

It is five o'clock on Friday afternoon. This hour, after the week's work is finished and before the Sabbath has begun, is popular in Tel Aviv for sitting in cafés or strolling along Allenby Road. The crowds move as though on an electric belt. Children draw their tongues lingeringly over pink ice cream cones. The little Yemenite shoelace vendor is doing a heavier business than usual and his ebony side-curls bob against his cheeks as he pushes through the milling crowd. There is an abundance of perambulators, wheeled by fathers as well as by mothers and monopolizing much of the sidewalks. Watch out for your shins!

We are sitting in the Shlosha Cushim, one of the popular cafés this summer. The silver-colored walls are dotted with drawings of Sudanese waiters in crimson coats. The orchestra is playing Bei Mir Bist Du Shon. A handsome blonde Viennese in mauve linen frock foxtrots by our table in the arms of a longhaired Russian. The waiter brings our fruit juice in a tall frosted glass, tinkling with ice cubes. "Bei mir bist du schon." So kiss me and say you understand—croons the orchestra in Germanized English. The Viennese and the Russian pass by again; they are carrying on a mild flirtation in broken Hebrew.

Suddenly a dull thud rises over the traffic and the baby perambulators and the syncopation in the Shlosha Cushim. It comes from the direction of the Tel Aviv-Jaffa border. It is a muffled sound. A newcomer to the country might not have noticed it. But to us, the sound is not unfamiliar. It was a bomb.

Word filters about among the tables. A bomb exploded on the border! There is great concern. Were there casualties? Who? How many? A few journalists at the next table make a dive for the telephone booth. A lorry of British soldiers with machine guns lumbers down Allenby Road. The orchestra begins to play I Kiss Your Hand, Madame. The Viennese and the Russian waltz by our table. The flirtation is obviously progressing.

And thus life goes on from day to day in Palestine. Soon it will be two and a half years since the nightmare began. At times one wonders how the Jews have maintained their sanity during these nine hundred days of uncertainty, death, destruction, and horror. The answer is the scene in Shlosha Cushim. The abnormalities of living are not allowed, insofar as possible, to penetrate the normalities.

In the towns the women go to the hairdresser to be given the latest mode in hair rolls. And crimson nail polish too, if it suits their fancy. Last night there was a reception in Haifa for a visiting American. In the middle, a few of the local guests quietly departed. Six Jews had been killed in ambush a few miles away. Tonight Dr. So-and-So gives a lecture in Jerusalem on the latest archeological finds in Iraq. In Tel Aviv a troupe of Yemenite dancers hold a recital.

The Mateteh ["broom" in Hebrew—a satiric Israeli theater of the time] had a premiere this week in the Beit Ha'am [community center] in Tel Aviv. There was S.R.O. [Standing Room Only]. There were new songs and wisecracks which soon will be known in every corner of the country. The audience rocks with laughter when, in one skit, a guide explains to tourists, "This is Jerusalem, the seat of the government during the day. At night, the government moves to Tulkarm."

Jews here know that they must laugh. If they stopped laughing the "government" at Tulkarm might prevail. So they laugh and try to go about the normal business of living. They go to see mystery films and Mickey Mouse. In Rehavia and Talpioth, they give "stuffed-shirt" dinner parties. They play bridge. At nine o'clock the game is interrupted to listen to the news broadcast. "The High Commissioner deeply regrets the death of Lieutenant So-and-So of the such-and-such regiment who was killed in action near Nablus...." And then the appalling list of Jews and Arabs whose death occasions less official "regrets."

Afterward the bridge players may indulge in political discussions. Or they may not. "I bid two clubs." The game goes on. Refreshments are served. There is a sharp "ping" in the distance. Shooting from the direction of Beit Hakerem [a neighborhood in West Jerusalem]. Or shooting from the Ahuza quarter. Or shooting on the Jaffa–Tel Aviv border. Ping. Ping. They follow in quick succession. Sometimes it seems as though the shots are whizzing by the house. "Won't you have another piece of cheesecake? I baked it myself." Ping. Ping. Ping.

Five new schools were opened in Tel Aviv this week. The municipal engineer showed us about. He is as pleased as punch with his yellow-tiled corridors, his parquet-floored gymnasium and his assembly hall in the Mizrachi School, which can be converted into a proper synagogue. Ping. Ping on the border. But when you are with the municipal engineer it would seem that Tel Aviv had nothing else to worry about except the comfort and enlightenment of little Tel Avivians.

This week the animals were moved from temporary quarters to the first Palestinian zoo. At six o'clock in the morning the lorry arrived to transport the leopards, the hyenas and the parrots. The founder of the zoo is Rabbi Schornstein, formerly Chief Rabbi of Copenhagen. He'll tell you that a love for animals must be inculcated in the young generation. Ping. Ping on the border. But Rabi Schornstein's chief worry is that an Indian maharajah has offered him the gift of an elephant which he can't accept because it costs five dollars a day to feed an elephant. And the children of Tel Aviv ought to have an elephant!

You board a taxi going to Jerusalem. If the passengers allowed themselves to think, they might wonder what were their chances for arriving safely. But they do not follow thoughts to logical conclusions. Several passengers do keep their eyes glued to the road and regard nervously the Arabs who are mending a road or loitering in front of an orange grove. But one passenger sleeps—and after awhile snores rhythmically. Another reads The Daring Young Man on the Flying Trapeze. And two young women knit.

"Do I knit two and purl three or knit three and purl two?" Her companion ponders over the pattern. The taxi nears the danger zone of Ramleh. "You knit two and purl three."

In the agricultural settlements…but this is a story in itself. There are no Mickey Mouses or bridge games or dinner parties. Watching and working. Working and watching.

So this is life in urban Palestine day by day. Folks sip grapefruit juice under parasols in the garden of the San Remo Hotel. And directly across the street, armed guards patrol one of the entrances to the city. Housewives read the black-bordered morning newspapers with hearts that would break if hearts broke. And then they have an argument with the vegetable seller for over-charging them two mils for pomegranates. Rabbi Shornstein worries about the elephant. The municipal engineer rejoices over his schools. The Viennese blonde flirts with the longhaired Russian. Ping. Ping on the border. And the Mateteh laughs at the whole shooting match.

"TRAPPED!" OR, "THEY WHO ARE TO LOSE THEIR PASSPORTS"

An article from Bar-Adon's personal archive
Another version published in *The Palestine Post*, April 8, 1938

Kahn accompanies a group of Jewish tourists from Germany in Palestine and reports the thoughts and feelings of one of those tourist, a widow of a painter, who, like the other tourists, can't take money out of Germany. She, like the others, is terrified to start life in a new country virtually penniless. Despite the Arab Revolt and its consequences, they sense the freedom in comparison to the terrible conditions for the Jews in Nazi Germany and feel trapped.

"This street is as fine as any in Berlin—just as fine." The woman who shared my seat in the bus looked out on the main thoroughfare of a new settlement bordering on the south of Tel Aviv. Her nose was pressed against the windowpane. A few houses, a stretch of sand dune and rows of meager saplings characterized the street which is "as fine as any in Berlin."

This was her first visit to Tel Aviv. She has been in Palestine two weeks. In another two weeks she will be on her way back to her home in Bavaria. En route to Tel Aviv we had stopped at Rehovot, Ayanoth, and other settlements. But even as she stood in the settlements she seemed to be viewing everything as unreal, unattainable, the "Promised Land" to be viewed from Mount Sinai but never to be actually reached.

The passengers in the bus were a party of German tourists. For many of them, like my companion, Palestine is unattainable, the "Paradise Lost." They are past middle age, and they cannot take money out of Germany; to start life again in a strange country virtually penniless is terrifying. This situation has existed for several years. But the new note of horror that has been added within the past month is making them pay hurried visits to Palestine.

With the increasing rise to power of Hitler, like an unleashed behemoth on rampage, they fear that their passports may be confiscated and they may never be permitted to leave Germany again. They come here to see children and relatives. It is a "Hail and Farewell" to—who knows what?

And so they come on their tours. They travel hurriedly from Tiberias to Tel Aviv in buses. They spend a night here and a night there. They gather blurred impressions of settlements and villages. They try desperately hard to remember whether Safad or Tiberias was the seat of the kabbalists, to learn the difference between a *kibbutz* [larger collective settlement] and a *kvutzah* [smaller collective settlement) and a *moshav ovidim* [partially collective settlement]. But in the end they retain only a confused impression of tents and chickens and grapevines. They refer to their notebooks to see if it was Ein Harod or Ein Geb that they visited yesterday—they know it was "Ein something." They are rushed from Ayanoth to Mikveh Israel in a space of half an hour while a tourist guide shouts facts, figures and explanations. It is all vague, muddled, but "wunderbar."

The Lesser Evil

The only clear impression they have is of freedom. Even when they are told that four Jews were killed on the road to Safad they feel the freedom in the air. What blessed freedom to be ambushed when Jews in other parts of the world slink off to commit suicide if they have the courage and wish they had the courage if they remain alive.

But we have digressed from my companion who is sitting with her nose pressed against the windowpane talking in disconnected sentences. She is more than middle aged. She is the widow of a Bavarian painter. He did landscapes in watercolors. They had lived for a while in Italy, and in other places, where he found inspiration for his work. She speaks three or four languages freely. She has a quick wit and the zest for life of one who has become so accustomed to enjoying the world in spite of itself that even tragedy cannot break her of the habit. She has come to Palestine now because it might be her last chance.

"When I go back, my passport will be confiscated and I will never get it back again. I had planned to go to America for the Exhibition next year. But that depends on whether one can get a passport. To get a passport or not to get a passport. That is the question!" She likes her little parody and laughs.

Then she presses her nose against the windowpane again. "Oh, to stay here. The freedom! It is terrible over there. Terrible. Terrible. You can't pick up a paper without seeing a caricature of Jews with long noses. I have never seen Jews that look like that. It is terrible. Oh, to stay here."

Then she talks on about Italy and her husband's watercolors. In those days you could go anywhere. Imagine, being able to go to Italy just because you wanted to paint watercolors? What do watercolors matter nowadays? Now you have to just be quiet and watch your step. She lowers her voice to a whisper and leans close to my ear as though even here she might be overheard by a Nazi agent, "Be quiet and watch your step." Wasn't that the correct American expression, "Watch your step?"

Messenger Duties

She would be busy the first day in Tel Aviv. She had brought so many greetings and presents from mothers to their children. In Haifa she had already given kisses and candy to the young people who eagerly awaited her at the harbor. Her duties as messenger were robbing her of precious time. But still—"Poor mothers. You see they may never get out of the country if their passports are not renewed this year. And their children may never get in again. I may be the last one to bring these personal messages. So I'll be busy in Tel Aviv tomorrow. To get a passport or not—that is the question."

SATURDAY NIGHT IN TEL AVIV

Dorothy Kahn
Tel Aviv
Palestine Review, March 4, 1938

Bar-Adon compares Tel Aviv's Saturday night to other big cities in the West and emphasizes the change in the city in the last couple of years.

A few years earlier, very limited entertainment options were available on Saturday nights, and now multiple types of entertainment have developed. She describes the new possibilities to demonstrate the rapid progress of the city.

In most parts of the world, Saturday night is distinguished from other nights of the week. It marks the end of the week and precedes the day of rest. People feel in the mood for celebration. It is not a matter of masses and classes. The masses may go to a cinema or dancehall and the classes to the opera or a nightclub. But Saturday night is set aside for going somewhere.

In cities the choice of entertainment is wide. In towns and villages, it may be limited to a soda fountain or saloon, as in America. However, one may presume that wherever a calendar is introduced, the desire for a "spree" on Saturday night is introduced with it.

Palestine's "metropolis," Tel Aviv, is no exception. The only difference is that Saturday night marks the beginning of the week instead of the end and follows rather than precedes the day of rest. After the quiet of the Sabbath, the population seeks entertainment.

Only a few years ago, Saturday night merry-making in Tel Aviv was impromptu. Outside of a cinema or two, the population created its own entertainment. The question, "Where shall we go tonight?" did not arise. One went unquestioningly to Allenby Road or the seashore for a stroll. One jostled with the crowd, greeted one's friends, and finished off the evening with tea and pastry.

But within the past year or two, Saturday night in Tel Aviv has begun to resemble Saturday night in any other large city. The traditional question, "Where shall we go tonight?" becomes as pertinent in Tel Aviv as in London—a choice of five places can be as difficult as a choice of fifty.

For instance, let us consider last Saturday night in Tel Aviv. First and foremost was the concert of the Palestine Orchestra. In view of the fact that this was its hundredth appearance, the event took on an added interest. During the day one gathered the impression that all Tel Aviv would be packed into the grounds of the Levant Fair when the baton was lifted. But actually the several thousands who attended the concert did not make a dent in the teeming throng of entertainment seekers. A large number went to see a Spanish dancer. Before six o'clock all tickets had been sold out for the film, *The Life of Emile Zola*. Long queues were trying to obtain tickets for *Captain Courageous*, and other cinemas were packed. On Nachmani

Street, one found hundreds milling around the Club Hapoel. When you asked what was taking place, you were told "box," which is Hebrew-English for a boxing bout and is pronounced something like "bux."

But neither the concert, Emile Zola, the Spanish dancer, "bux" nor the hundred and one other things which are in progress in other parts of the city affect the Saturday night street throngs. From seven o'clock till long after midnight the highways and byways are electric. Even the street throngs of Tel Aviv have changed within the past few years. One rarely meets one's friends now, except by appointment.

The promenade is no longer bounded by Allenby Road and the seashore. There are areas, such as the upper end of Pinsker Street and Dizengoff Circle, that have a lay of their own, complete with shops, restaurants and cafés. They are smaller and quieter replicas of the heart of the city. They have taken on the air of the business section or the residential section of a large city. The American might be reminded of West Philadelphia or Jackson Heights.

The center of movement is still Allenby Road. Cars speed up and down and as many as a dozen buses collect at the seafront terminal at one time. The illuminated shops are inviting enough to make window-shopping a worthwhile pastime. There are restaurants and cafés galore to suit the tastes of all and sundry. There are special shops for pastry and for coffee, for sausages, and for vegetable dishes. A cosmopolitan note is supplied by the girl who stands in a window frying *latkes* in the same way that hotcakes are made in the New York "Childs."

The fact that Tel Aviv is developing "districts" like any metropolis is most evident on Saturday nights. The shoddiness of the seafront becomes more and more apparent as the rest of the city assumes a more attractive and sedate face. The carnival "Blackpool" atmosphere of the seafront cafés, with their blaring radios and gramophones, is conspicuous enough to set this area aside from the rest of the city. Thrown into relief by a glaring electric bulb is the wan, weary face of the hot-corn vendor. O. Henry would have made her the heroine of a pathetic story.

About ten thirty there is a lull in the streets. The after-dinner strollers and café sitters have gone home. But a half-hour later the streets take another long breath. The concert and the cinemas are over. People are dropping into cafés for a cup of coffee and a late snack. Saturday night has still a few hours to go.

CHAPTER FOUR

"Our Cousins"—on the Arab Population of Mandatory Palestine

Dorothy Bar-Adon's archive contains a full-length, unpublished manuscript devoted to materials concerning the Jewish-Arab conflict, or what has come to be called the Arab-Israeli conflict. Having given up her American citizenship and having received a British passport as a resident of Mandatory Palestine, Bar-Adon believed that Arabs and Jews would eventually find ways of peacefully sharing the same territory, via mutual understanding, and without attempting to expel one another from the land. The common Semitic identity of Arabs and Jews, in Bar-Adon's view, would enable both peoples to create a shared life.

As she gained experience in covering events in Palestine, however, Bar-Adon concluded that stronger forces than the local Jewish and Arab populations were preventing the two peoples from living in peace. The leaderships of the neighboring Arab countries did not allow peaceful coexistence. The British Mandatory authorities severely limited Jewish immigration to Palestine; immigration continued, but was considered by Great Britain to be "illegal."

With the hope of increasing understanding between Jews and Arabs, Bar-Adon wrote not only about the Arabs of Palestine but she also she travelled to Transjordan, Baghdad, and Damascus in an attempt to understand the forces motivating Arab objections to Jewish settlement in Palestine. Based on her personal contact with Arab people, Bar-Adon attempted to outline possible solutions for the Arab-Israeli conflict. Bar-Adon's stance vis-à-vis Arab people was based on respect and sympathy, and this despite her occasional use of terminology that is unacceptable in the twenty-first century (e.g., "primitive"). She gave special attention to the reality of Arab women's lives.

The following is the editors' attempt to provide data that will make Bar-Adon's thoughts more accessible to a reader with limited knowledge of the period. We do not, of course, pretend to provide a full historical overview of the events that Bar-Adon witnessed, and of which she wrote, but rather to mention certain events with which Bar-Adon would have expected her readers to be familiar.

During the period of the British Mandate, the Jewish population grew from 10 percent in 1917 to 30 percent by 1948. Conflict between Jews and Arabs increased, both as a result of the growth of the Jewish population and as a result of circumstances on the international stage. The Mandate powers in the Middle East—in order to moderate nationalist tendencies in neighboring countries—gave limited rights of independence to Iraq, Syria, and Transjordan. The Arabs in Palestine feared that a Jewish majority in Palestine would mitigate against Arab independence in Palestine.

Bloodshed in the form of attacks on the Jewish population dates back to the Nebi Musa celebrations in April 1920; these attacks lasted four days and resulted in 7 Jews killed, 200 wounded. The 1921 May First demonstration in Jaffa lasted four days and left 47 Jews killed and 140 wounded, 48 Arabs killed and 73 wounded by the British army and by Jewish defenders. As a result, the government of Great Britain established the Haycraft Royal Commission of Inquiry, whose main conclusions (October 1921) were the limiting of Jewish immigration to Palestine, separation of Transjordan from the proposed Jewish "national home," and turning Transjordan into an Arab monarchy under the rule of King Abdullah.

Beginning in August 1929, the Yishuv suffered pogroms, as well as conflicts resulting from disagreements as to Jews' right to pray at the so-called Wailing Wall in Jerusalem (the Western Wall). These conflicts spread, leading to attacks on Jews throughout Palestine, culminating in the massacre of 67 Jews in Hebron; the Jewish community had been residents in that ancient city for hundreds of years.

During the 1930s, events on the local and international levels impacted the Arab national awakening in Mandatory Palestine: Fascist regimes were established and strengthened in Europe, and Italy, and Germany displayed aggressive tendencies which British and French appeasement did little to moderate. By 1935, when some sixty-five thousand Jews immigrated to Palestine in one year, and the Jewish "national home" was perceived as an established fact, the ground was prepared for what became the Arab Revolt against the British Mandatory authorities in 1936–1939. The aims of the revolt were:

1) Ending the Zionist settlement of the land by destroying the Jewish economic infrastructure and starving the Yishuv.
2) Forcing the British government to abandon its commitment to the establishment of a Jewish "national home" in Palestine, as mandated by the Balfour Declaration of 1917.
3) Establishing an Arab state in Palestine, governed by Palestinian Arabs.

The Revolt led the British government to institute changes in policy: the White Paper of 1939 greatly cut back Jewish immigration to Palestine and limited the rights of Jews to purchase land. Many of Bar-Adon's articles relate to these events.

FOREWORD

1936
Inhabitants of the Rock, pp. 1–4
Unpublished manuscript from Bar-Adon's personal archive

Kahn relates how she decided not to include any material on the Arab population in Palestine in her autobiography, Spring Up, O Well, published in 1936, despite her interest and attempts to get to know them, because she felt that the Jewish population was not ready to hear anyone who had not yet lived in Palestine during riots and violence. She then does experience them and decides to address the question due to her passionate belief that the two nations are related and that they both must and can find a way to live together.

In my first book on Palestine, Spring Up, O Well [Kahn's autobiography, published in 1936 in the United States and England], I told something of the lives and feelings of the four hundred thousand Jews who have returned from the ends of the earth to their home, "as of right and not on sufferance."

Of the million Arabs who were already inhabiting this home [the Arab population of the land of Israel at the end of the 1930s], I said almost nothing. When an Arab cameleer happened to trudge across a page, I made way for him. When a lithe brown Arab boy playing a flute leaped gaily into a paragraph, I made way for him too.

For Arab cameleers and Arab flute players can be charming. And it would be a dour book indeed that pictured Palestine without a single tinkle of a camel bell, held in place by the blue beads that bring good fortune to the cameleer, the camel and the sons of the camel.

But the cameleer and the flute player pushed their way into the book because they were irresistible and not because of any assistance on the part of the author. For I had grimly determined not to treat with the moot "Arab question."

This determination did not emanate from any grandiose belief that the four hundred thousand were more important than the million. Nor did it emanate for lack of interest in the Arab. The Arab had interested me more than the Jew. I had known Jews before I came to Palestine. I had not known Arabs.

Therefore Arabs presented the challenge of the unknown. I applied myself to trying to probe this unknown man who is my neighbor, my Semite cousin, and who shares this country.

Free social contact between Jew and Arab in Palestine is infrequent and difficult. But I battered the barriers whenever possible. I ate tender lamb meat in the palace of the Emira of Transjordan and foul goat cheese in the mud hut of a *fellah* [Arab peasant] woman. After a few years I felt that I was beginning to know and to understand the Arab.

This slight knowledge I planned to put into *Spring Up, O Well*. Then I lost my courage.

I lost my courage because of one sentence. The sentence was, "But you weren't here during the 1929 riots" [demonstrations and violent riots in late August 1929; 133 Jews were killed by Arabs while 110 Arabs were killed by British police who were trying to suppress the riots]. For whenever I voiced the slightest opinion to Jews about Arabs, I was met with this rebuff. Gradually I realized that one was not entitled to hold any views about Arabs until one had lived through a riot. Perhaps the rebuff was justified. I could see Arabs giving me scented sprigs of jasmine or red pomegranates. They had done it. But Arabs amuck with daggers, I could not see. I had read about it. But I could not see it. Perhaps the rebuff was justified, and I should wait to put into words what I felt about my Semite cousins.

So I lost my courage to write about the million and confined myself to the four hundred thousand.

As I write this, machine guns are booming in Lifta Village, a few miles from Jerusalem. Curfew law [During the 1936–39 Arab Revolt the British applied defense emergency regulations including curfew laws] is in force in Jerusalem and lorries carrying police and troops tear noisily through the otherwise noiseless streets. Wheat is being burned in the north and orange trees are being uprooted in the south.

I am living through the riots of 1936. I've been living through them for ten weeks now. I saw the Jews bury their dead, chanting, "El Maleh Rachamim" (God Full of Mercy). I saw the Arabs bury their dead, chanting, "Allah Akbar" (Allah is Great). I think I've earned the right to talk about the other million.

I can do little more than talk about them. I cannot write a political treatise because I know so little of politics. The cold-blooded consideration of the "Arab question" means less to me than the hot-blooded consideration of the Arab as an individual.

Neither can I write an ethnological treatise on the Arab. For to me he is not primarily a picturesque or romantic product of the East to be surveyed, studied and reported upon.

The Arab is my close neighbor. He is my fellow citizen. He is the man with whom a few months ago I broke bread. He is the man who today is spilling the blood and burning the crops of my people. He is the many with whom a few months from now I hope I shall be breaking bread again.

No, to me the Arab is not a dashing figure on a white steed. It would be more romantic if I could consider him as such. Nor is he the "Arab problem." It would be less complicated if I could consider him as such. He is a man. He is the man with whom fate has destined I should share this country and the future of this country.

He is a man. He is a Semite. He is my blood relation. What is my feeling toward him? What is his feeling toward me? Why does he periodically rise up to kill me? Is it his fault? Or my fault? Or the fault of the British Mandatory power? When will he stop rising up to kill me and to destroy the fruit of my labors?

I shall not attempt to answer these questions that are being asked today in Palestine, in London and everywhere in the world where there are Jews. I shall simply elaborate upon the questions themselves and shall set forth a deep belief in the possibility of the reorientation (in all senses of the word) of the Jew and the Arab in Palestine.

Amid the machine guns and the bombs and the talk of Royal Commissions [the Peel Commission of 1936–1937, formally known as the Palestine Royal Commission, was a British Royal Commission of Inquiry set up to propose changes to the British Mandate for Palestine following the six-month-long Arab general strike; it recommended partitioning the country], this belief may sound like a futile whimper, less even than a cry in the wilderness. But the Semite bond antedates the machine guns. Who knows if it will not postdate them?

MAHMOUD BEY

Probably the end of 1933
Inhabitants of the Rock, pp. 1–7
Unpublished manuscript from Bar-Adon's personal archive

Bar-Adon remembers a conversation with an educated town Arab and her gratitude when he told her frankly that although he liked her as an individual, he didn't like her as part of a race he believed was invading his country. Whereas she had felt frustrated and helpless in the face of anti-Semitism in the past, in this case she felt she did have answers.

Ever since I knew that the Jews were resettling Palestine, I knew that they were faced by the "Arab problem."

I arrived in Palestine with a hotchpotch of ideas about these Arabs, gleaned from sporadic reading of Lawrence, Gertrude Bell [T.E. Lawrence, a British army officer renowned especially for his liaison role during WWI and the Arab Revolt against the Ottoman empire; Gertrude Bell, 1868–1926, an English writer, traveler, political officer, administrator, archaeologist and spy] and Zionist tracts.

Some Arabs wore flowing headgear. They had a consuming love for their camels to which they gave lyrical names. They made a rite and ritual of hospitality. They had a code of honor and a code of revenge. They ate flat loaves of bread and black olives. Some of them were homosexual.

Some of them sold land to Jews and then agitated for restriction of land sales to Jews. Some of them resented the Jew because he was a colonizer and then resented the Jewish Labor Federation's creed that Jews must not employ Arabs but must work themselves in order to preclude the possibility of Jews becoming colonizers. Some Arabs had dark eyes. Their white teeth flashed. They drank a great deal of very black coffee from very tiny cups and a white colorless liquor called arak.

With these incohesive notions, I boarded the ship in New York and found myself, a few weeks later, jogging through Jaffa and gazing at the back of a gharry driver—my introduction to Palestinian Arabs.

It was not an unusual back. But the head sat rather jauntily on the neck. The kaffiyeh was wrapped rather jauntily around the head. And most jaunty of all was the red rose stuck behind the ear of a pathetically dilapidated horse.

This rose gave the whole ramshackle contraption a certain undeniable dash and gaiety. The driver cracked his whip as though he were master of a victoria and prancing steeds. And I felt like a princess galloping off to high adventure—perhaps to a handsome commoner hiding outside the palace gates.

I've never quite gotten over this feeling of high adventure when riding in a ramshackle Arab gharry. Even if I'm only going to the cobbler's, it seems that something unexpected will happen before we return.

Simple Arabs usually put a flower behind the ear of their horses or their mules. And the more mangy the animal, the more gay is the flower (or appears to be). If they drive automobiles, or buses, or lorries, they stick a flower in the windshield.

All this has nothing to do with the ponderous "Arab problem." But I like the jauntiness of people who put roses in the ear of a dilapidated horse or in the windshield of a creaking lorry. It has nothing to do with their ethics or standard of civilization. It has only to do with their primitive joy of living, which also makes them put red scarves on their heads, yellow sashes around their waists, and dance a debka while waving a handkerchief.

I'm less afraid of the primitive when it knows joy than of the civilized when it doesn't. I never could believe that people who still know the deep joy of a flower, bright colors and dancing with a handkerchief were really bad. They can be easily misled, roused, incited to be bad. But the primitive cannot be bad in the deliberate way that the civilized can be bad.

So I liked the jaunty back of this simple Arab on the first day I came to Jaffa. I still like the simple Arab, even today when I fear the part of him that has been incited.

It was a few months later before I became acquainted with an educated, town Arab. His English and cut of his suit testified to his education abroad. We were eating ices in a casino in Tel Aviv, fronting the sea. He talked for several hours and he bought me a mixed bouquet from a passing vendor, which he presented with tremendous grace and charm. It was as though he were laying all the gardens that ever had been, including the Garden of Eden, on the table before me, and for me alone. This was my first encounter with the charm of the Arab of which I shall speak in later chapters, because it is so conspicuous a part of him.

Three years has passed since this talk with Mahmoud Bey. Most of the conversation is vague now. But I remember a few sentences clearly.

"As an individual, I like you. I want to be hospitable. My house is your house. But remember, as an individual! As a race, I don't like you because I believe you are invading my country."

I was flabbergasted and dabbled with the ice to hide my confusion. Only a few months ago I had arrived in Palestine aglow with the fervor of a homebuilder. There was, I knew, an "Arab problem." But I thought it existed chiefly in English parliamentary circles or at Zionist congresses. Otherwise, it seethed underground. It lived in dark places, like anti-Semitism in other countries. The last I expected was for an Arab who was my host, and a charming host, to say, "As a race I don't like you." And then proceed to tell my why.

At first I was flabbergasted. Then I was jubilant. I was jubilant because for the first time in my life I had met a man who disliked the Jews, knew exactly why he disliked the Jews, and whose reasons were to be respected.

Mahmoud Bey did not start with the detestably annoying prologue so familiar to Jewish ears, "Some of my best friends are Jews," because, being a Semite, he had never been schooled in the rudiments of anti-Semitism.

Nor did he find it necessary to remark that, "Some Jews are peculiar, but you're so different from the others." Mahmoud is less interested in the small differences between us—a pitch of voice, a lift of the nose which comes from being out of the ghetto—than in the large sameness between us that makes us regard Palestine as our rightful home.

So Mahmoud doesn't charge us with being dirty or wily or the instigators of the Great War or the power behind the financial crisis in America.

He isn't revolted when we talk with our hands because he talks with his hands too.

Mahmoud Bey doesn't like Jews as a race because he believes they are invading his country. This was the simplest, most terse, most straightforward reason for disliking Jews that I had every heard. It made me want to shout for joy. It made me feel that I had really come home! It made me feel as much at home as all the flag-waving by Jews in Tel Aviv had made me feel at home.

For where else but in this native land could a Jew meet men who dislike his race and who could give such a clearcut, clean, answerable reason?

Anti-Semitism has usually rendered me speechless, ashamed, and utterly defeated. What could you say to a man or to a country who inferred that you were dirty, unscrupulous, engineered wars, and sometimes murdered babies for Passover? The charges were so indefinite. Your answers had to be indefinite too. You could say that your forebears had been scholars while their forebears were still savages. You could remind them that the Jews had given the world the Bible. But the world is tired of being reminded of this gift. And some Jews are becoming fatigued with harping on their ancient glory. So anti-Semitism left one ashamed of oneself and more ashamed of those who were making the vague, unanswerable charges.

But you could talk to Mahmoud Bey. He didn't render you speechless or ashamed. Here was a Semite disliking other Semites. He doesn't dislike you for the family traits, which he also shares. He doesn't dislike you for the shape of your nose, which you can't change and have no desire to change. He makes definite charges.

By what right had you come to Palestine?

By the right of the Balfour Declaration [a letter from the United Kingdom's Foreign Secretary Arthur James Balfour to Baron Rothschild stating that Britain favors and will support the establishment of a national home for the Jewish people in Palestine] and under the sanction of Feisal Ibn Hussein himself who signed the Pact of 1919 [a short-lived agreement for Arab-Jewish cooperation on the development of a Jewish homeland in Palestine, signed on January 3, 1919 by Emir Faisal (son of the King of Hejaz) and Chaim Weizmann (later President of the World Zionist Organization) as part of the Paris Peace Conference], the Arab-Jewish treaty of friendship.

What was your excuse for interfering with the liberty of the Arab people?

I need make no excuse. The Arabs had been under the heel of Turkey. Now they were a British Mandate. Jews had never entered into the question of Arab liberty.

How dare you come from America to crowd the Arab out of his own land?

I was not prepared to agree that Palestine was the Arab's own and exclusive land. And the charge that I was crowding the Arab out was ridiculous. My people were draining swamps and introducing intensive agriculture. In the Jezreel and Hepher valleys, hundreds lived now in plenty where one lived before in want. Through love and patience and courage, we are refructifying a desolate, neglected, underpopulated wasteland. Is the Arab poorer, or any more crowded, because land that a few years ago bore only *tares* (weeds —which is a word derived from the Arabic *taraha,* meaning "rejected") now bears wheat and apple trees?

Mahmoud and I were still talking, discussing, arguing when the sun set over the Mediterranean. My flowers had wilted and he presented me with another bouquet. He made bitter charges. But they were charges. There was no beating around the bush. So I answered. We both remained obdurate and unconvinced. But it didn't matter. Here was a man who had clean, healthy, definable, respectable reasons for disliking Jews. Therefore I could answer. I didn't have to plead that two thousand years ago my people wrote the Bible and extolled peace.

The sun had set now. We were both tired of talking. We sat in silence, I brooding over the fact that, for the first time in my life, I had me an avowed enemy of my people toward whom I could feel warmly. Outside of Palestine I had met honest friends of the Jews. I had never met an honest enemy. A crescent moon climbed over the crags of Jaffa, like a symbol, sealing my friendship with this honest enemy.

Later I was to learn that there are few Arabs in Palestine who are sincere enough nationalists to dislike or fear the Jews as Mahmoud Bey. The leaders continue to sell land to Jews while they are agitating against land sales. The effendi dislikes the Jews when he fears that he is loosing his death grip on the *fellahin* [Arab peasant farmers] or when foreign powers tell him to and pay him for doing it. The fellahin dislike the Jews (or pretend to) when the effendi tells them to.

And yet, even when I met with the hatred of Mahmoud Bey, I had found it a clean and honest hatred, compared to anti-Semitism that breeds in dark places.

A few years later a Jew remarked to me, "The Arabs must be our cousins. You can think of everyone else as a *goy* [a gentile]. But you can't think of an Arab as a goy."

His words summed up my meeting with Mahmoud Bey. A *goy* means not so much a non-Jew as a non-Semite. If you change or forget your religion, you remain a Semite. Even Hitler knows that. Anti-Semitism can be cultivated among non-Semites. But laws of logic prevent Semites from becoming anti-Semites. Therefore the hate of the Arab should not be confused with anti-Semitism. This hatred when it exists is honest and an honest Jew should be prepared to meet it honestly.

So my conglomeration of impressions from Lawrence, Gertrude Bell, and Zionist tracts began to be straightened out.

UMM TALLAL

Inhabitants of the Rock, pp. 142–144
Unpublished manuscript from Bar-Adon's personal archive
Earlier version in *The Palestine Post*, "Umm Tallal the Emira in Drawing Room on Her Son's Wedding Day," November 29, 1934

Kahn describes a reception given by Emira Umm Tallal on her son's wedding day. (Emira is a title of high office, used throughout the Muslim world; Umm Tallal was the mother of Tallal, who was the father of Hussein, king of Jordan.) It was a festive occasion attended by royalty and slave girls who danced for each other and then feasted. The wedding, attended by fifteen hundred people, took place the next day.

The interest that people evince in a royal bride cannot be eclipsed by any other feature of the wedding, even if the groom is as important of a figure as Emir Tallal, eldest son and heir apparent of Emir Abdullah of Transjordan. And so, though the men of Transjordan according to the tradition of this part of the world were the most important figures in the festive nuptial ceremonies at Amman, it was to their wives, sisters and daughters that they were compelled to look for an answer to the burning question, "What does the bride look like?" And the air in Amman was alive with stories of the bride's lustrous back-bobbed hair and dark, thick-lashed eyes. Indeed, as privileged ladies were to discover, the young bride, brought only several days ago from Egypt, proved to be everything that a daughter of Emir Jamil and relative of King Ghazi [of the Hashemite Kingdom from 1933 to 1939] of Iraq was expected to be.

Wives of important people fortunate enough to be invited to the palace by the emira, one of the wives of Emir Abdullah, who is known as Um Tallal (Mother of Tallal) came from all parts of the country to meet the bride. At five o'clock on Tuesday afternoon, an antechamber to the throne room was filled with all the hubbub that accompanies last-minute preparations when a crowd of women is about to embark upon an adventure. In the next room was the royal family.

To the Western eye, the dinner, which began at five o'clock and did not conclude until after ten, was everything that an Eastern royal wedding feast should be, from the numerous black slave girls who removed one's wraps, down to the quartered sheep and delectable Damascus sweets.

The first few hours of the reception proved that all women do not chatter like magpies. Chairs were drawn up in a circle, and after all had kissed and touched with their foreheads the hand of Umm Tallal they sat in repose and apparent meditation, broken only by simultaneous rising to their feet as each member of the royal family appeared. There was King Ali's [King of Hejaz and Grand Sharif of Mecca from October 1924 until December 1925] wife, wearing a white-fitted gown, and lots of little princesses, far too many to keep straight. The breathless moment, of course, was when the bride entered, in a smart frock that bore the traces of either Cairo or Paris. In her wake came Emira Haya, the sister of the groom who, according to tradition, wore a gown almost identical to that worn by her new sister-in-law.

The slaves, their brilliant-colored dresses in sharp contrast to their dark skins of gleaming ebony suddenly appeared with Arab musical instruments, and the entertainment, provided by the guests themselves, began. There were many Oriental dances to the accompaniment of singing and hand-clapping. A number of the performers stopped in the middle of their "act" and ran bashfully back to their places, somewhat abashed by the impressive figure of Umm Tallal seated in their chair before which they were dancing. Then there was a comedy number with one woman exercising the privilege of the harem to poke fun at the men. Appearing in trousers and kaffiyeh, she went through a number of antics which vastly amused Umm Tallal. The Circassian women executed their native dance which the bride watched with solemn attention. One of the ladies whispered that the bride herself had been seen to dance beautifully before her wedding, but now such levity is, alas, forbidden.

Then there was a call for an American dance and a slave girl returned from some corner with a gramophone (that may have seen better days) and a number of "jazz records." All the princesses attentively looked at the solo foxtrot, which I did, and the applause was abundant.

Dinner was then served and the rest of the story of this night is just plates and plates of roast sheep, rice and nuts and other Eastern tidbits.

The next morning camel meat was piled five feet high in preparation for the great midday feast given by Majed Pasha Adwan in honor of the wedding. About sunrise the slaughterers and chefs began to prepare the luncheon, of which 1,500 people partook. Four camels and fifty bushels of rice were prepared in huge cauldrons in the "desert kitchen," improvised not far from the Palace.

The donor personally supervised the entire process of preparation. While the aroma of the steaming rice and boiling meat filled the air, the part of 1,500 guests waited on the ground under the huge brown tents that had been especially erected for the occasion. A few meters away stood five camels, the gift of another sheik, innocently unaware that tomorrow they in turn will be stewing for the feast. The host supervised the last rite of literally shoveling the content of the vats onto one hundred large copper trays, which were alternately conveyed to the waiting crowd. The feast ended with the usual festive and colorful sword dance.

"NABLUS SOAP"

Zif Zif, pp. 111–113
Unpublished manuscript from Bar-Adon's personal archive
Earlier version in *The Palestine Post*, "Nablus Soap Is Best," June 5, 1935

Kahn writes about her visit to the Nablus factory that hand made and cut "the best soap in the world." "The Master," who had learned the trade from his father (who had learned it from his…), oversaw his three sons.

"Is this the soap factory? Are you manufacturing soap now? May we watch?"

We address our question to three men who were seated near a large cauldron that was bubbling like a miniature Vesuvius in action. They stopped their simple midday meal long enough to tell us that we must wait for "The Master."

Where and who was this intriguing Master of the Kingdom of Soap? Then we noticed a slight figure bent in prayer on a nondescript couch not far away. Neither the loud bubbling of the cauldron nor the sudden intrusion of chatterbox sightseers had disturbed the remote dignity of the pious "Master."

After he had finished his rather prolonged supplications to Allah he took his place cross-legged on a special chair reserved for him and nodded his willingness to answer our questions. But he was not inclined to be garrulous. The remote dignity seemed to trail with him, even after he had finished his prayers and, sitting cross-legged like an ancient potentate, he invested soapmaking with great mystery; as though to say that anyone who didn't know all there was to know about soap didn't deserve to be told.

There is one fact that is established at the outset and everything else is commentary, "Nablus soap is the best in the world." Everyone from the Master down to the smallest boy shoveling olive pits into the fire tells you this as though it were the alpha and omega of all existence. They have heard rumors that there are people in America and Europe who take this soapmaking business seriously. But this in no way affects their deep conviction that "Nablus soap is the best in the world."

It is fifty years since the Master was first initiated into the secrets of soap manufacturing in this very room. His father had taught him and his grandfather had taught his father. No one knew exactly when soapmaking had been introduced into his family. Fifty years had wrought not a single change in this room except that he had developed from apprentice to Master; that he had three sons who were now grouped about him, the mainstay of the factory; and that soda was mixed with olive oil instead of a hard substance that, when he was a boy, was taken from the nearby hills as a principal ingredient of the soap.

The bubbling cauldron is almost a one-man show, constituting the first and almost the last process. Here the olive oil and soda are brewed until they reach the proper consistency to be taken upstairs.

We followed the Master's sons up a pair of old stone stairs into a large arch-ceilinged room. Here was a Little Egypt replete with pyramids, pyramids of glistening soap which stretched from ceiling to floor. Yesterday had been cutting day. The contents of the cauldron were now in pyramids while drying. This soap, however, is only the common variety. The Master's sons brought for our inspection the *piéce de résistance*, colored balls and cubes of soap that delight the eye as well as the laundry.

All of this is made completely by hand, even to the cutting of the thousands of cubes. Therefore it must be sold by weight, as the cakes may not be of uniform size, although, to the inexperienced eye they all look as alike as peas.

The last point of interest takes us underground. Here the fire that boils the oil and soda is fed constantly. Waves of heat bathe your face as you descend the rickety steps. But the two little gamins seated on either side of the oven are impervious. In time to their own lilting Arab tune, they throw handfuls of olive skins and seeds into the hungry fire that must be kept blazing.

By using the refuse of the olives, the fuel problem is solved. The children tell you that they are accustomed to this heat. For hours on end they sit thus, singing and tossing in handfuls of fuel. They too are convinced that "Nablus soap is the best in the world" and putting pits on the fire is more of a rite than a chore. In this dim light and grimy air they appear as nothing more than animated voices and fists.

The Master is an executive now. The actual work is in the hands of his sturdy sons. So, when we ascend we find him as we left him, sitting cross-legged and contemplating the seething substance as though he could divine the secret of all things in the green-gray eddies.

One takes leave of the Master with the feeling that if one's sons were journalists, and if his son were a journalist, he might return and find the olive oil and soda sizzling away in the same way in the same spot under the happily contented eyes of those who know that "Nablus soap is the best in the world."

THE BRITISH

Probably written in 1936
Inhabitants of the Rock, pp. 37–43
Unpublished manuscript from Bar-Adon's personal archive

Bar-Adon sees the British as the base of a triangle—the Jews and the
Arabs are the other two legs. She commends the Mandatory Power for

its delicate handling of a difficult situation. If the British do mingle with the population, they usually prefer the Arabs since they are the more exotic and different, with the touch of servility the British are accustomed to from their experience in other parts of the Empire. The Jew is too similar and familiar, also irritating in his preoccupation with building a homeland and in his incessant questioning of orders.

The British are the base of the triangle upon which the two legs are standing. This base can serve either to bring together or to keep apart the two legs. It is natural that the legs should coincide at the vertex. And I believe this has happened in Palestine. Where Arab and Jew have met on a friendly basis, it has been of their own doing.

I can neither criticize, analyze nor even comment upon the British Mandatory power. The Mandatory seems to operate along the same general lines as the Empire. And empires and ways of empires are as strange and wonderful to me as to most American-bred folk. I have heard stray phrases such as "carrying water on both shoulders" and "divide and rule." But nothing concrete comes out of these stray phrases beyond the vague impression of castles and pawns. There is a great deal of moving about. The pawns are always raising a hue and cry. And in the end, the Empire triumphs. There are also servants of His Majesty's government who serve the Empire in remote outposts of civilization and provide material for engrossing stories by Somerset Maugham [British playwright, novelist and short story writer]. Sometimes these servants drink much whiskey or become involved with native women to forget. But they remain loyal to the Empire through thick and think and in the end the Empire, somehow, triumphs.

I know only what everyone who lives in Palestine knows too; that the British Mandatory power has had a mammoth and delicate task to perform. Whether the task is being performed for the sake of the Arabs, the Jews, or the Empire is beside the point. Establishing a Jewish homeland is a unique and historic undertaking. And in proportion to the importance of the undertaking, there have been the difficulties with the undertaking. Britain has managed to balance water on both shoulders, even though it spills over a bit now and then. It is doubtful if any other nation in the world could have succeeded so well.

And perhaps by holding the two legs of the triangle apart, the base has performed its particular function. Perhaps it is entirely the business of the Jews and the Arabs themselves whether or not they have the wisdom to coincide at the vertex. The Mandatory remains an impersonal, more or less mechanical, instrument of which the Jews and the Arabs send their protests and their demands, which are "seriously considered."

In times of peace, His Excellency the High Commissioner inspects the crops in the Jewish settlements and he inspects the crops in the Arab villages. In times of rioting, he visits the injured Arabs in government hospitals and the injured Jews in the Hadassah hospitals. This, I suppose, must be a minor part of this vague operation known as "carrying water on both shoulders." To one who believes that nothing is more important than the fusing of the two populations, the whole performance seems at times discouraging; one can imagine that in fifty years from now another high commissioner may be inspecting other Jewish and Arab crops and visiting other Jewish and Arab wounded.

But the entire experiment in Palestine would have been impossible without this base to hold the two legs of the triangle apart or together. And probably it would have been impossible for the Mandatory to function effectively except as a mechanical instrument. Such an instrument is best able to deal with what goes on in heads. As for what goes on in hearts, this should be dealt with by the Arabs and the Jews themselves.

It is easier to talk about those who are administering and serving the Mandate than about the Mandatory power. When I first arrived in Palestine and was still wide-eyed enough to ask general questions, I remember asking a British constable who was on duty at the Arlosoroff murder trial in Jaffa whether he preferred Jews or Arabs. He replied, "I prefer Arabs because when you tell them to do something, they do it. When you tell a Jew to do something, he asks you 'why.'" (This, of course, was three years before the present disturbances.)

Since that day, I have speculated a great deal about the triangle. But I have never forgotten the forthright answer of the constable and I have often wondered if there is much more to be said to explain why there is so little social intercourse between the British and the rest of the population. People who do what you tell them to do become boresome. And people who persist in asking "why" become irksome. It is cozier to stay within one's own circle than to be bored or to be irked.

Actually, there is little reason for the Englishman to rouse himself from the coziness of his own circle. He came here to do a certain job, whether he is a constable or a high official. He is doing that job. He is interested in Palestine in the same way as he is interested in all parts of the globe that concern Britain. But this fate is not bound up with the fate of Palestine. Next week or next month he may be transferred to India or the Barbados. Then Palestine will be but a headline in the newspapers and a barren spot on the shore of the Mediterranean where Jews and Arabs are squabbling. No one can blame the Englishman. If Palestine were not my country, I should wonder myself why the Jews and Arabs are making so much noise about it.

There is little necessity for the Englishman to want to associate with the natives. There is more necessity for the natives to want to associate with the Englishman. We are all—Jews and Arabs—painfully far away from understanding the British mentality. And since our destiny rests a great deal with how that mentality functions, it would be well for us to become acquainted by the dignity, humor and human qualities of these men who are talking about us so familiarly somewhere in London. But, unfortunately, many of the Englishmen we meet here are no more than human editions of Hansard's [printed transcripts of parliamentary debates; named after Thomas Curson Hansard, an early printer and publisher of these transcripts]. Sometimes they impress us by the things they say or do. But few of us know why they say or do these things. We never quite know what makes the wheels go round in an Englishman. Jews and Arabs of the higher circles exchange pleasantries with them at garden fetes or on the King's birthday, or at the High Commissioner's dinner table. It doesn't seem to go much beyond these pleasantries.

There is probably more intercourse between the Englishman and the Arab than between the Englishman and the Jew. I believe the constable in Jaffa supplied the reason. Mixed with the charm and the graciousness of the Arab, even the most important Arab is a gram or so of servility. This may not be conscious or recognized by either party. But, be it ever so subtle or ever so slight, it is there. The Englishman may not ask for or demand this servility. But at least, he knows how to treat it. He is accustomed to it in the colonies. He regards it as his due from all natives and he accepts it with the same grace as a beautiful woman accepts small favors.

Also, the Englishman who comes out to the colonies looks for the picturesque and the exotic. He likes to have lambs slaughtered for him and he likes to roll rice into small balls and eat it with his fingers, even if the sauce drips down his cuffs. All this is part of the pageantry of coming to the colonies. He may think he has outgrown this pageantry. He never quite does. The picturesque compensates, in part, for the discomforts in these sorts of places. Otherwise, they are a dreary, depressing, inadequate imitation of the West. That's what Tel Aviv must be to the average English-man. At least, that's what Tel Aviv would be to me if I were an Englishman.

The constable also answered the question why there is so little inter-mingling of Jews and English. The Jew has always asked himself "why" even when he was in places where he daren't ask aloud. Now he is at home and dare ask aloud. So he asks anybody "why" about anything. And no Englishman in a colony likes to be asked "why" by a colonist.

I think this "why" that sprouts out of the eyes, ears and mouth of the Jew confuses the Englishman a bit. Here is a brand new type of colonist. How exactly is one to deal with him?

Even in the informality of a drawing room this colonist is puzzling. He isn't different enough from an Englishman to be interesting, as an Arab can be interesting. And yet he isn't exactly like an Englishman. He is ridiculously wrapped up in this business of a homeland, sometimes tense about it, sometimes fanatical. He is grateful to the Englishman for having made the homeland possible. He realizes that without him it would probably have been impossible. It is a debt that he will not easily forget. But at the same time he is proud. He is as proud as the Englishman is proud. Despite his gratitude to the Englishman, he regards Palestine as his home. He will live for it in times of peace. He will die for it in times of trouble. And at all times he will persist in asking "why" about it.

No doubt if many of these same Jews and Englishman met in England, there would be a common intellectual meeting ground. But it's different in Palestine.

Add to this the gregariousness of the Jew, and the picture of airtight social compartments is complete. The Jew is accustomed to being herded together for one reason or another with his fellow Jews. It has become second nature to him. He has even learned to like it. He has not been in Palestine long enough, nor under favorable enough conditions to lose this herding instinct which comes from being on the defensive. He likes to talk to his own people. They share his problems, his joys and his fears. He would like to know the Englishman. But under the existing conditions, this requires an effort. He retires instead to the coziness of his own circle.

So here is the Englishman, the stolid base of the triangle: sometimes drawn to the Arab by the picturesque and then withdrawing because of boredom; and a bit baffled by this new kind of colonist, the Jew who is proud and who persists in asking anybody "why" about anything.

THE ARAB

Probably written in 1936
Inhabitants of the Rock, pp. 43–61
Unpublished manuscript from Bar-Adon's personal archive

According to Kahn, the burden of creating a relationship between the Arabs and the Jews rests on the Jews as the ones coming into the country. She stresses the differences between the town and the village Arab.

She admires the hospitality, generosity, and dignity of the village Arab but feels that the illiteracy of this generation would prevent any closeness with the educated Jews. The town Arab is torn between his own culture and the West—sometimes he rejects his own culture's positive values and adopts vulgar ones from the West. He protests the sale of land to Jews, only after selling his own. An attempt to learn more from an American-educated Arab woman fails when that woman flatly denies (perceived) discrimination against women in her society, barring the possibility of open discussion.

The burden of the duty of establishing relationships rests with the Jew who is returning to Palestine. One would hardly have expected the traditional hospitality of the Arab to extend as far as making actual advances toward the incoming people, externally so different from himself. I cannot see where the Arab could have done more than wait with folded hands for these advances to be made. And in this respect the Jew has sometimes fallen short because he has had to expend his energies in so many directions.

Because of the marked class cleavage, we must consider the town and village Arab separately.

The village Arab may mar the charm of his flowing garments by adding a shabby European cloth coat or a pair of brown brogues. He has listened to the radio so often in coffeehouses that the unseen voice is no longer a grave mystery. But despite these surface flourishes, he remains an unadulterated Easterner.

I have been in Palestine only three years. I think my experiences are not unlike those of other immigrants. Like most Jews, I have been obsessed with busyness. I have looked at much and seen little. I have not learned Arabic. The things that I have learned, many people know without coming to Palestine. I know that one must always accept coffee when it is proffered by an Arab, even if he wipes out the cup before you drink with the dirty hem of his *abaya* [a simple, loose overgarment]. I have learned a bit here and a bit there about the Arab.

The principal thing that I have learned is how much I must still learn. I am still of the West. I have come back to Palestine. He was already here. And when my first flush of busyness subsides, I must learn about him. He will not learn about me unless I teach him. He peers at my bobbed hair and free ways, his wonder tinged with amazement. Otherwise he pursues the tenor of his ways, not very perturbed by the fact that I have come from America to settle in Palestine. My coming is far more momentous to me than to him.

In times of peace, he has the composure of the East. If he were an American, he would formulate solutions to complexities before the complexities arose. Being an Easterner, he is slow to sense complexities and does not create them. If I and my ways do not collide with him, he does not collide with me. When, however, his leaders tell him that I have desecrated mosques and murdered babies, he believes them and sets out to murder me. He does not know me well enough to have faith that I would not desecrate a mosque and have no interest in murdering babies. It is partly my fault that he does not have this faith. Learning the ways of this Easterner and teaching him mine is a mammoth task and a sacred duty. I am busy, but I dare not be too busy to realize that he will not take the initiative.

What are the chances for executing this duty?

I reiterate that I do not know the Arab well. I have been to his festivals. I have slept in the tents of his wives. I have ridden in his buses to Jericho, all tangled up with chickens and melons and cacti fruit. I have brushed past him. And I have emerged with the impression—which can be no more than impression—that I like the simple Arab.

Jews who have been here longer and who know the Arab better may refute me. I may be speaking from the depth of my ignorance. But many Jews who have been here a long time tell me that they like the simple Arab too. And the longer they have been here, and the better they have known him, the more sure they seem to be that friendship between the Arab and the Jew is a possibility and a probability.

The village Arab, aside from being an unadulterated Easterner, is a simple man. I cannot see where he is different from simple men the world over, except for his particular and peculiar headgear or traditional customs. A Russian journalist once told me, "Our peasants are peculiar. They will take you into their hovels and will share with you their bread and vodka. But while you sleep, they may steal everything—even your shoes. But you cannot be annoyed. They don't realize that they are doing anything wrong. And at heart they are such good people."

I wonder if, after all, the Russian peasant is so peculiar. I wonder if all simple people are not peculiar to us who have long since stopped being simple and have become very complex. They have a naiveté that confounds us. They have a confusing code which involves sharing and also involves the survival of the fittest. This code prompts them to offer us shelter and bread and, sometimes, to steal our shoes while we sleep. But at heart they are good people. Being naive with the naiveté of a child, they are quick to sense kindness or insult and to respond. They have no prejudices. And they laugh and cry and hate and love without malice aforethought. This same naiveté, which prompted them to share their bread with me a few months ago, is prompting them tonight, as I write this, to kill British constables and to burn the wheat of Jewish settlers.

It seems to me that the same rules that apply to simple men, in general, should apply to simple Arabs in particular. And, as far as I can see, these rules do apply. I remember the day I rode to Hebron in an Arab bus. It was orange season and everyone on the bus was eating oranges. The floor was a jungle of peels and the juice was gushing in miniature fountains down chins and across wrists. The last thing one felt like doing was eating an orange. But when the Arab occupying the same seat proffered my companion and me his sack of fruit, there was nothing to do but eat an orange. And when, with superb gallantry, he offered to peel it (after wiping his knife on a filthy sack) there seemed nothing to do but have it peeled. My companion, meanwhile, was frantically peeling her orange with her fingers, fearing lest his gallantry and his dirty knife extend to her. She was a tourist. So it didn't matter. But I wasn't. So it mattered. It mattered very much that I accept this gallantry with the same graciousness as the gesture was made, although I might formulate a secret hope that soon he will learn not to clean his knife on his filthy sack.

It is always like that when you're with simple Arabs—some filth and much charm and warmth and spontaneity, all mixed together. I've looked for hate in the mixture—deliberately looked for it. I've been told it's supposed to be there. I've simply failed to find it. I have tried to be a realist. And knowing that hate has much to do with realism, I have looked for hate. I have long since discarded rose-colored glasses. Wherever I go, I search for this hate because if it is there, then it is high time that I knew about it.

Many times I've searched in Ramallah when I went to buy pottery, and in Bethlehem when I went to buy mother of pearl brooches, and in Hebron when I went to buy glass, and in Nablus when I went to see the Samaritans. I've searched Jericho and Tulkarm. I've searched in trains and buses. I've searched on the shores of the Dead Sea and in the desert beyond Be'er Sheva.

I have failed to find this hate, except sometimes among the schooled town Arab, whom I shall discuss later.

I think that if men and women looked at me with hate in their eyes, I'd recognize it as soon as the next fellow. But I can't put into their eyes what I haven't seen. And I've seen only what one usually sees among simple people—a conglomeration of filth and warmth. And in Palestine, this warmth seems to include Jews as spontaneously as it includes anybody else.

Usually we more complex organisms, who neither share gracefully nor steal the shoes of our guests, are not called upon to mingle very closely with these simple folk. If we mingle at all, it is to observe them politely through pince-nez, as did the Russian journalist; but we Jews in Palestine are called to mingle very closely. And despite the naive virtues of the simple Arab, establishing relationships is difficult.

There is no opportunity, for this generation at least, to enjoy the slightest bond of mind or intellect. The Jews, including the village Jew (or especially the village Jew) has been cultured and horticultured to a fine point. The village Arab is illiterate. In most cases, the Jew has encompassed the world and come back to simplicity. The Arab clings to his simplicity because he knows nothing else. Though they reach the same spot, they are at the opposite ends of the poles. The Jew is not capable of coming back to peasantry as the Arab understands peasantry. In the next generation, or the next after that, the village Jew may be less complex and the village Arab less simple. But this doesn't reduce the gap today. And this gap of mind is painful to the Jew as it is painful to few men. He has put so much of his life into books. What is he to say to this man who cannot even read a book? So there are almost a million men here to whom the Jew cannot speak—even when he knows Arabic.

But meantime where is the language of the heart. The simple Arab will not take the initiative in establishing a relationship. He is not even aware of the necessity. But he will not bar the way. He will share his sack of oranges with the Jew and he will accept our sack.

Sacks of oranges. Such little things. Such small drops in the bucket of the complicated "Arab-Jewish problems." Perhaps small. Perhaps as large as the bucket. For who has ever drawn the line where small things end and large things begin?

The town Arab is quite a different species of man from his village brother. It is not solely busyness that has kept the Jew from being able to reach him. Nor is it that the Jew prefers a simple man to an educated one. For, as I have said, the Jew is so immersed in his books that he must pick his way back to the simple man. I believe that the thing that is baffling the Jew is that the town Arab today is neither cultivated nor wild, neither tamed nor untamed, neither simple nor complex. He is at the crossroads of many things. How is the Jew—how is anyone—to reach him?

The town Arab may have been converted to Christianity and attended the Friend's School in Ramallah. He may have graduated from the American University in Beirut. He even may have studied in England.

In most cases his father did not. He is the first generation to taste of higher Western education and to be thrown into a new environment. The learning and the environment may be in his head. But they have not had time to be absorbed into his bloodstream. At times they rattle him. He suffers all the proverbial dangers of a little knowledge.

This frequently results in his becoming a hybrid product, combining the East with a smattering of the West. A combination of Eastern and Western influences should be sought. But he is not yet sufficiently discriminating. The West is apt to mesmerize him. Too often he relinquishes some of the good things of the East and adopts some of the bad things of the West. He has not yet the wisdom to pick and choose, to separate the wheat from the chaff. He is too quick to distance his own and to allow himself to be wooed and won by the glamor of the new. But he never takes more from the West than the glamor, the superficial or the distinctly bad. Sometimes he is like a parrot who only picks up swearwords. He is neither here nor there. In his effort to be smart, he becomes a smart aleck. In the same way that adolescent boys must pass through that "difficult stage," he is passing through a difficult stage in his general development.

I think this hybrid stage must be trying for him. He is not to be censured. One meets with the same thing in Baghdad and Damascus, and probably wherever East and West are colliding. The education process is always gradual. The fact that it has begun at all is cause for rejoicing rather than censure. At the same time, it is extremely difficult for the Jew who must find a way to reach him and to talk to him during this transitional period. If only we could wait until he passes through this "difficult stage" and comes out safely on the other side. But we cannot wait. We must talk to him today. And I believe this hybridness is one of the principal factors that has kept us from reaching him. At the present moment, he doesn't know exactly what kind of a man he is personally or politically. Neither do we.

This quality of being neither here nor there reveals itself in small ways and large ways, from the cut of his suit to the variety of his nationalism.

Sometimes he displays an excessive admiration for anything Western in order to stress the fact that he has studied in Beirut or London. In this event, he prefers speaking English, even poor English, to Arabic. He abandons his naive dress and is not yet able to choose his western clothes in good taste. In his home he discards low stools and divans in favor of garish, overstuffed furniture.

One of the most pleasant homes I have ever seen belonged to the Arab servant of a friend of mine. We visited him on his wedding day, traveling an hour on horseback from the main road to reach his little village. A rug, stools, and plenty of cushions comprised almost the whole of the furnishings. The square, box-like rooms of a Western house need decoration to make them livable. But the Arab rooms, with their graceful arches, nooks and deep window ledges are their own adornment. These houses must have been conceived by some wise architect of the East who knew well the climate and conditions of the country but who knew nothing at all about overstuffed furniture and bric-a-brac manufactured in Japan.

It seems rather a shame that the Jews have not adopted these Arab houses—it is doubtful if they can improve upon them. And it seems more of a shame when the Arabs destroy, by improvement, the beauty that is their own heritage.

The clothes and the home of the hybrid Arab are unimportant externals that in no way concern the Jew. Yet they serve as a key to important internals that must concern the Jew if he is to bridge the present gap. They explain and give physical body to the loosening of spiritual moorings; dignified, splendid, Oriental moorings that should be too proud to creak before the West.

The honor, pride, and above all else, dignity of the thoroughbred Arab needs no elaboration. This dignity was based on traditions that did not countenance compromise. This Arab was guided by tradition even down to the tune that he beat when he ground his coffee. He knew his friends. He knew his enemies. They knew that he knew.

This is not to be interpreted as a lament because the educated Arab does not sit cross-legged in the desert and grind his coffee. It is natural that he should want his coffee prepared for him in the best fashion provided by the cafés of Jerusalem, Tel Aviv or Haifa.

But it is a lament that he does not hold onto the best of his own spiritual traditions—the honor and pride and dignity of the coffee grinders—until such time as he fully adopts the traditions of the West. But that is his business and he seems to be tending in that direction. At all events, he cannot continue to vacillate. He must come back to the East, or go completely West, or fuse the best of the two wisely.

The same hybrid impulses that prompt him to put a suite of overstuffed furniture in a vaulted room are responsible for his politics. Of late, he has become a dilettante in nationalism. He looks wistfully in the direction of Mussolini. Sometimes he sends his children to Italy to thoroughly imbibe the ways and means. But because he is a dilettante with only a smattering of the West, the constructive phases of Mussolini's program, which have benefited at least his own people, completely escape the Arab.

In recent years, the influential and opulent Arab has not lifted a finger to better the condition of his people. Not a single educational, scientific and cultural or health institution has sprung up in Palestine through the will of the Arab people. Now and again there are rumors of a university or vague references to "funds" which, owing to inner dissention, come to naught. It is only in times of rioting that these "funds" materialize. The educated classes cannot say that they do not want these things. They want them and they use them for themselves. But to give them to those less opulent than themselves is a social trick of the West that they have not yet learned.

Of late years one has heard much of the lessening of beggars and penury in Italy. In a series of articles on Palestine by Mr. St. John Ervine [Irish author, writer, critic and dramatist], one got the impression that there was nothing else here but Arabs whining for *baksheesh*. Mr. Ervine said, "I am not ready to believe that a ruling race can come out of a people whose infants' first articulate word is not *Allah* but *baksheesh*....When I see Arabs displaying some of that pride that is, I am continually assured, the badge of all their tribe, I shall begin to believe in their nobility."

I wish that Mr. Ervine could have met with me the thirteen-year-old son of Sheikh Mithgal Pasha in Transjordan, already a man, already a Crown Prince of the desert in his own right, more interested in showing his splendid horsemanship to his guests than in collecting baksheesh. There wasn't a whine in his taut brown body.

But the educated Arab has renounced this freedom and pride of the desert of his own free will and not through the coercion of the British Mandate or the Jews. He had renounced it before they came to Palestine. Often he proclaims himself less attracted by what remains of the desert tradition than is the tourist. Well and good. But he has taken away the dignity of Mithgal Pasha's son and replaced it with the whine of baksheesh. Either the child must have the dignity of the untamed, or he must have the advantages of the tamed. As long as he remains a diluted hybrid, he will whine, and the Westerner—be he Mr. St. John Ervine or the Jew—will be obliged to seek for that ancient nobility.

In times of peace, the influential Arab busies himself with land transactions and other personal and private business. Sometimes he winters in Cairo and summers in Lebanon. And his people whine unless they are cared for by government funds, now plentiful owing to Jewish immigration. In times of riots, he summons his "people" to fight for a cause that he has never troubled to define to them.

It is this kind of dilettante nationalism that makes it difficult for the Jew to approach the town Arab. For it is a nationalism that seizes like a vulture on the degradations of Italy and Germany and any other parts of the West that have anything to say about nationalism. But of the constructive forces that are these countries' only excuse for being, they remain completely unaware.

Meantime, the Jew has come home with an overwhelming love for the country. Nationalism to him, as far as Palestine is concerned, can only be translated into terms of long-needed trees and wheat and grapes and cities, into terms of hospitals and schools and laboratories. He does not expect even the town Arab to know as much about these things as he knows. But if only the town Arab would show that he wants to know....

There are in Palestine a few town Arabs, like Mahmoud Bey, who are nationalists and at the same time idealists. They preach the non-sale of land to Jews and, I believe, they abstain from selling. Jews respect this type of Arab, even when we disagree most bitterly with the premise of his argument.

We respect him because he knows what he believes and is willing to sacrifice for that belief when the need arises. We understand him because he functions as we function. We Jews need land. And yet time and time again I have heard Jews complain, "The leaders agitate against the sale of land. But they all sell their own land." Paradoxically enough, this selling of land disturbs the Jew despite his terrific land hunger. It disturbs him because he finds that his Arab countrymen, with whom he must reach an understanding, are vacillating. And this vacillation leads them to betray their own people. They have relinquished ancient tribal loyalty and have not yet learned modern national loyalty. And if they betray their own people, whom will they not betray?

Unfortunately the number of Mahmoud Beys [Bey—Ottoman or Turkish title for chieftain, traditionally applied to the leaders of small tribal groups] in Palestine is shockingly few. The number of educated Arabs, who have started to agitate about land sales after they succumbed to selling their own land at exorbitant prices, is shockingly many.

I do not desire to delve into the fine points of politics in Palestine. I mention the sale of land only because it is so characteristic of the relationships, large and small, between town Arabs and Jews.

Had the nationalist Arab consistently refused to sell his land to the Jews, a different solution to the carrying out of the Mandate would have been sought several decades ago. Had the nationalist Arab objected to the influx of Jewish immigration and capital a long time before the newcomers had settled themselves in their homes and before the six million pound surplus had piled up in the government treasury, the Jew would be less confused by the Arab outcry.

But the tactics of the town Arab confuse the Jew and postpone understanding tactics. At best, they are unpleasant. The Jew had hoped to have been done with them when he came to Palestine. His position was simple enough. He had been given the right to have a homeland in Palestine. He rallied funds from Jews, rich and poor, throughout the world. He moved in bag and baggage and put not only his nose but also his body and soul to the grindstone. He was not prepared for tactics.

If he had to encounter opposition, he would have preferred it to be the honest, hostile, opposition of a Mahmoud Bey. But the tactics of a hybrid town Arab, who himself does not know what he wants, are difficult to meet. And I think that it is this undercurrent of tactics, more than anything else, that has made social contact difficult.

There are, or course, some pleasant relationships between town Arabs and Jews. It must always be borne in mind that the Arab is usually hospitable and charming, no matter when or under what circumstances you meet him. So there are friendly interchanges of opinion at rotary club meetings or in the course of business dealings, especially since the Arab has the Eastern knack for mixing business with pleasure. In Jerusalem, where a number of Jewish tenants rent houses from Arab landlords, one frequently hears, "Our Arab landlord and his family are delightful."

And in this way, acquaintanceships have sprung up. There is the elaborate interchange of compliments and pleasantries. Sometimes one family is invited to tea. Unfortunately, these acquaintanceships usually remain acquaintanceships, based a good deal on the proverbial Arab graciousness that none can withstand.

There is still too much strain and too little spontaneity. Inviting Arabs to tea or being invited by Arabs is still somewhat in the nature of an event; still something to mention to one's friends afterward. No doubt it is the same in Arab circles. There is as yet little vestige of those deep bonds of friendship that can link people together tightly enough to transcend politics and memoranda.

The Muslim custom of keeping their women in the background helps to make social intercourse less free. Jews are still a bit embarrassed by this "man's world." If they plan to invite Ibrahim Bey, there is some uneasiness in the household. Has Ibrahim Bey a wife or wives? Is she a Muslim? Is she ever seen in public? Should she or should she not be included in the invitation?

Some deep friendships have grown up. And when they have, they often prove themselves of fabric strong enough to withstand hard wear. One of the blessings of every riot in Palestine has been that it unearths such bonds. Out of the blood and horror of the 1929 slaughters [during the week of riots from August 23 to 29, 133 Jews were killed by Arabs and 339 others were injured], numerous instances emerged of Jews and Arabs risking their lives for each other. And no doubt when the smoke of the present [1936–39] disturbances clears away, history will have repeated itself.

Such ties reveal themselves in times of stress. Why not in our day-to-day existence?

Why? I do not know. But I believe that when the Jew tries to know this town Arab, he is able to get just so far and no further. Then he bumps up against this disconcerting hybridness. If he bumped up against honest hostility, he would meet it. But he bumps up against a man who is no longer of the East, not quite of the West, and not very sure in which direction he is tending.

This hybrid quality, as opposed to the dignity born of self-assurance, was illustrated in a story told to me by a Jewish executive. One day, while driving, he passed an automobile that had been in an accident. He took the injured occupants to the hospital. One of the men whom he had helped was an influential Arab sheikh. When he recovered, the sheikh sought the Jew out and was extravagant in his gratitude. The incident resulted in a deep friendship which ripened with the passing years.

On his deathbed, the sheikh sent for the Jew and with characteristic simplicity asked him to "act as a father to my son." The Jew accepted his fosterfatherhood.

Years passed. The busy executive and the growing boy kept in close touch. "And now?" I asked.

"Well, now it's difficult. Whenever there are disturbances, I don't see him. He is a bit of a nationalist. Before the 1929 riots, he came to me for advice. What could I say to him? I could only remind him that now he is a man. He is an Arab and must behave as an Arab in the way that he believes right."

So now and again there is this chasm between the fosterfather and his protégé. For the young man has not attained yet that self-confidence, that dignity, that bigness of soul that had raised his father so far above and beyond movements.

I remember an encounter that I had with the wife of a prominent Arab attorney. I wished to discuss with her the status of Arab women in Palestine. Hitherto my relations with Arab women has been confined mostly to simple Muslims who wistfully admired my modern jewelry and were pleased when I remarked that their own hammered silver earrings were more beautiful. So I looked forward to my meeting with Mrs. Y., who had studied in America. I wanted to push beyond the romantic veils of the harem, and Mrs. Y. could help me.

I came to her office and we plunged into the subject. I was hungry for information and my eager questions tumbled over each other. But an unpleasant clash came when I mentioned the fact that the fellahin women walk beside the donkeys while their husbands ride. She was incensed. She felt that I was insulting her people. And then she flatly denied that women do walk beside their husbands.

I was taken aback. We were not theorizing. We were talking facts, and I had seen Arab women walking alongside donkeys more times than I could remember. They are as much a part of the Palestinian landscape as olive trees and cacti.

Had Mrs. Y. replied, "That is the way of the East and we like our way," there would have been no quarrel. No one has ever proved that the Western treatment of women is superior to the Eastern. Perhaps women in purdah are shut out from as much evil as good. Who is to judge?

Or had Mrs. Y. declared that the position of fellahin women is not enviable but it is on the road to improvement, there would still have been grounds for discussion.

Under the circumstances, I could only gulp down my coffee, hurriedly finish my cigarette and flee. I had no way of meeting this smoldering resentment of hers that made it appear as though the fellahin women walking on the roads were a figment of my antagonistic imagination.

Here again was the hybrid—the lack of pride in the East, and the intangible resentment against the Jew and the West.

Before I left, however, Mrs. Y. invited me to come to have tea at her home. I said that I would. I thought that I would. But somehow I never did. I cross-examined myself. Was her invitation sincere or was it mechanical Arab cordiality? Did she really want to see me again? How could we talk in the face of this unreasonable resentment of hers? Would the tea hour be as strained as the interview had been? By the time I finished the self cross-examination, there was no spontaneity. So I postponed going until another day. And I never went.

This is just a stray encounter but more or less typical of what often happens when we Jews try to slip across the frontiers. I have tried many times and met with one kind of barrier or another. Other Jews have never tried and cannot tell you exactly why they have never tried.

I recall a recent conversation with a Jewish woman who had lived here for some fifteen years. She was expressing some opinion about the Arab population and I interrupted with, "Do you know many Arabs personally?"

Miss G. was taken by surprise, reflected for a moment and admitted, "Well, no. Practically none." Then she corrected herself, "Yes, I know my Arab landlord of course. I like his family, especially his young daughter. Once she came to my house for lunch. I liked her."

I tried to pin Miss G. down. Did she intend to remain here for the rest of her life? Yes. Didn't she feel any curiosity about these people among whom she has lived for fifteen years and with whom she intended to remain?

I could tell by her surprise that it was probably the first time she had been pinned down. Her replies were halting, "Yes, they are my neighbors. Of course.

I never had any prejudice against them. I like them when they're nice, just as I like anyone else. But I have always had my own friends, just as I had my own friends in England. I never avoided meeting them. It just never happened."

So that's it. A Jew can live in Palestine for fifteen years and just never happen to meet an Arab. Or you can try to make it happen and find a Mrs. Y. who discourages you.

I don't know how we Jews are going to slip over these frontiers. All I do know is that we have to slip over these frontiers—every last Jew who intends to remain in Palestine. Even if it means planting less vineyards and building less cities, we've got to tackle these frontiers. A Jew living in England can afford to remain within the warm circle of her own friends. A Jew coming to Palestine cannot. The circle must be widened to include new friends of the East.

It isn't easy. It would be easier if the Arabs would stretch forth a hand. But the gap must be bridged. If they don't help, the Jews must do it themselves. It isn't easy.

But nothing in Palestine is ever easy. You have to move a boulder to find room to plant a potato. And you have to slip over frontiers to get to a man.

So here is the triangle.

The Jew obsessed with a busyness that shuts out all the world but renaissance.

The Englishman carrying out the Mandate like a capable hand moving chess pawns.

The simple Arab ready to share his sack of oranges and ready to accept those of the Jews.

The town Arab who is passing through that "difficult stage."

THE TRIANGLE

Probably written in 1936
Inhabitants of the Rock, pp. 29–37
Unpublished manuscript from Bar-Adon's personal archive

Bar-Adon feels that very little progress was made in building "peace and understanding" between Jews and Arabs because neither side had accepted the vital necessity of doing so. She understands the Arab refusal to show gratitude toward the Jews for the "gifts of the West" that they brought (which would have come eventually). Again she insists that the Jew must be the initiator in breaking down barriers, although she understands that perhaps this has not happened because he has been overwhelmed by the task of building the country: Tel Aviv, the agricultural settlements, hospitals, roads, etc.

How far have the Jews and Arabs gone toward achieving an understanding?

The basic blood bond prevents natural hatred and provides the foundation for this understanding. But the structure that will ultimately rise on this foundation has hardly been begun. Occasionally bricks and mortar have been brought. But the great task of building still lies ahead, with all of its mountainous difficulties and all of its inestimable rewards to both sections of the population.

This structure will have to be built with infinite patience, deep wisdom and fine appreciation for the delicacy of all human mechanisms.

The first requisite, however, is the conviction on the part of the builders that the structure is necessary; and the realization that it will not spring up out of the ground like a mushroom.

As I write this, the riots of 1936 are in full swing. The Jews and the English are mouthing hysterical slogans about the need for "peace and understanding." The Arabs are too roused to mouth anything beyond the age-old battle cry of death and destruction.

The "peace and understanding" slogans have nothing to do with the ultimate structure. Peace and understanding, if they are to be interpreted as lack of hostility, could be secured cheaply. If the Arab leaders had been restrained from prostituting the newspapers for purposes of incitement, probably we would have had peace. If the British bayonet had been more apparent on April 19, probably we would have had peace. But this is a negative peace.

The basic peace, existing between one Semite and another Semite, we have already. But this too is a negative peace. It is there because it happens to be there.

The ultimate structure must be the kind of deep peace and rich understanding that comes of a shared culture and that will bring more abundant living to Jew and Arab.

One must struggle and wait and work toward this kind of understanding. Once it has been established, the Arab agitator may lose his taste for agitating and may spend his energies in more constructive fields. If he does not, he will find it more difficult and perhaps impossible to inflame the Arab masses against their Jewish neighbors.

Why has so little progress been made in the building of this structure of peace and understanding? Tel Aviv is twenty-six years old and the first BILU settlers came from Russia to Jaffa fifty-four years ago.

Fifty-four years is a long time in the life of a man. In the life of men and nations, it is trifling. It was not to be expected that these Semite peoples, separated for centuries and exposed during that separation to diametrically opposed forces, would have become completely reunited in fifty-four years.

Notwithstanding, more steps toward reuniting could have been taken in more than five decades. There are numerous reasons why they have not. Perhaps the basic reason is that none of the people involved has looked squarely in the face the crying necessity for fusion.

This may sound paradoxical. On the surface it may appear as though the major consideration in Palestine has been the "Arab-Jewish problem." In times of upheaval, this is certainly true. In times of peace, it is true in a political rather than a social sense. And human beings will probably never reach the point where politics outweigh society.

Whether or not there is a legislative council, whether fewer or more dunams of land are sold to Jews, whether a thousand more or less immigrants come into the country, are all beside the point as long as Jews and Arabs live in narrow, prescribed circles and fail to intermingle freely.

Why has there been so little social intercourse between Jew and Arab? Who is to blame?

The marked increase in the Arab population in the vicinity of Jewish settlements and comparative decrease in towns like Nablus and Gaza testify to the fact that the Arab is ready to accept the gifts of the West.

I say "gifts of the West" pointedly. I abhor the argument that Jews have brought gifts. I don't blame the Arabs for abhorring it too.

I distrust righteous, magnanimous gift-bearers. And usually I don't like to receive gifts, even if they happen to be gifts that I need or want. I like honest give and take. But I don't like gifts. I see no reason why the

Arab should like to receive gifts either. And worse still is to be reminded of those gifts.

Jews inside of Palestine neither think nor talk about the "gifts of the Jews." They realize that the Jews have brought from the West what they needed to build a healthy country. They planted trees, made roads and built hospitals because they wanted them and needed them. They are pioneers and harsh realists. They do not believe for one moment that they would have done these backbreaking things for the Arab population. This would have been preposterous. But, having built these things, it would have been equally as preposterous to have closed them to their Arab neighbors. From a purely selfish point of new, it would be foolish to foster sick people in a healthy country.

So the Jew inside of Palestine takes a different view than some people outside of Palestine who sometimes foolishly refer to these "gifts to the Arabs." The Jew here is too much of a realist to view himself as a philanthropist or a benefactor. He brought certain things to Palestine. They were good things. It is natural that the Arabs should have partaken of them. It could not have been otherwise.

Being a realist, the Jew in Palestine does object, however, when Arab leaders or sentimental English tourists infer that the things the Jew has brought are not good, or that the Arab has not partaken of them to his benefit. The things he brought came from the West and, at all events, would have come here eventually. The Jew was merely an instrument that brought them more quickly. The Arab masses, when not incited, have accepted these gifts of the West.

And yet, in some ways, I believe that the Jew has failed to discharge his duty. Since he was returning to Palestine, this duty was tremendous, in some ways overwhelming. It was, of course, a self-imposed duty. It was a condition of the declaration that gave him Palestine as a Homeland. But the Jews have imposed a number of duties on themselves, such as returning to the Arabs a part of the land that they purchased and made fit for cultivation.

This duty meant that he must not stop at transporting the gifts of the West; he must not stop at throwing open his doors. He must teach the Arab to know the man who has transported these gifts; he must coax him, when necessary, to enter the open doors. He must not only invite him to participate in the Levant Fair at Tel Aviv [an international trade fair held in Tel Aviv in the 1930s]. He must coax him, educate him, until he is able to understand the importance of becoming a vital part of the trade fabric of the country. Yes, the Jew must coax him if necessary. This is no time for petty pride. All this the Jew must do. A tremendous duty!

And yet, under normal circumstances, I think the Jew would have discharged this duty of examining and becoming thoroughly acquainted with his fellow countrymen who were already occupying the country. But the return of the Jew has not been accomplished under normal circumstances. From the moment he set foot in the country, he was faced with staggering difficulties and problems. No busier person can be imagined than a Jew coming to Palestine! And this busyness has been one of the prime factors that has kept him from devoting himself to getting to know his Arab neighbors better.

I want to explain this busyness. It is difficult to put into words. Probably never before have men and women been so absorbed in any task as have the Jews in the resettlement of Palestine. For centuries they have waited and prayed for this return, and when the Balfour Declaration gave them the right for which they had prayed, they devoted themselves to the upbuilding with a zeal that beggars description. To properly explain this busyness would entail the explaining of modern Jewish Palestine.

To understand this busyness, one must know the dynamic, thriving phenomenal city of Tel Aviv, with its 150,000 inhabitants and its theaters, schools, hospitals, factories and art museum. Only then can one realize why inhabitants of Tel Aviv have been so frightfully busy since they began putting tents on sand dunes twenty-six years ago.

Every ounce of strength of almost every man and woman, living in Tel Aviv has gone into the birthing of the all-Jewish city. Without this combined strength, the city would not have been built. And the Jews needed a city in their homeland.

There are today thousands of Jews living in Tel Aviv who know as little about an Arab as an Englishman living in Manchester or an American living in Timbuktu. If their Arab fruit vendor cheats them out of a piaster's worth of grapes, they conclude that all Arabs are sly. If their Arab fishmonger brings them a bouquet of roses, they conclude that all Arabs are delightful. During times of peace, they think little more about the Arab than they do about the Icelander. In time of rioting, they fear him because he murders.

I do not hold a brief for this kind of airtight, insulated living. But I think I know why the Jew in Tel Aviv lives this way. He is absorbed in a task as few other men have ever been absorbed. And if he were less absorbed, he would not have built Tel Aviv in twenty-six years. And the Jew needed a city. After centuries of homelessness, he deserved one.

One must walk through the local products pavilion of the Levant Fair. Here one sees silks, leather bags, razor blades, refrigerators, biscuits, perfumes, and fertilizer—all made in Palestine.

English ladies, like Amy Fullerton, who published diaries in the eighties [1880s] of their visits to the Holy Land, record how they were obliged to bring to Palestine the simplest articles, such as tea and sunglasses. Were these ladies to stroll through the Levant Fair, they would understand better than we why the Jewish manufacturer has been so busy.

One must also know the agricultural settlements. How the Jewish pioneers turned swamps into orange groves, wheat fields and tomato patches is now a well-known saga that hardly bears repeating. It was a gigantic task. It sapped men's energies and even their lifeblood. Every vine, every blade of grass, every tree that is blossoming and bearing fruit in these stony wastelands tells the story of the busyness of these pioneers.

They came to the barrenness of the Jezreel Valley or to the isolated outpost of Tel Hai. They faced the task of refructifying the unfriendly soil. And they were plunged into a busyness that made them forget everything in the world, except the vagaries of rain and sun and wind and crop.

Sometimes they forgot kith and kin whom they had left in other parts of the world. Sometimes they forgot to eat when they had not enough to eat in their terrific struggle for a new life. Perhaps it was not well that it should have been so. But there was no other way. Palestine only could have been revived by these strange, ideal-intoxicated people who were content to be busy. So busy that they forgot all else—sometimes even forgot the other part of the population.

Strangely enough, despite their busyness, closer relationships with Arabs are enjoyed by these colonists than by any other sections of the population. These relationships, however, have not been tended or cultivated. They grew up in the way that good things have of growing up among simple people. The Jewish colonists dug wells. And the Arabs, who had been accustomed to lugging their water for miles on muleback, began to use their wells. Jews were invited to Arab festivals in nearby camps. Sometimes they went through picturesque peace rites. I saw Arabs joining in the hora dances at the May Day celebration at the Dead Sea. I saw Arabs seated around the Passover table in the kibbutz of Givat Brenner.

The early pioneers had to make the modern language from the ancient one. The newcomers today have to learn the modern language. It is a difficult language. It keeps them busy—too busy to learn Arabic. But their children, to whom Hebrew is a mother tongue, are learning Arabic in the schools, and for these children it will be less difficult to know their Arab neighbors. The renaissance involved the establishing of schools, a university, newspapers, theaters; in fact all of the necessities and amenities of life that accumulated over a long period of time elsewhere.

And it must be borne in mind too that the Jew came from the West to the East. He had to contend with the ordinary physical difficulties such as disease and change of climate. Never before have a people, scattered, broken and crippled by centuries of wandering, attempted a renaissance. Therefore, this people have suffered backaches, headaches, and heartaches. They have much to show for these aches. And they may also have to show a few sins of omission and commission. It is understandable.

Once before, the Jews withdrew from the world for forty years and remained in the desert between Egypt and Palestine in order to become changed from slaves to freemen. Perhaps we are witnessing this withdrawal again. This generation of Jews, who are too busy to raise their eyes from their crops and their cities and their factories, are in the desert again—the desert of transition.

SEVEN FAT YEARS

Probably written in 1936
Inhabitants of the Rock, pp. 29–37
Unpublished manuscript from Bar-Adon's personal archive

The title refers to the seven years of comparative peace and prosperity between the riots of 1929 and 1936. Despite the high level of violence between Arabs, there were few attacks on Jews, evidence of the basic blood bond between two Semite peoples. The village Arab had to be incited by the newspapers and led to believe that his basic rights were being usurped by the Jews.

The wonder is not that the "return of the native" has been punctuated by uprisings. The wonder is that these uprisings have been so few when the differences between the two populations confronting each other in this tiny patch of territory are taken into consideration.

Palestine enjoyed seven fat years of comparative peace and prosperity between the riots of 1929 and 1936. Few nations of homogeneous populations can boast such tranquil internal relations during those stormy years of general economic depression and civil strife. Arabic newspapers, which are in the control of a handful, are hotbeds of unbridled incitement. And yet the sheikhs and the leaders must practically carry the masses to battle by the scruff of the neck or browbeat them to revolt by intimidation. This is not the natural uprising of a people consumed with hate against alien new-comers by whom they are being oppressed, down-trodden and dispossessed.

No other Eastern country has been subjected to a sudden onslaught from the West in the same way as has Palestine. And yet, at no time, even in 1936, has there been a spontaneous rising up of Arabs against Jews.

For seven years, from 1929 to April 1936, Jews and Arabs lived and worked together side-by-side in isolated sections of the country, and there were practically no attacks by Arabs on individuals or settlements.

This was not owing to the insensibility of the Arab masses. Arabs in Palestine are not to be confused with Chinese coolies or Indian untouch-ables. Overpopulation, which can turn semi-starved millions into pathetic clods, has never plagued Palestine. Even in times of oppression and pov-erty, the Arab had a place to pitch his tent or to build his mud hut. His few sheep and goats could find stubble between the crevices of the rocks. He is naive and gullible. But he is also alert and alive. He has not been crushed to insensibility. He is not so far removed from the desert that he does not retain a distinct sense of possession. He would not sit by passively and watch his few needs being filched from him by newcomers. He sits passively only when he knows that his black olives of yesterday have been supplanted by meat and potatoes.

Nor can his passivity be said to be owing only to the British bayonet. Physical evidences of the bayonet have never been too conspicuous in Palestine, as witness the dearth of troops in 1929 and the imported soldiers from Egypt in 1936. The simple Arab is not very remote from marauding and murdering. His passions run high. The moral effect of British occupa-tion could not have staved off individual attacks.

This can be proved by the crime sheets. Stabbing of one Arab by another Arab is so frequent that local newspapers dispose of the most grue-some cases in a few lines. An Arab woman being stabbed by her husband is not news. If she is unfaithful, she is apt to be stabbed. And her lover as well. An Arab will stab for less, as judged by Western standards. He will stab his neighbor whom he believes has dishonorably defrauded him of a shilling. It is his code of honor and revenge. Even the British bayonets and criminal courts cannot abolish entirely this deep-rooted code. The Arab knows how to deal with his avowed enemy first and take Western codes and punishment into consideration afterward. This reversion is understandable. Crime sheets from all Arab towns and villages in the country testify to the continuance of this code of honor and revenge.

And the present disturbances of 1936 are testifying to the fact that the Jews are not exempt from this code. If led to believe that his rights have been violated by the Jew, he will murder him in the same way that he will murder his unfaithful wife or his neighbor who has robbed him of a shilling. No one expects this code, rooted in the bones and blood of the Arab to evaporate as soon as he learns to operate an automobile or to use an automatic cigarette lighter. And no one should expect this code that applies to his wife and to his brother to exempt the Jew.

But first he must be led to believe that his rights are being violated. He is not dull. He is not stupid. And yet he has never arrived at the conclusion that his rights are being violated. Always he has had to be led to the belief. While he jogs along the dusty road on the back of his patient mule, his keen eyes see much. And yet year in and year out he has failed to see danger or avarice in his Jewish neighbors. He has tended his vineyards and his fig trees and left the Jewish settler to tend his in peace.

These seven fat years cannot be discounted lightly, especially since they followed on the heels of the 1929 blood orgy. The Arabs are not insensible. They settle private and personal accounts, despite the British bayonets. They attack the Jew when led to believe that their rights have been violated. How then, are we to explain these seven years?

The explanation seems to hark back to the note in the voice of the Jew that the Englishman in his Surrey cottage could not understand, back to that indefinable something that distinguishes a Semite from a non-Semite, back to the simplest and strongest bond in the world—the blood bond.

It is not natural for an Arab to hate a Jew. And nature usually prevails. Nature can be trammeled, stifled, perverted. But usually she will prevail. Therefore, if the Arab is provoked, or if he believes his rights have been assailed, he will attack the Jew. But he will not hate the Jew merely because he exists, as does the anti-Semite. The Arab is familiar with the color of the skin of the Jew. He is familiar with the slant of his nose. He is even familiar with the syllables of the Hebrew language. Because they are so like his own. His "salaama" is very like the "shalom" of the Jew. He is aware of these links and feels even more than he is aware of.

German refugees have arrived in large numbers during the latter part of these seven years; another direct impact with the West. And yet the Arab did not rise up. Probably he knows that he can best digest that part of the West that he desires when it is fed to him by Semites.

No mechanism is more delicate than the human being and no task more trying than the adjustment of human beings to other human beings. When two men are stranded on an island, fighting for their very existence, there is as much chance for bitter discord as for accord. It may arise because one man is irked by the way the other man shells his coconuts.

Thousands of Jews have poured into Palestine. They have brought the strange and wonderful contrivances of the West. When and where has there been such a dramatic meeting of human beings? When and where such fertile ground for bitter discord? Not the kind of artificial hate that is whipped up like a spectacular typhoon. But the kind of hate that eats into people's vitals day and after day and spreads poisoned vapors that would confound even the British bayonets. Such hate, which would have proclaimed itself whenever a Jew passed an Arab on the road, would have been understandable in the process of the adjustment of two such different human beings. Such hate would have been no wonder.

But these seven fat years are a wonder. They are more important in a historical sense than the present disturbances. They may mark the beginning of a fusion of East and West. They transcend statesmen and portfolios and memoranda.

Lately we have heard much of the force of anti-Semitism. These seven fat years speak, in accents clean and undeniable of Semitism, of that blood bond between Jew and Arab that prevents a natural hate.

MUEZZIN OR HASID

This article expresses Bar-Adon's central belief in the closeness of Jews and Arabs:

And I believe that there is a bond of brotherhood between the Semite Jew and the Semite Arab…

On the night that my friend couldn't tell a muezzin from a Hasid, I felt closer to the heart of the Arab-Jewish problem. It was only something I felt in my bones. But anti-Semitism is usually based on what people feel in their bones. Why shouldn't Semitism be based on the same thing?

That night didn't bring me closer to the solution of temporal difficulties. But it made the problem seem less immense and the gap less yawning than statesmen and memoranda had led me to believe.

September 1936
Inhabitants of the Rock, pp. 12–18
Earlier version in *The Palestine Post*

This is the comradeship of any thirsty men in any dry land. I maintain that the comradeship of the Arab and the Jew has even a more solid foundation. They are not only two thirsty men but also two Semite men.

The question of how far the Jew has become alienated from the East during his wanderings is debatable. Most American, English or Russian Jews, even though they return to Palestine, do not consider themselves, at a superficial glance, Semite in the way that the Arabs or Yemenite Jews are Semites.

I cannot speak scientifically about the corpuscles in the blood or the cells in the brain of a so-called American, English or Russian Jew. How much of him still belongs to the East, I do not know. Nor have I graphs and diagrams to prove my case.

I know only that the Jew, whether he has tried to maintain his identity or whether he has tried, as in Germany, to assimilate, has stuck out on the world's anatomy like a carbuncle (and I use the word safely as meaning either a precious stone or a malicious tumor).

The world, despite its wideness, has never quite found room for the Jew. It has given many and varied excuses for not finding room for him. The chief reason, which it does not give because it does not know it, is a note in the voice of the Jew. The world has never understood this note and therefore has feared it greatly. Call this note a sob. Call it mysticism. Since living in Palestine, I have learned to call it Semitism.

I may be indulging in fancy. But I believe that the way the stars sit in the sky here, and the way the sun strikes back from the sand, has something to do with this note that an Englishman in a Surrey cottage couldn't understand, even if he wanted to.

The Arab has this same note in his voice when he praises Allah. The Arab who has not been condemned to wandering has this note in his voice.

Can it be then, that this note in the voice of the Jew comes not from persecution and wondering, as is supposed? But that it comes from the way the stars sit in the sky in Palestine and the sun strikes back from the sand?

Can it be that the particular and peculiar geography of this part of the world puts a man in a certain juxtaposition with nature, which catapults him to strange depths and strange heights?

A man who lives in a land where the stars seem to jostle on his shoulders like opals is, perhaps, a different creature than the man who lives where the stars proudly stud distant planets like diamond chips. It is not possible that this intimacy of the stars and this heat of the sands have been crystallized in the note of the Jew from which the rest of the world shies.

The Arab has remained in this part of the world, and the note has remained in his voice. The Jew has trudged around, carrying this note with him, his blessing and his curse. Now some Jews have come home again. They have brought this note with them. It mingles with the note of the Arab. I cannot believe that the fusion will birth discord.

Arab leaders, Jewish leaders, British parliamentarians and the League of Nations may emphasize discord. But there is a force in these notes that may ultimately transcend statesmen, a simpler and stronger force, the force of blood, the force of two people who have known and responded to a land where stars jostle the shoulders of men like opals.

I remember the morning when this theory was welded into fact. Or perhaps the theory was born on that morning. I was walking with a friend through the streets of Jerusalem at about four o'clock. As I was turning into my gate, we heard a voice. It was a voice with that strange note that the Englishman in a Surrey cottage couldn't understand.

"He is a muezzin calling from a minaret," I said.

My friend answered, "No, he is a Hasid reading prayers in the cellar of some synagogue."

We were both stubborn and finally had to settle the question by following the sound to its source. The air is so clear in Jerusalem that, although the voice seemed close at hand, it led us far afield.

Meanwhile we argued and the further we walked, the more impatient my companion became, "Don't you think I know a Hasid when I hear one? Didn't I study in a yeshiva [institutes of talmudic learning] in Russia? Many a time I chanted just like that man until morning. I tell you, he is a Hasid."

We pursued the elusive sound through a maze of narrow, silent streets, I looking up for the minaret, he peering down into the cellars. Sometimes the sound stopped. Then it rose again, from nowhere and from everywhere like a sob encompassing the sleeping city.

Day was breaking, with the customary suddenness of dawn in Palestine, when we came within sight of the minaret and the muezzin calling to Allah with the intimacy of one who has lived close to the stars.

We had walked far to discover whether this chant that was hovering over Jerusalem at dawn came from an Arab or a Jewish throat. My friend was a bit sheepish. Hadn't he been a Hasid? Didn't he know a Hasid from a muezzin?

He didn't.

This similarity between Jew and Arab (more especially the Muslim Arab, although conversion makes a slight fundamental difference) has often been remarked upon. It is more marked when witnessed.

I remember the day I walked into the courtyard of the El Azar Mosque in Cairo. Thousands of students from all parts of the world came here to take the twelve-year course in the Koran. Squatting on the ground in the vast courtyard were Muslims of all ages. Young lads, with delicately chiseled brown features; old men with white beards, sensitive nostrils, and furrowed brows. Some gathered in groups around one man who read aloud. Others sat alone, swaying back and forth over the book. The air was weighted with the low droning of those who read aloud.

For twelve years they study here—and yet they must know the Koran by heart before they enroll. I could have remained for a long time looking at these students with their fine Semitic heads.

But my companions from Palestine were impatient. One of them explained, "This is not new to us. We lived like this ourselves in yeshivot in Russia."

I remember, too, a certain dawn when coming from Egypt to Palestine in a third-class carriage. One could sleep only fitfully on the hard, wooden benches. I awakened just as the dawn was streaking across the desert. In the uncertain light, I saw an Arab on his wooden bench, at the other end of the carriage, praying to Allah. I was traveling with members of the Jewish Labor Federation. These young people have abandoned traditional religious forms. Less emancipated Jews would have been donning their prayer shawls and adjusting the straps of their tefillin, preparatory to greeting the day with prayer.

I first saw an Arab drop to his knees in simple, unceremonious piety in a public park in Jaffa. He was a gardener. At prayer time, he laid aside his trowel and faced the East. The next time I saw such prayer was in the laundry room of the King David Hotel in Jerusalem. I was touring the hotel and happened to come into the laundry at noon. The Arab employee was kneeling in a window ledge. And the next time I saw such prayer was in a soap factory in Nablus. I had come to watch the primitive soapmaking methods. I found the "master" of the shop kneeling in a corner, not far from the bubbling cauldron.

I have met this same simple intimacy with God among Jews, even in America. I have seen Jews put on their tefillin at dawn in the sleeping car of the Chicago Limited.

For the Muslim and the Jew there is no intermediary between God and man. The rabbi and the sheikh are, in the last analysis, teachers. There is no confession to the priest.

Oh, the stark simplicity of a Muslim prostrated on a rug in a mosque, or of a Jew with his body pressed against the stones of the Wailing Wall. The hate that sometimes eddies around the Dome of the Rock and the Wailing Wall is false, artificial and infinitesimal compared to the magnitude of this shared simplicity. It is primitive and therefore noble. It antedates the time when man created from fear the medicine men and intermediaries. It goes back to the purity of the beginning.

It is Adam talking to God or Allah.

True, both the Muslim and the Jew in Palestine are moving further away from traditional religious forms. Young Jews are to be found in meeting halls rather than synagogues on Saturdays, and young Muslims turned back to the mosques in large numbers only recently when some mosques were turned into virtual meeting halls, being the platform for airing national grievances. But Semite characteristics, whether expressed in religious forms or through some other channel, remain fundamentally unchanged.

These praying Jews and Arabs may have nothing to do with the "Arab-Jewish problem" as statesmen view it. True, they have nothing to do with the important portfolios containing important memoranda on important questions such as restriction of sale of land to Jews, restriction of Jewish immigration and the absorptive capacity of the country.

But one begins to lose faith in these important portfolios with their memoranda. They are doing so appallingly little toward easing the headache of the world. Washington is cluttered with memoranda while America stinks with poverty. Geneva was swamped with memoranda while Italy tramped into Ethiopia. There are memoranda and more memoranda, and Hitler continues to crucify the Jews in Germany.

Whither memoranda?

Perhaps in the last analysis, men and the passionate divinities and degradations of men are all the matter. And these divinities and degradations are complicated, but not unusually changed, by memoranda. Changes are made at the source, within the men. Perhaps there are more gleams of truth outside of portfolios than inside. I believe there are.

And I believe that there is a bond of brotherhood between the Semite Jew and the Semite Arab that has nothing to do with portfolios or memoranda. If assisted, but not strangled by important memoranda, this bond will make itself felt.

On the night that my friend couldn't tell a muezzin from a Hasid, I felt closer to the heart of the Arab-Jewish problem. It was only something I felt in my bones. But anti-Semitism is usually based on what people feel in their bones. Why shouldn't Semitism, be based on the same thing?

That night didn't bring me closer to the solution of temporal difficulties. But it made the problem seem less immense and the gap less yawning than statesmen and memoranda had led me to believe.

PENELOPE POSTPONES

Written after 1936–1939 riots
Inhabitants of the Rock, pp. 8–11
Unpublished manuscript from Bar-Adon's personal archive

Kahn reflects on the need for Jews and Arabs to understand each other and on how it would be possible were people not incited to hatred and violence.

Since this meeting with Mahmoud Bey, I have spent weeks and months turning over this question of Arab-Jewish relations as though it was a ball. When the light fell this way, peace seemed possible. When the light fell that way, it seemed that, with Jeremiah, we cried for peace, peace, when there was no peace.

Sometimes, when in Tel Aviv, that all-Jewish city which is an unadulterated patch of the West, understanding between these two peoples appeared to be remote.

East is East and West is West. Jaffa is Jaffa and Tel Aviv is Tel Aviv. They are separated not by a few meters of beach but by centuries.

In Jaffa, husky Arabs leap joyously into the waves in their nakedness. They sit in coffeehouses, smoking nargilehs and gazing stolidly out to sea.

In Tel Aviv, Jews parade in lido bathing suits. They sit on terraces of hotels and talk of the drama, books and tomorrow.

> Will the Jew ever understand the richness of this stolid silence of the Arabs?
> Will the Arab ever understand the richness of this talk of tomorrow?
> Will the Jew ever understand the wisdom of living sparingly?
> Will the Arab ever understand the wisdom of living eagerly?

I had never asked myself whether the Jew would learn to live and think like the Arab or whether the Arab would learn to live and think like the Jew. This seemed neither necessary nor beneficial to either people. But understanding? That is imperative.

Here I must say clearly what I shall reiterate in the remainder of the book.

I believe that the fact that Jews and Arabs are Semites pull them closer together than any temporal differences of opinion pulls them apart.

I believe that there is no need for the Jew and Arab to learn to "tolerate" each other in Palestine for, as Semites, they already possess the basis for a deep understanding and even affection.

I believe that understanding between Jew and Arab will come, if enmity is not artificially simulated from without.

I believe that despite the uprisings of 1921, 1922, 1929, and 1936, the following phrase from the pact of 1919 is as true and as meaningful today as when signed by King Feisal and Dr. Chaim Weizmann, "mindful of the racial kinship and ancient bonds existing between the Arabs and the Jewish people, and realizing that the surest means of working out the consummation of their national aspirations is through the closest possible collaboration in the development of the Arab State and Palestine...."

I believe that none of the diseases affecting and infecting Arab-Jewish relations are congenital or chronic. In varying measures, the Jews, Arabs and English are responsible for them; the Arab masses by their gullibility, the Arab leaders by their corruptibility; the Jews by their preoccupation with upbuilding, which left little time or energy for the important duty of becoming acquainted with their neighbors; the English by thwarting any attempt to foster friendly relations between the two sections of the population.

I believe that the Jew has much to learn from the Arab. The Arab has much to learn from the Jew. A fusion will come, whether it will be in ten years or a hundred years. And this fusion of East, as retained by the Arab, and West, as carried back by the Jew, will mark an epoch in the history of peoples.

I have said that in Tel Aviv, one was conscious of a gap caused by centuries of living apart and developing in different directions. In the agricultural colonies, these centuries evaporate, and one realizes that the differences are decoys. They are the decoys erected everywhere by a wily civilization for the purpose of separating peoples.

For civilization is like Penelope who told her suitors that she would forget Odysseus when the work of her loom was completed. But unraveled her handwork by night. She postpones the coming of understanding by this unraveling of the work of her loom. Artificial hindrances are manufactured. Thus civilization is postponed.

In the colonies there are no decoys. An Arab from a neighboring village strides into a Jewish settlement to ask for water. The day is hot. *Chamseen* winds blow from the desert and the sun beats down without mercy. The pioneer fetches water. The Arab slakes his thirst greedily with this nectar of Palestine.

The Jew from Tel Aviv may have little to say to the Arab from Jaffa. But there is no need for talk when the eyes of this Jew and Arab meet over a can of cooling water on a chamseen day. For they both understand the meaning of water in Palestine, he who thirsts for it and he who has made it to flow again in this parched wasteland.

Parliaments may decorously discuss "Arab-Jewish relations." Their rhetoric is like the tapping of a woodpecker in a tree compared to the thunderous silence of a Jewish pioneer and an Arab fellah sharing a can of water on a chamseen day.

SPRING OF JASMINE

Inhabitants of the Rock, pp. 81–91
Unpublished manuscript from Bar-Adon's personal archive

Kahn stresses the importance of Arab charm, which she considers inherent, and its effect on human relations and politics. She quotes Henrietta Szold who said that "it made the wheels of daily living go

*round more easily." Kahn gives several specific examples of this charm
and generosity and explains why, due to his past history and present
preoccupation with building the homeland, the Jew has neither the time
nor the energy to cultivate charm. She ultimately criticizes the British
for not attending the real problems in Palestine, bewitched as they are
by the charm.*

One day I was descending one of the hilly slopes of Ein Karem [a neighborhood west of Jerusalem]. I stepped to the side of the path to allow
a small donkey to pass. Seated on the donkey was a fellah, his long legs
almost touching the ground. In his hand he carried a single pink rose. It
was a perfect flower. His fingers were cupped lest a slight breeze ruffle the
petals. The donkey was dilapidated and drab. The fellah was ragged and
none too clean. But the flower was perfect.

Over the roofs of the little whitewashed cottages, I watched the
donkey making the tedious descent down the stony path, the rider holding
on with one hand and guarding his flower with the other. He drew up in
front of an inn and, with a gracious bow, presented the rose to the English
proprietress who was standing at the gate.

I don't know how this Englishwoman felt when she received the rose.
I know how I felt under similar circumstances. I know how I felt the day
that Mahmoud Bey gave me the mixed bouquet. And to this day I feel the
same way when an Arab presents me with a single blossom.

It is as though you have never received a flower before. It is almost
as though you have never seen one before. It is as though this flower was
grown for you. It is almost as though nature had made the seed for you.

Away with our decorous flower shops, with their lilies and gladiolas
spread out "for sale" like lovely maidens in a slave mart. After an Arab has
presented you with a blossom and the blessing of Allah, you will never
want to traffic in flowers again. You will be convinced that flowers are not
meant to be bought and sold. They are above barter. They are meant to be
presented with a gracious bow and elaborate blessings.

Besides adding a picturesque touch to the already picturesque scene
of Ein Karem, what has this mangy fellah on his mangy donkey carrying
a pink rose to do with the Palestine problem? He personifies Arab charm.
And I believe that it is impossible to survey the Palestinian scene without
taking Arab charm into full account. For this charm effects human relationships, and therefore the political problems of the country as much as

any conference that ever was or ever will be held in Government House on the hill. Arab leaders and Jewish leaders can trek up to Government House as often as they like with puckered brows and memoranda. But the mangy fellah carrying the pink rose still remains as important to the general scene as anything in their portfolios.

On that day in Ein Karem, I arrived also at the same inn and was met by the English proprietress. My companion was an artist. For a long time we had been sitting on a rock on the top of the hill. On one side stretched the magnificent hills, caught in the hard whiteness of mid-summer heat. On the other were the whitewashed cottages and trim little gardens of the Russian sisters and monks tucked away on the ledge like dollhouses.

My companion had been trying to catch the scene in colors. I had been trying to catch it in words. But the magnificent bareness of Palestine is not to be subjected by palette or dictionary.

So we arrive at the inn hot, tired, and wearied by a strange beauty that sometimes gluts one's soul because it defies expression. We didn't present the proprietress with roses. My companion wanted very English tea. I wanted very American coffee. We were weary. And we weren't very charming. Probably we weren't less charming than other Westerners. But in Palestine we aren't compared to other Westerners. It is the Jew versus the Arab. And compared to that fellah, I don't think the English proprietress found us very charming.

What an English proprietress who manages a small inn in Ein Karem thinks may be unimportant—but multiply it by what some tourists and clergymen and British high officials think—and it becomes important. For frequently a pink rose in the hand of a mangy fellah can do more to elicit sympathy for the Arab cause than all the swamps the Jews will ever drain can elicit for the Jewish cause.

Not only does this charm cloud the vision of the susceptible, but also sometimes it even postpones understanding between Jew and Arab. For the Arab is a superlatively charming fellow. And the Jew is definitely lacking in charm. Therefore the Jew is sometimes perplexed by, or suspicious of, the Arab's charm. And the Arab is apt to look upon the Jew's lack of charm as a personal insult or as gross arrogance.

I have used the word "charm" many times in describing the Arab. I know of no synonym for this quality that usually accompanies the simplest Arab like an aura. I have heard it spoken of as being "artificial" or a "pose." I believe that it is neither. I believe that they are born with it as surely as they are born with their skin and ten toes. The daughter of the janitress of our office building has it. She is five years old. She lives in a tin hut behind the office. She has the bearing of a little princess and charm enough to subdue a tiger before his supper. I think she got that charm when she got her sloe eyes.

I've met this charm in many places. It doesn't perplex me. I'm not suspicious of it. I like it. It makes life easier and very pleasant. Buying firewood is pleasant because the Arab proprietor of the shop is charming. Having shoes mended is pleasant because the Arab shoemaker is charming. I once had an Arab scavenger who carried away the day's refuse with charm. I like it. I like it so much that I never stopped to analyze it.

One day Miss Henrietta Szold [a Zionist leader and founder of Hadassah] summed it up. We were driving to the north to visit a children's farm. Three or four women who live hermetically sealed lives in Jewish quarters were discussing the Arab question. One had had an Arab washwoman who had stolen some of the children's play suits—the same old story ending up with the declaration that Arab charm is cloying.

Miss Szold, who was sitting in the front seat and apparently not listening, turned around suddenly and asked, "Do you use a sewing machine, Mrs. X?" Mrs. X. replied that she did. "That's what Arab charm does," replied Miss Szold. "It makes the wheels of daily living go round more easily."

So call it oil. The oil of the East. I met it in the house of the mayor of Nablus. A resident of Nablus had won a large sweepstake prize, and I had come to interview him. The mayor had sold him the ticket, and we met in his home. Nablus is supposed to be fanatically anti-Semitic. Perhaps they didn't mean to be gracious. But I can still remember the warmth of the brothers and cousins and the old lady who was ill in bed. The winner of the sweepstake ticket is the owner of the soap factory. So I left the house with my car piled high to the ceiling with soap—there were cubes and balls of soap in all colors and sizes. Some were solid, and some were speckled, and there were enough to lather all Jerusalem. There were farewells and much laughter as I tried to arrange myself between the soap. And I left Nablus feeling warm.

I met with the same thing in Ramallah. I had come to see an old woman who makes lovely pottery without a wheel. I didn't know her name or her address. So I went to the mayor. The mayor, and the hunchback man who he commissioned to take me to the house of the potter, and the potter herself were all charming.

It was no trouble for the Mayor to find me a guide. It was no trouble for the guide to trudge several miles. It was no trouble for the potter to have me invade her premises and deluge her with questions. Coffee appeared as if by magic in her primitive dwelling. Nothing is trouble for an Arab. And if it is, you are never the wiser. Call it oil. Call it what you will, it makes life easier and more pleasant.

I remember meeting this charm one day in the village of Silwan. I was exploring with a professor from the Hebrew University. We stopped an Arab to ask a direction. He directed us and then invited us to come to his house for refreshments before continuing on our way. My companion was reticent. If you stop a man in London and ask a direction, he doesn't invite you to his home. He has lived in Palestine for some time, but he was still a bit baffled by the charm of the Arab. But I was already scrambling up the hill in the foot-steps of my self-appointed host. His house was ours. I was taken to meet the woman. Chairs were brought to the terrace. The traditional coffee and ciga-rettes appeared. The usual procedure. And yet it never seems mere etiquette. It is as though the host and the entire household and the house itself had been waiting all their lives just for this moment when you would be their guest. The coffee beans were grown—for you. The tobacco in the cigarettes was cultivated—for you. The romance of the East wears thin quickly. The mere fact of drinking coffee with a sheikh no longer holds any special zest. But I don't think the charm of these people wears thin.

We sat on the terrace for some time, watching the sun set over the Old City. Then our host accompanied us to the edge of the village. On the way home, the professor delivered himself. He had enjoyed the visit. But it was the first time he had ever done such a thing. Isn't it odd for a stranger whom you stop on the road to invite you into his home? Perhaps such invitations are only formal and it is presumptuous to accept?

I agreed with him that it was odd. But so many of the Arab customs are odd to the Jew. And perhaps his invitation was formal, and perhaps it was presumptuous for us to have accepted. But to me, Arab charm and hospitality are too warm to be analyzed and picked to pieces. I would as soon analyze the song of a thrush or the scent of a pine tree as to analyze the impulse of that old Arab in Silwan. Perhaps I'm being naive and simple. But when they open their homes to me, I walk in and hope someday they'll walk into mine.

Looking back on many incidents, they seem hardly worth recording. Just snatches—moments—and yet they trail pleasantly back like a sound or a color or a scent.

There was the day I tried to buy an especially curly lamb in Jericho. We had completed the bargain. But just as I was walking away, the child of the family began to sob and to pull at my skirt. So I couldn't have the lamb after all because the child wanted to keep it. And the mother was so genuinely grieved for me that I went away not caring whether I had the lamb or not.

There was the man who was stamping sesame seeds with his bare feet. I had stepped into his little den in the Old City at about midnight to watch the blindfolded camels walk round and round the huge cauldron. He was knee deep in sesame seeds. He beckoned me to a stool. The dirty den, the camels, the two broken down horses—the entire place and all the sesame seeds and the sweet smelling oil—were mine.

And then there was the Arab woman who lived in a little hut on the edge of a cliff in Safed. I stopped for water. She gave me the water and then, just as I was leaving, she gave me a sprig of jasmine from her garden.

One sprig of jasmine.

What about the Jews? The plain fact is that usually they are not charming. Someone has said that it is not possible to say that one man is "kind" and another is "wise." Every man has the same ingredients in his make-up. It is a matter of which predominates.

We might say, therefore, that charm is not a predominating characteristic of the Jew.

There are numberless reasons for this. He has had to fight. Fight for his body and soul. He has had to run. He has had to fight again. And run again. He has had no particular reason through the centuries to trust mankind. Sometimes he has sunk completely into his books and his soul and his God. He has lost touch with mankind. He has not known the broadness of fields and sky and desert. He has been cooped up in dark places. And sometimes he has had to run so quickly from one dark place to another dark place that he hardly had time to catch sight of the sun.

Yes, there are numerous reasons why the Jew was not charming when he came to Palestine. And there are numberless reasons why he has not had time to cultivate charm since he arrived. Some of these reasons are explained by the busyness that I have already described.

Almost every Jew in Palestine today is putting up a grim battle of one kind or another. He used to be curator of a library in Berlin, and now he's selling secondhand books. Or he's trying to keep his restaurant in Jerusalem as clean as his restaurant in New York used to be, and his employees don't know what he's talking about. He's trying this, and he's trying that. He's trying above all else to build a homeland.

And it's grim business, this building a homeland. I'm not feeling sorry for him. He wants no pity. He's enjoying it. He's reveling in it. But, nevertheless, it's a grim business, and he hasn't the inner calm of the fellah riding on his donkey with a pink rose in his hand.

The Jewish taxi driver and plumber and plasterer may not be charming either. He's putting up a grim battle, too. He's trying to put labor back where it belongs. He's fighting for the dignity of labor. The Arab taxi driver can afford to carry your luggage upstairs for you. But the Jewish taxi driver will be apt to advise you to hire a porter. This isn't very charming. But it's an important part of his grim fight for the dignity of labor.

In the communal colonies there is a hospitality that transcends all hospitality I have ever known. Here there is the literal sharing of bread with any and all strangers who come to their gate. And there are always beds for strangers, even if the members of the kvutzah tired from a hard day in the fields, must sleep on the ground. Anyone may come to a kvutzah and stay as long as he wants. And he dare not offer payment because money has no part in the life of the kvutzah. There is hospitality in these kvutzoth that beggars description. And yet, one would not say there was charm. That is, not the same kind of charm as that of an Arab village.

For the pioneers who live in the kvutzoth are grim men and women. With their hands they are fighting to bring grain and fruit out of rocks. And with their souls they are fighting to bring a new order into a sick world. They are fighting for the simple biblical creed that every man should work according to his ability and receive according to his needs. It is doubtful if, in all the chaotic weary world today, there is any other such group of human beings, putting up a grim fight for the brotherhood of man in its truest sense.

And yet these people are not charming in the way that the Arab is charming. When you come to see them, their home is yours, no questions asked. But they do not behave as though they had been waiting for you, and only you, to arrive. They haven't been waiting for you. They've been working in the sun all day. Perhaps six months ago, they were doctors or teachers, and they're not accustomed to working in the Palestinian sun. Their hands are blistered, and their backs are aching. And even if their hands aren't blistered, they weren't waiting for you to come. For you are not important to them. They are not important to themselves. Nothing in all the world is important except the task and the creed to which they have dedicated themselves.

You may catch glimpses of eternal truth and beauty in these kvutzoth that will make life outside seem cheap and grasping and tawdry. Or you may miss it and see nothing but grim men and women to whom you are most unimportant compared to their cows and their search for a new way of life.

I think the Jews would rather be charming than grim. I think someday, in Palestine, they will be. But first they have to get done with this engrossing business of laying the groundwork for a homeland. Not that there is not joy among the Jews in Palestine. There is more joy to the square foot than is usually seen outside of Palestine. But even this is rather a grim joy. It is the joy of work accomplished and of work yet to be accomplished. It is not the simple, charming joy of a pink rose.

It seems to boil down to this. The Arab is an exceedingly charming fellow. The Jew usually is not charming at all.

The charm of the Arab is delightful. It is the oil that makes the wheel of daily life go round more easily. Perhaps it would be best for the Jew to recognize this charm as an integral and lovely part of the nature of his neighbors and to emulate them when they can.

And perhaps it would be best for the Arab to accept once and for all the lack of charm of the Jew, to realize that the Jew does not mean to be insulting or arrogant. The Jew has many fine characteristics. But charm does not predominate in most Jews.

And perhaps it would be best for some of the tourists and clergymen and British officials to stop weighing, consciously or unconsciously, the Jew and the Arab on a scale based on charm.

Perhaps it would be best for them to realize that charm is one characteristic of which the Arab has full measure and the Jew has very little. Best for them to stop thinking, consciously or unconsciously, "But the Arab is such a charming fellow and therefore Jewish immigration should be restricted."

For the problems of Palestine are too momentous to rest on the charm of the fellah who came down the hill on a donkey carrying a pink rose.

THE WOMEN OF PALESTINE

Probably written 1936–1937
Zif Zif, pp. 192–199
Unpublished manuscript from Bar-Adon's personal archive

Kahn describes the differences between the various female populations: the bedouin living the same nomadic life her foremothers lived; the Arab peasant woman, whose situation is scarcely better; the Muslim

woman, still bound by tradition but also exposed to Western influence;
the Christian Arab woman, emancipated in many spheres of her life;
the urban Jewess, committed to building the homeland; and finally the
pioneer women, working side by side with the men in her community—
the woman of the future. Hopefully, the lives of future women will reflect
the best of each sector.

There is perhaps no other canvas on which is so vividly depicted the woman of the past and the woman of the future as Palestine. Walking through the streets of the cities and the narrow lanes of the villages, one can see within a few paces the dramatic epic of woman's progress, from the earliest stirring of time, unfolding in a living picture.

Here is a chalutza striding down the road with all the pride and courage of a woman who is building a homeland shoulder to shoulder with the men. She sits in the councils. She works out of doors in the scorching summer sun and in the bleak winter winds. She shoulders a gun when the colonies are attacked to protect the groves and fields which she has helped to make flourish in the stony wasteland. So thoroughly has she emancipated herself that she may be rightly called a woman of the future.

On the same road we pass an Arab woman of a bedouin tribe. Her face is completely hidden beneath the tremendous load of wood that she miraculously manages to balance on her head. She wears strings of silver coins which are stretched from her ears to her nostrils, between which tattooing is visible. Mentally and spiritually, as well as physically, she is as untouched as though she has had no contact with civilization. She wanders over the hills of Palestine as did the nomads in biblical times, unaffected by the intervening centuries.

Between these two extreme groups of women, one finds several stages of development among the strangely diversified population of the Holy Land. There is the Arab fellah who is a bit more advanced than her bedouin sister. There is the Muslim woman who, although still bound by tradition, is showing signs of eventually succumbing to the Western influence. There is the Christian Arab woman who is definitely emancipated in various phases of her life. There is the Jewish woman of the cities who, while leading a less strenuous life than the chalutza, shoulders all the burden that even the urban phase of a pioneer country imposes.

Preceding all growth, there is the wrenching period of conflict between the old and the new. It is through this period that the woman of Palestine is now passing. The British Mandate, bringing in its train an ever-increasing influx of Jews from all parts of the world, has changed the face of the Holy Land. The Arab woman, who has been drowsily nodding amid lackadaisical Orientalisms, awakens after centuries to find that a breathe of the Occident is sweeping through the land with a precipitude probably unmatched in pioneer history.

Yesterday there was little to disturb the stagnant serenity of a country whose only glory was her past. But overnight, cities have been built on sand dunes. And roads to join these cities. And on these roads, buses and automobiles race by caravans of camels. And there are shops where latest model gowns may be purchased. And sanitary butcher stores with electrical refrigeration. And there are things more strange, such as adult education, prenatal care, preschool child clinics. All these and more the British government and the Zionists are pouring into the withered lap of the Holy Land.

Is it any wonder that the native woman is confused? In another part of the world she might quickly regain her bearings and follow in the wake of her emancipated sisters. But the East moves with the same slow gait as the camel. Traditions are as deeply rooted and seemingly as permanent as the grand bare hills of the country. It is therefore not to be wondered at that the mass of Arab women remain virtually unchanged. Indeed it is the light of the ironbound traditions that have encompassed these Eastern women for countless centuries; it is amazing that any Western influence has managed to seep into the confines of the women's quarters.

We have already met the bedouin woman on the road. We may see her again when she comes to town to buy her meager supplies. Water is not plentiful in the Holy Land, but she has not learned to make use of what there is. Even during the rainy season when all vegetation and animals enjoy a long needed douche, she and her family present the same filthy exterior. You will catch sight of her trudging patiently behind the donkey on which her husband is riding. Or you will see her helping to pitch the tents of a bedouin camp in some forsaken hill. You will recognize her children in the city streets picking up dung to be sold for fertilizer. A scene in Jericho depicts well the present position of the bedouin woman. A caravan of camels has just come into the village after an all night journey. The man and the camels lie down in the road, exhausted, to rest. The women place clay jugs on their heads and plod toward the fountain to replenish the water supply. Returning to the sleeping group, they set about making a fire over which they will roast the kebab (meat) that their masters will want, piping hot, when they awaken. The lot of the bedouin woman, from the time she marries at the age of thirteen or fourteen, is one of drudgery and complete subordination, but she is doubtless not too unhappy since the seeds of discontent have not been sown.

The position of the fellah woman is, socially, not much more advanced. She too married at an early age, and, as one of her husband's wives, devotes herself solely to his wants. However, because she is established in a home, no matter how wretched, she is within the reach of the constructive British and Jewish forces. She comes to hear of the Hadassah [Women's Zionist Organization of America] health clinics and sometimes makes use of them. When she brings her produce to market in Jerusalem, Haifa or Tel Aviv, she sits beside her huge basket of cactus fruit or oranges—a picturesque figure in her brightly embroidered dress—and watches the Western world march by. She is not yet a part of this world, but she may yet be.

In the ranks of the urban Muslim women, one finds a rustle of transition. A few years ago the Muslim woman resembled a bulky black tent, garbed in her many cloth wrappings and thick veil. But today many of the Muslim women are scarcely conspicuous. Their black coats are cut along smart and fitted lines and their gossamer veils are only slightly more concealing than the veils worn in the name of fashion by Western women. Frequently they can be seen lifting their veils when making a purchase, a liberty only recently adopted.

A few advanced Muslim families are sending their daughters to schools of higher education, after which they enter the teaching or nursing professions. At a recent graduation exercise at the Jerusalem Girls' College, Muslim girls comprised about one third of the class.

These are the beginnings of what may later prove to be a revolutionary movement in the world of Muslim women. But as yet, the life of this group remains fundamentally unchanged. The woman is never seen in the public streets unless accompanied by another woman, and during the evenings when her husband is smoking his nargileh and drinking Turkish coffee at one of the many Arab cafés, she is confined to her home. The fate of the fairly well-to-do Muslim woman today is not enviable from the Western point of view. In contrast to the lower-class woman who is little more than a beast of burden, she leads a life of complete idleness that is deadening. She cannot meet her husband's friends. Indeed, even today a man may not inquire about, or in any way allude to, the existence of the wife or wives of a Muslim. Therefore, the Muslim woman, whose sole diversion is shopping for fine silks in the bazaars, soon becomes fat and—we are told—devotes much of the day to gossiping in the women's quarters of the houses.

The nationalist propaganda that the Arab leaders are spreading throughout the country, in an attempt to curb the British policy and to stem Jewish immigration, is awakening a few groups of Muslim women. During the protest demonstrations the women marched through the streets in public parade with the men. Delegates of the Arab Women's Federation even went so far as to appear before His Excellency the High Commissioner to enter vehement protests against the killing of the illegal demonstrators by British police. Special dispensation for these political activities are, accorded to them, by nationalistic-minded sheikhs. This letting down of the bars of Islam for political purposes may lead to further emancipation along other lines when the nationalistic wave has subsided.

The Christian woman is the most advanced among the Arabs. She has adopted the Western mode of dress; her social position is comparable to that of women elsewhere; her domestic life is stable since polygamy does not prevail; her entry into the business and professional realms is taken for granted, even by the Muslim men.

We left the Jewish chalutza striding down the road. Her skin is blackened by the sun; she is wearing a blue blouse and shorts, beneath which one sees her sturdy bare legs. Before coming to Palestine you might have passed her in the streets of London, Paris, Berlin or New York. She was a teacher, lawyer, or journalist; today, she is a peasant—a new type of intellectual peasant who lives in the kvutzoth that have been established throughout Palestine.

The group that she represents, although comparatively small, is making a unique contribution to the annals of womankind. Throughout history, women have played their part in the stirring and difficult pioneer periods of all countries, suffering deprivation and facing danger. She has done all this and more. She has helped to create a new social order that she believes approaches the philosophy of life laid down by the early Hebrew prophets.

Communal living is characteristic of life in the kvutzah, personal property having been abolished. Each member of the group goes about her tasks with a tireless energy that is fed by a passionate belief in an ideal.

To the tourist, the children of these chalutzoth appear as a new race of people—bright eyed, intelligent, and healthy as they chatter in biblical Hebrew. The children, living together in a well-built communal house, receive the most scientific care and education, although the adults may be living on thin soup and black bread.

There is no phase of life in the kvutzah in which the woman does not participate. Her voice is heeded in the council that governs the colony. She takes her place behind the plow and does her share of the agricultural work, which is more demanding here than elsewhere since the rocky soil has lain barren for centuries.

Volumes have been written—and more will yet be written—testifying to the rich drama supplied by the women during the early stages of the resettlement of Palestine by the Jews. The list of heroines who died for the cause in that soul-trying period is long; women who faced and succumbed to the malaria infested swamps and the attacks of savage native tribes.

Conditions have changed in the last decade. The kvutzoth can claim dairies and citrus groves that are as flourishing as any in the world. The swamps have been dried up by the planting of eucalyptus trees. But, despite the progress made, the lot of the chalutza is still a difficult and precarious one. Living in these outposts in the most remote sections of the country, she realizes that, if the political kettle should again boil over, she will be required to defend her colony and her children against the easily aroused Arab tribes.

The Jewish woman in the city has resumed her living along much the same lines as in Western countries. She has always been accorded recognition—witness the biblical Judge Deborah. It is not then to be wondered at that she takes her place in the professional, business and political world of the Jewish National Homeland. Equality of the sexes is one of the fundamental principles of the Histadrut, which is one of the most powerful factors in Palestine. Therefore, within the urban as well as the rural communities the woman enjoys full and equal rights with regard to occupation and general status.

The German women, Hitler refugees who are daily streaming into Palestine, deserve commendation for the manner in which they are adjusting themselves. New restaurants and shops of all kinds are being established by this group, so recently and so rudely uprooted. Wives of professional men who cannot immediately reestablish themselves here are providing for the temporary upkeep of the family.

These are the women of Palestine. Conflicting ancient and modern standards and differing Occidental and Oriental philosophies are the materials that are being woven on the loom; who knows but that, from these colorful and chaotic threads, the pattern of a new woman, who will combine the best of the East and the best of the West, may be spun.

THE RETURN OF THE NATIVE

1936–1939?
Inhabitants of the Rock, pp. 19–23
Unpublished manuscript from Bar-Adon's personal archive

The "native" in the title refers to the Jew whose roots are in the East, but who has lived for many generations in the West, and now brings technology and knowledge with him to rehabilitate Palestine, which had been neglected under Turkish rule. Here, therefore, as opposed to other places in the East where modernization is a gradual procedure, it is rapid and dramatic. But Bar-Adon wonders why it has to be accompanied by violence.

Because the Arab and the Jew are Semites, the gap between them is less yawning than statesmen would lead us to believe. But the gap is there. It is the gap caused by living apart for centuries, during which time the Arab in Palestine has lost much of the glory of ancient Eastern civilization while the Jew has plucked the fruits of modern Western civilization.

Superficially, no more different species of animals could be imagined than the present-day Arab and the present-day Jew. Superficialities, if spectacular enough, can dominate a picture, and the inventions and contrivances of the West are spectacular.

The Jew is fundamentally an Easterner. His life forces spring from the East, and in the East, perhaps, he is destined to fulfill himself again. But, except for those Jews who have remained in this part of the world, he comes as a messenger from the West. On top of his Eastern soul, things have accumulated—the things he learned in London, Cape Town, and New York. They are good things. But they are also charged and powerful things, apt to confuse the Eastern mind. There are things that today are fighting malaria in the Huleh swamp, which, prior to Jewish purchase, had been abandoned to a few reed-dwellers, papyrus, and water buffalo. They are the things that probe trachoma, build cities, and establish world trade.

The Jew returns to Palestine not only in the guise of an energetic Westerner but also of an ultra-energetic Westerner. At his worst, he is accustomed to living vigorously. In Palestine, he is at his best, and his vigor is a flame. He calls every muscle of mind and body into full play. He has returned home, fatigued with being buffeted about the world. But this fatigue is transmuted into terrific energy when he is faced with the challenge of rehabilitating Palestine.

The Jew plumbs the Dead Sea for minerals; he puts grapevines on hilltops; he makes a city sprout in sand dunes. He plants. He plows. He plasters. No sun is too hot. No rain is too penetrating. No swamp is too malarial. He has returned home. He has found that home dilapidated and neglected. It must be renovated and clothed again in glory. Planting a tree is a form of religious ecstasy. In all things, he is driven forward by a force beyond himself.

To witness this performance is breathtaking. Upbuilding is usually a slower and more gradual process. Even the energetic West has time and time again expressed surprise and bewilderment at the accomplishments of the Jew in Palestine. Those who oppose the principles of Zionism have not withheld their amazement at the achievements of Zionism.

If the energetic West is amazed, then how could we expect the lackadaisical Arab to take for granted the Goliathan strides of his Jewish neighbors? The Arab peers through Oriental eyes at tractors, laboratories, well borers, trade fairs; he peers sometimes with wonder, sometimes with jealousy, sometimes with hatred.

What was the condition of this Arab when he began peering at these bewildering Western inventions? The extent to which Palestine had been allowed to become run down by the heel of Turkish rule is already history and has been faithfully recorded by travelers to the Holy Land who salted their accounts of delight at visiting sanctified sites with complaints against lepers at large, vermin, and lack of transportation. It is only when irked with the British regime that the Arab leader feigns to look back with nostalgia to the time of the Turks. The fellah does not share this nostalgia. The squalor and poverty of pre-war Palestine, is too well known to need elaboration.

This then was the kind of Jew and the kind of Arab who met in Palestine; the former was bolstered by the inventions of the West and driven forward by the zeal of a zealot; the latter was deadened and phlegmatic after years of oppression.

The Jew could not discard the trappings of the West. They were good. Therefore they had to be fused into the woof of the whole.

And this fusing of the East and the West in Palestine is high drama. Never before has Occident and Orient met on such a close and intimate basis. The potentialities for development in uncharted and undreamed of directions, for nurturing a distinctly new form of culture, are vast, provocative and challenging.

The Jew and the Arab have not lived together long enough nor examined each other closely enough to properly evaluate these potentialities. They cannot move far enough away from the canvas to get a prospective. Perhaps in this, as in so many things, it may be some poet, some worthless dreamer and prophet who will someday point the way to this fusion that practical politicians, fumbling with important portfolios, are too busy to see.

The impact of Orient and Occident in Palestine is dramatic because it is unique. In other places the West seeps gradually into the East. Native headgear was abolished by law in Iran. Doubledecker buses were recently introduced to the streets of Baghdad, after much ado and negotiation in England. Thus, slowly the West creeps Eastward.

But the Jew had no time to let his Western inventions seep into the East. At first he carried the water from great distances on mule back. But as soon as he could, he dug wells and made canals for artificial irrigation. At first he harvested his crops as best he could. But soon, he got combines. And he brought apples trees from New Jersey. And special citrus trees from California. He learned which breed of cow thrives best in the Palestinian climate and why certain diseases infest the chicken coops. He crossed continents for seedling and build laboratories to study a destructive bug.

No, there was no time for the seeping process. A long pent-up love and energy had been unloosed. And today, when the Jew looks at Tel Aviv or the fertile Jezreel Valley, he is amazed at the work of his own hands. How can the Arab be expected to take it for granted?

Sometimes the West has come in the person of a trader or soldier to conquer the East "for its own good." In that case there was no need to establish basic understanding, no need for fellowship between the colonizer and the colonized. There was need only that one knew how to issue commands and the other to obey.

But the Jews have not come as traders or soldiers. Their position is less romantic and more complex than one of Kipling's empire builders. The Jew cannot stop at feeling warmly indulgent toward the "native." For, he too, is a native. He has not come to make pacts or to make barter or to make anything else with these natives. When he needed land to live on, he paid for it as though the rocky soil were gold ore. He has never tried to simulate the purchase from the Indians of Manhattan for twenty-six dollars and a few strings of beads, for he did not come to exploit the natives. He came to live with them and to talk to them as one native to another native. There must be fusion, or there will be nothing at all.

So far we have the picture of the Jew returning to his ancient home, bringing the trappings of the West. He could not properly assimilate in the West because he is a Semite. Yet, his Semite cousins are confused by and sometimes distrustful of these Western trappings.

How far have the Jews and Arabs gone toward achieving an understanding?
And why should the "return of the native" be punctuated by uprisings?

THE "MAUROTH"

Dorothy Ruth Kahn
1939
Larnaca, Cyprus
An article from Bar-Adon's personal archive

Bar-Adon summarizes the three years of violence and questions the failure of the British to restore order, concluding that it is the result of deliberate "divide and conquer" policy. She claims that the events were in no sense an uprising of the Arab people against the Empire or the Jews. She notes that there are signs that the British are finally committed to restoring order, and she highlights the suffering of both the Arab and Jewish populations. She mentions the "sunrise to sunset" settlements (including Ein-Hashofet, named in honor of the Supreme Court Judge Louis D. Brandeis) and the Palestine Philharmonic Orchestra, which was founded during this period, and stresses the contributions of women during this period.

April 19 will be the anniversary of the outbreak of the 1936 disturbances in Palestine. During this period, life for us has been intense; therefore it is difficult to believe that only three years have lapsed since that first bloody morning of shooting and stabbing in the streets of Jaffa. The dead were brought back for burial in the neighboring city of Tel Aviv. We believed that, as in the case of the uprisings in 1920, 1929 and 1933, peace would be restored within a few weeks by His Majesty's government. But the disturbances of 1936 proved to be more than a fortnight's eruption. When the smoke of battle clears, doubtless it will be discovered that the course of history in this strange, volcanic country—smaller in area than the state of Rhode Island—has again veered.

The term "disturbances" has been retained, perhaps owing to the British flair for understatement. But other terms have been applied, depending on temperament or political views. Arab terrorists, in quest of recruits from the villages for their bands, have called it a "holy crusade." American journalists, in quest of headline stories, have called it a "war." Jews, unwilling to admit even to themselves that this was more than a tempest in a teapot, clung optimistically to the Hebrew word *mauroth* meaning "incidents." Arabs, wishing to minimize banditry and emphasize patriotism, have used the term "revolt" to imply that their countrymen were up in arms against the Empire rather than the Jews.

Whether the occurrences in Palestine have been a "war" or a series of "events," they have assumed large proportions, reminiscent of ancient times when a falling rampart in Jerusalem had its repercussions in the kingdoms of Rome, Greece, Cyprus, Persia, Egypt and Assyria. Since communications have compressed the modern world, shots in Jerusalem during the past three years had their echoes in Geneva; 10 Downing Street; the Palace of Emir Abdullah in Amman; the White House in Washington, D.C.; the residences of Herr Hitler and Signor Mussolini and the palace of the Emir of Saudi Arabia.

The Arab kings, the American government which was a signatory to the Balfour Declaration, and Italy and Germany, who wished to embarrass England by a continuation of unsettled conditions in the Mediterranean, have all had a finger in the pie—which might be specified more accurately as a mincemeat pie.

The cause of the disturbances is no longer as pertinent a question as the cause for the continuation of them. The proper answer to this question can only be given by the empire that manipulates the strings operating the puppet show. The naive outsider (and one living in Palestine can be as remote from the actual pulse in London as one living in New York) can only pose the simple question, "Is it possible that the British Mandatory Power could have failed to restore order in a pigmy strip of territory during a period of three years?" Granted, the peculiar geography of Palestine with its hills, wadis and caves, has always favored the bandit. Even the picturesque, twisted olive trees are ideal hiding places for arms. Granted too, the rebels are known to have received financial assistance from outside sources. Still, the idea that England was unable to restore order in three years is ludicrous. Therefore the naive outsider must come to the conclusion that maintaining the disturbances were part of the British policy, a policy known as "divide and rule" or "muddling through."

Being an ex-American and accustomed to the simplicity of a country whose interests do not extend beyond its own borders, I cannot criticize this policy. Despite some years of residence in Palestine, the complex mechanisms of Empire politics, as seen from close range, still amaze and bewilder me. It is quite possible that this policy of "muddling through," of prolonging for three years an unpleasant business that might have been scotched in three days, will prove in the long run to have been best for all parties concerned. Britain is an old hand in such matters and Solomon has said, "Better is the end of a thing than the beginning." We have not yet seen the end.

One fact is self evident: at no time during these three years has there been an uprising of the Arab people as a whole in Palestine or neighboring countries against the Mandatory Power or the Jews. Had there been anything bordering on a serious uprising, the Jewish population of only four hundred thousand souls (completely unarmed in 1936) would have been massacred in the twinkling of an eye.

There is no doubt that the slight rumblings heard in 1936 could have been quickly squelched had government taken decisive action. At the time, Sir Arthur Wauchope was high commissioner and popular with all elements in the country. His vacillation and inability to end the troubles was traced to his distaste for injuring any factions involved. He has been compared to the kindhearted man who, when taking his dog to a veterinarian to have his tail amputated would say, "Please don't do it all at once. I can't bear to see him suffer. Cut it off a little at a time." As a result of this vacillation, a situation arose comparable to gangsterism in Chicago, except that the misbehavior of the Arab "Al Capones" resulted in more serious and far-reaching damage.

A most concise analysis of the situation was given a fortnight ago in a statement by the British War Office who admitted that, "The total number of permanent active rebels in the whole country does not exceed 1,000 to 1,500 men split up in small bodies under the command of various leaders. Small parties of rebels combine by night for such activities as sniping and sabotage, which have become a recognized and remunerative racket. Although mainly the effendis have supplied the administrative capacity, they have not gained any real control of the fighting leaders and in fact they continue to be terrorized by the fear of being "bumped off." They may give advice but they cannot give orders; orders come direct from the mufti [the religious leader of the Muslims of Palestine] and his associates. Even in large towns there is little sign that the educated classes combine to give general support to the gangs."

Therefore, with the mufti playing the role of Al Capone and with Britain leisurely "muddling through," terrorism held sway for three years. British police, soldiers and civil officers, as well as Jews and Arabs paid with their lives for the "muddling." There was no road, town, village or city (except Tel Aviv, which has a concentrated Jewish population of 150,000 souls) where life and property was not menaced. The hills in the region of Jericho and the Dead Sea were again infested with bandits, as in biblical times. Jewish shepherds of Galilee were murdered and their flocks stolen. At times the audacity of the rebels and the meekness of Britain assumed farcical proportions—such as when the Arab towns of Bethlehem, Jenin and Nablus were "conquered" by the rebels who ousted or murdered law-abiding Arab officials, hoisted the rebel flag, and took over the courts, post offices, banks and police stations.

A few months ago the rebels also took possession of the Old City of Jerusalem and raised the flag over Damascus Gate. I stood on the roof of a nearby house, listening to the clicking of the army machine guns, which answered the snipers who were firing from the parapets of the mosques, and watching the planes circling over the Tower of David. Eventually the British troops entered the gates and "recaptured" the city from the bandits. The picture of a handful of villagers defying government was high farce—but at least it provided the foreign newspaper correspondents with one of the best stories of the disturbances since "Jerusalem Besieged"—always front-page stuff.

Within the past months it seems to have become evident that Britain desires to restore order. Those measures that could have been applied more successfully three years ago are now being enforced. The arms traffic is being partially controlled by a law requiring all male drivers and vehicle passengers to carry traveler permits. Last week an ordinance was announced forbidding everyone except Europeans and Jews from crossing the Syrian-Palestinian frontier (Syria having been one of the chief sources for gunrunners).

Paradoxically enough, although the Arabs have been on the offensive and Jews on the defensive, the Arab population as a whole has suffered as much as, if not more than, the Jewish. Firstly, the need of the Jews for a home has become increasingly desperate within the past three years. This meant that, in the face of any odds, they were determined to push forward with the upbuilding of the land. Urban areas have expanded, new factories set in motion and agricultural settlements established in the most isolated and dangerous places. The need was too great and the tempo too swift to permit demoralization within the Jewish ranks. In addition, the Jews had the comfort, at least, of knowing who their enemies were.

On the other hand, the moderate Arab (and there were thousands) who was opposed to the methods of his countrymen was forced into an intolerable position. If he did not respond to the extortioners' demands, he was taken to the "courts," held in the hills, for trial. In this way hundreds of the moderate and courageous Arabs who sincerely desired to reach an understanding with the English and the Jews, and who bravely opposed the terrorists, have lost their lives. Thousands of them with their families have fled the country and are now living in exile in Beirut, Damascus, Cairo and Alexandria.

Since the wealthy Arabs have left the country and commerce with the Jews was stopped, the condition of the poor Arab can be imagined. Illiterate, he depends on the Friday sermons in the mosques for information. There he only learns from the sheikhs (mouthpieces for the mufti) that the Jews "want to burn the Mosque" [Al-Aqsa Mosque in Jerusalem. the third holiest site in Islam]. Having seen no evidence of incendiarism in three years, he is bewildered. Naturally, he does not distrust his countrymen, and yet for the Jew who brought him nothing but increased prosperity, he feels no instinctive hatred (as proved by the War Office report that, after three years of continued provocative propaganda, the rebels have only one thousand recruits). Therefore, his simple mind can only grasp the fact that owing to mysterious circumstances, it is more difficult for him to earn the few piasters required for his bread and olives. Frequently, for economic reasons alone, he is forced to join the bands in the hills, one of the few paying "enterprises" left to him.

The port of Jaffa (the ancient port of Joppa from which Jonah set sail) is again as sleepy as when Mark Twain wrote his *Innocents Abroad*, although in 1936 Jaffa had become one of the leading cities in Palestine. After Jaffa became unsafe in 1936, the city of Tel Aviv (five minutes distance) was given permission to construct a "jetty." The jetty evolved into a thriving port that now handles as much traffic as the harbor in Haifa. The Jewish businesses located in Jaffa in 1936 had to be transferred to Tel Aviv for reasons of security. Jaffa has declined into a second-rate Levantine port town, and former boatmen and porters employed at the port, carriage drivers, hucksters and bootblacks who made their living in Tel Aviv are existing in penury. After a landmine had been laid on the Tel Aviv beach on a crowded Saturday morning and a bomb had been exploded in front of the San Remo Hotel at teatime, it was considered unsafe to allow Arabs to circulate freely in Tel Aviv. Therefore the innocent and ignorant Arab who once supported his family on what he earned by driving a carriage on Saturdays (when Jewish carriage drivers do not work) pays the price for his gangster countrymen.

So much for politics. Behind the curtain of Royal Commissions, Round Tables [a conference on the partition of Palestine; began on February 7, 1939 and lasted until March 17, 1939] and prolonged confabulations, a drama has been enacted that—like the "covered wagon" era in America—will only be properly recounted in later years by historians who can see events in retrospect.

Although Palestine is among the most ancient countries in the world, the modern Jewish section is among the new territories that came into existence only after the World War. Therefore the word "pioneer" may aptly be applied. In view of centuries of neglect under Turkish and Arab rule, this country, which once supported a flourishing population of millions, has reverted to a veritable desert. In parts, the brackish tributaries of the Jordan had made the soil salty. Wells and springs had dried up until even survey authorities pronounced the land arid. Although the dyes of Lod and the fine linens of Beit She'an were renowned in ancient times, there were no industries in Palestine before the war except soap, wine and Hebron glass. The diaries of pre-war travelers contain amusing accounts of how they brought their own tea, candles and sunglasses from England when visiting Palestine.

So, in the last three years, we have relived some of the drama of early American history—developing the country with one hand and defending ourselves against attackers with the other. As always, during such pioneer periods, women have played an important role. In the first place, it was impossible for a woman to stay behind the "front lines" even if she wanted to. Actually there were no front lines. In the above-mentioned War Office report, it is pointed out that, "Throughout the country the active rebel and peaceful citizen are inextricably mixed." An American journalist who came here from Spain told me, "I was never so nervous in Spain as I am in Palestine. There, at least, you knew where the battlefronts were."

This meant that the most timid woman became, willy-nilly, a soldier of sorts. She traveled about in buses with iron-barred windows. An armed guard sat next to the driver. But even this was not full protection against sniping, bombs and landmines—she was never quite sure if she would return from her visit to the beauty parlor or the dressmaker. On occasions, bombs were thrown into schoolyards, so she darned her stockings or baked her cakes wondering if her children would come home safely in the afternoon. Her husband, whether a teacher, farmer or carpenter, was also in constant danger. The actual casualties for a three-year "war" have been comparatively few. But the murder of one to ten or twenty Jews almost every day has been as nerve-racking as water dropping on a stone. The suspense and insecurity over such a long period has been more trying—especially for the women who wait at home—than a quick and more terrible slaughter would have been.

But it is amazing how adaptable human beings are to any set of conditions. Going to market under armed guard has become the normal rather than the unusual thing.

Last week I was traveling from Rehovot to Tel Aviv in a new type of bus that is completely lined with metal, having only peepholes for ventilation. It gives the effect of a war tank and, naturally, interested the children. I overheard a five-year-old in the seat ahead of me ask her mother in Hebrew, "Why do we have these buses?" The mother, engrossed in her newspaper, replied off-handedly, "Because the mufti wants us to." "He doesn't want us to catch cold?" persisted the youngster. "Yes," replied the mother, lost in the morning news.

But the women's role has not been limited to her historic one of "waiting." Her contribution began soon after the 1936 outbreak when two Jewish nurses, serving in the Jaffa Arab hospital, were murdered in the hospital grounds.

A few months later the women in agricultural settlements demanded their right to assist the men in defense. After some discussions, the right was granted. The first woman to take over the watch on the water tower of a settlement, Ramat Hakovesh, was shot dead (apparently not knowing the art of crouching behind sandbags). Since then, women have not been spared participating in every form of atrocity. About half a year ago, a man and his wife and two children were kidnapped in Atlit and taken by the band to the hills. The children were later returned in safety, but the man and his wife were never heard from again.

Strangely enough the Palestine Philharmonic Orchestra was born and developed during this hectic three-year period. The first concert under the baton of Toscanini was held six months after the outbreaks began. There are a host of amusing stories to be told of how the seventy-five musicians (most of whom had been former leaders in Berlin, Vienna or Budapest) toured the country under armed guard. Sometimes the bassoon players would stick their instruments out the window and blow long blasts to frighten away the terrorists. Here again women took their chances with the men. It is said that the pretty harpist never had a quiet moment when the orchestra was on tour for fear that her precious French harp would suffer at the hands of the snipers.

One of the most dramatic events during the uprising has been the establishment of the "sunrise to sunset" settlements. Owing to insecurity, it was impossible for the Jews to start agricultural settlements in the normal way. Therefore they migrated to the new sites at sunrise, accompanied by several hundred farmers from neighboring settlements. They brought with them partially constructed shacks and walls (resembling the Sears Roebuck collapsible houses). They worked at high speed all day, and before sunset they had put in place the four wooden defense walls, watchtower, dining shack and tents. When completed, the compound resembled the early American barricades. These settlements now number several hundred and are located in various parts of the country from Dan to Be'er Sheva. Here again the women play important roles. The settlements are located in dangerous spots, some on the Transjordan and Syrian frontiers. Usually five or ten women accompany the original forty settlers. They do the cooking and other household jobs, under most primitive conditions. As soon as the farming begins, they assist. Owing to the frequent cutting of telephone wires, there is now a Morse code system joining the Jewish settlements. In most cases, it is the women who sit in the watchtowers at night while the men are on duty below. From the towers they operate the light projectors and give or receive the necessary signals from neighboring settlements.

As I write, the pictures of hundreds of young women whom I have seen in isolated outposts flash through my mind. I remember a dozen living in a place called Ein Geb, which is located on the shores of the Lake of Galilee, near the Syrian border. The only neighbors are bedouin tribes, and assistance in time of danger could only come from across the lake.

The usual quota of women is also living in the settlement at the end of the Dead Sea where the Jews are mining potash. This is one of the lowest spots in the world, and the heat during the summer (and most of the winter) is almost unbearable. Women are also living in the new settlements bordering the Huleh swamp, which was only recently purchased and is still malarial. Here and on the Lake of Galilee, the women assist with the fishing.

One of the most hazardous settlements in the country is Ein-Hashofet, located in the heart of the hills and connected with civilization only by a small mud road, impassable during most of the rainy season. This was settled mostly by Americans and was named in honor of Judge Brandeis [associate justice of the Supreme Court of the United States from 1916 to 1939; the leader of the American Zionist movement in the United States, 1916–20] (*Ein-Hashofet* meaning "Well of the Judge"). It is strange to come into this remote, wild place, surrounded by the black tents of the bedouin, and be greeted by lusty American slang and see young women from Detroit and Chicago walking around with rifles across their shoulders and cartridge belts around their waists. In these dangerous places, licenses to carry arms have been issued by the government to everyone, even the women.

Although these new settlements are more spectacular, the women in the older, established settlements have equally difficult tasks. With the men having been on watch for three years, a large portion of the farming falls to the women, in addition to their household duties. I remember spending a few days in a small farming settlement called Kfar Hess and seeing my hostess start out with a lantern to milk the cow at nine o'clock in the evening, after she had washed the dishes and helped her son with his arithmetic. Her husband worked in the fields during the day and was on watch at night.

Many of these settlements—like the American settlement of Ein-Hashofet—are inhabited by young people who are equipped mentally and physically to face the hazards and the challenge. But some of them are inhabited by middle-aged people who were forced by circumstances into "pioneering." Such is the settlement of Shavei Tzion (Return to Zion). They are situated in the dangerous but once fertile valley of Beit She'an. They are a German Jewish community that migrated last October en masse from the town of Rexingen in the district of Stuttgart. Behind the wooden defense walls, you will find gray-haired *hausfraus* [housewives] bending over primitive Primus stoves or mixing their *kuchen* [coffeecake] batter on upturned orange crates.

This, in brief, is the story of Palestine's women during the past three years when they took their places behind stoves, brooms, hoes, sandbags, rifles, and in watchtowers, as the occasion demanded.

WHY ZIR'IN'S REFUGEES CAN'T RETURN YET

Dorothy Bar-Adon
Merhavia
An article from Bar-Adon's personal archive
Earlier version in *The Palestine Post*, August 19, 1948

Bar-Adon explains why the Israeli government opposed the return of the Arab refugees to their villages. She examines the situation from "the worm's eye" point of view of their Jewish neighbors, using the example of Zir'in, a village located on a ridge above Merhavia. That strategic advantage would preclude the return of the Arab inhabitants, who had fought against their former neighbors despite decades of peaceful relations. She clarifies that in war, one side wins, and the other must accept the consequences of losing.

The Count [Folke Bernadotte, Count of Wisborg; a Swedish diplomat chosen to be the United Nations Security Council's mediator in the Arab-Israeli conflict of 1947–48. He was assassinated in Jerusalem in 1948 by the militant Zionist group, Lehi, while pursuing his official duties] seems rather hurt because the Israel government is "not inclined to permit" the refugees to return. He "appreciates Jewish misgivings on security grounds," but he thinks the danger to Israel would be "slight."

Now, the Count is a busy man who flies around a great deal and sees things along broad lines; the bird's eye view. We who don't fly around and who would be living next door to these refugees, should they return, have the lowly worm's eye view. But it's also a view. Therefore we see these Arab refugees in clear-cut outlines as individuals, as neighbors, as men who lived across the road or just beyond the pine grove or on the other side of the wadi; in contrast to those of the bird's eye view who see them as "the Arab refugee problem" composed of so-and-so many souls (approximately) who cost such-and-such pounds (approx.) to maintain daily on starvation (approx.) rations in order to ease consciences (approx.).

In order to consider these refugees as individuals and to consider their proposed homecoming from the worm's eye view, let's look at Zir'in [an Arab village near Merhavia—the Jewish settlement where Bar-Adon lived]. I've written about Zir'in on previous occasions. I do so again on the pretext of Thoreau who wrote, "I should not talk so much about myself if there were anybody else whom I knew as well." As our close neighbor we knew Zir'in well. And Zir'in being typical of tens of Arab villages, I've used it for close-ups when the scene became too panoramic and bird's eye.

So you may recall that this historic village of Jezreel, where the Kings of Israel was crowned, maintained friendly relations with our village for some thirty years without incident, even during past disturbances. There were times when I became quite lyrical about Zir'in, comparing it to a "cameo" set on the mountain; that's what it looked like. Then the delicate cameo began sniping. And if the Iraqis had taken the notion, our village and others would have been in direct and easy cannon range. Yes, we were close neighbors, uncomfortably close with all the strategic plums in Zir'in's basket.

People here didn't believe, as I wrote at the time, that the fellahin of Zir'in were responsible for the much publicized arrival of the Iraqi general and his troops. In fact, some of them had previously complained, like the other villagers, that if the British would guard the borders, hell "wouldn't pop in Palestine."

None of us know how many of our former good neighbors left the village before the Iraqi general's arrival, nor how many volunteered or were coerced to remain behind, fighting until the night when, after losses to our troops, the stronghold fell. One thing we do know is that on the night of the first unsuccessful attempt to capture Zir'in, the barbaric war cries of the women, urging their men on, were plainly heard by our soldiers. We assumed that the women were of Zir'in and not Iraqi A.T.S. personnel [Auxiliary Territorial Service—the women's branch of the British Army during World War II].

Visiting Zir'in after its capture wasn't a pleasure jaunt. Their own counterattacks had added to the original damage. There was all the emptiness and gapingness of a battered village. Stray cats and donkeys wondered in and out of houses where we had once sipped black coffee and talked of "shalom" through the nargileh smoke. An elaborately beaded makeup bag, made especially for a bride's mascara, hung forlornly on a caved-in wall. Saddest of all was the paralyzed woman whose family had deserted her in the rush. Mumbling about the will of Allah, she sat under a pomegranate tree, her day broken only by the meals brought to her by the Jewish troops. Of all the impressions of that wry day, the memory of the woman left behind under a pomegranate tree, stayed on.

There was sadness that day, the sadness of a deserted village, of destruction, of fellahin torn from their fields. But sadness was hardly the predominating emotion. We'd have been saints or liars if we said so. The predominating emotion was relief. Only here on the spot could we realize the horrible potentialities of this "delicate cameo" who had been sniping at us from a height. Only as we walked over the ground and surveyed Zir'in with other eyes than in the lyric past when we came to eat roast lamb—only now could we thank our lucky stars for the ultimate victory. Our losses were not, as the wishful thinking of the Arabs caused them to write then, "Oh Jewish mothers, if you could see the bodies of hundreds of your sons strewn in pieces on the rocks around Zir'in," etc.,—but the number was high for the subordination of a small village whose strength lay in her height.

And now comes the bland proposal that the Arab refugees be allowed to return to their homes. The idea mayn't sound too preposterous to those in high places when it's couched in that highfalutin "rehabilitation" language. But when you reduce it to its simplest root, Zir'in—and every single Jewish town and village had its personal Zir'in—it's unthinkable that anyone should not consider it unthinkable.

We knew the fellahin of Zir'in. Our farmers helped them in agricultural matters. Those of us with a weakness for that delightful vegetable, *bamya* [okra], had to cultivate our own this year. We miss our *tchina* [tahini] and the spicy bean [cardamom] that adds piquancy to the coffee. It's too bad that the fellah couldn't continue to sell us the bamya and coffee spice. And he'd probably prefer bringing us the bamya to doing whatever he is doing at the moment. It's certainly too bad that anyone with the broad wheat fields he had should be troubled now about where his next *peta* [bread] is coming from. It's too bad. But frankly we're more relieved than sad. If he wasn't living under an olive tree, we might have been. If he wasn't the refugee, we might have been. We prefer it this way. If we said otherwise, we'd be saints or liars. That's war. That's the worm's eye view.

Neither the fellahin nor we were responsible for the spectacular arrival of the Iraqi general in Zir'in. But one thing is certain. The notion of reinstalling Zir'in as a sniping cameo over our heads is fantastic. The blood of every Jewish soldier who fell there in order to ensure the fields in this part of the Emek would cry out against it, to say nothing of those still living here.

When the children used to say, "Zir'in is sniping down on us again," we answered casually, "Really?" or "You don't say." The casualness was part of the general "carry on" act, put on for ourselves as well as for the children. But one's sense of humor and casualness and "carry on" wears thin. We are not prepared to accept with open eyes the Count's "slight" danger.

We can regret that our once good neighbors are living under olive trees somewhere and hungry. We regret too those of our soldiers who will never be hungry again because they fell on the slopes of Zir'in. We can regret a great deal. But still, the idea of such a menace being established on the mountain over our heads is fantastic.

The onus for "rehabilitation" rests squarely with those who opened the borders to the Iraqis, thereby setting the first stone rolling in this whole catastrophe. What do the British intend to do about it? For the whole high-sounding "Arab refugee problem" is only Zir'in multiplied, complicated, and soaked with sudden British crocodile tears.

We who were good neighbors can feel more poignantly for the fellah whom we once called by his first name than England who brought him to this present plight. For us he isn't the "Arab refugee problem"; he's a man with a name with whom we had no quarrel. It's sadder to think of a man with a name living under an olive tree, hungry, with his wife and children with names, than to think of the "refugee problem" living under an olive tree, hungry. And more than once we inquire with concern, "I wonder how so and so is faring now." I think most often of ten-year-old Fatma with the dark eyes and chubby cheeks. It happened like this. American jitterbugging of a sort and Arab hoochy of a sort can be made to coincide at a given point. So, at a wedding we managed a twosome. Fatma was delighted to follow me like a shadow for two whole days. Where is she now? Often her dancing feet and dark eyes protrude from the bird's eye "Arab refugee problem" in a very personal, worm's eye way.

But the idea of Fatma's father being "rehabilitated" over our heads at this stage in the game is fantastic. In other words, the average man—devoid of Britain's beatific fairplayness—would answer any invitation to rehabilitation at his expense for the benefit of Britain's keeping face. "So sorry, old fellow, but—"

CHAPTER FIVE

Jerusalem: A City Not Yet Divided

INTRODUCTION

Until 1948 Jerusalem was not a divided city; only with the 1949 cease-fire accords, which ended the War of Independence, was the city divided between the Kingdom of Jordan and the newly established State of Israel. When Kahn lived in Jerusalem during the 1930s, the city was the center of the Mandate Government.

ALL DAY HE GRINDS HIS COFFEE [LOCAL COLOR]

Zif Zif, pp. 30–31

> *Smells on David Street in Jerusalem are as mixed up as the people, the animals, the stalls and the sounds. There are odors emanating from sizzling kebab [meat cooked over flames], damp sheep entrails, nargilehs [hookahs], and the very pink roses being arranged into small bunches by a peasant woman on a step. And yet, at one particular spot, there is an odor that never fails to disentangle itself from the others with the distinction of time-honored aristocracy. It is the odor of coffee, rich and fresh and tempting. So follow it to its source and discover Ahmed Ali, the blind coffee grinder who, for thirty-years, has been discovered on and off by all habitués of the Old City.*

In his dim little hole-in-the-wall shop, Ahmed has managed to imprison much of the romance and poetry with which the East has endowed the commonplace coffee bean. All of the odes and lyrics that Easterners from Sultan to bedouin have sung in praise of coffee seem to revive with poignancy in Ahmed's modest stronghold.

Ahmed Ali grinds coffee. As he grinds, his strong arms weave great circles with the wheel. His husky body bends forward, giving him the effect of a genie breathing a magical incantation over each grain of his precious mixture. His eyes are half-closed, his beard black and rather unkempt; his half-bared chest is hairy and expansive.

In the meager light one is transfixed, watching the flow of movement produced by this monarch of the coffee bean, whom the gods seem pleased to have made sightless so that they may shut out all else but the sound of his eternal grinding and the odor of his nectar.

Ahmed does not permit his spectators to stand long in admiring silence. He senses their presence above the thrum of the machinery and facetiously demands *baksheesh* (a donation) for his performance. Now the ice is broken. The fantastic figment is alive and relating the story of his life. Thirty years ago, when he was a boy, fourteen years old, he became blind. It was hard to find work in the village, so he came to the Old City to grind coffee.

He has been grinding ever since. Twelve hours every day, he is at his wheel. For this work he receives ten piasters a day. But he does not complain because somehow it is sufficient to maintain his family of five children.

The lights and shades and curious winding windings of the Old City, he has never seen. But he knows them. He boasts that you could not lose him in any part of the ancient labyrinth of narrow lanes. Indeed, he is as enamored with the life that flows through the Street of the Chain as the man who devours it with his eyes.

"Here come some soldiers," he says while the distant sound of the marching feet of a contingent coming to the mosque for the Nebi Musa festival [a seven-day-long religious festival celebrated annually by Palestinian Muslims] is still quite indistinguishable to the average ear.

Ahmed Ali is pleased when you want to buy a few piasters worth of his coffee. With the pride of a craftsman-artist he weighs it on his crude scale. "I have given you too much," he comments, preparing to return the extra measure to his stock. Then, with great abandon, he secures the bag with its extra portion and hands it to you remarking, "Yes, it is too much." But, *ma'alesh* (it doesn't matter).

THE INVASION OF THE "SUNDAE" [LOCAL COLOR]

Zif Zif, pp. 52–53
Earlier version in *The Palestine Post*, January 23, 1934

There are numerous treasures in the Jerusalem Young Men's Christian Association. Rows upon rows of fascinating scarabs, graceful urns of early Greek origin, priceless Hebraic seals, cases of intriguing clay relics of the stone and iron ages, rugs from Persia and a queen chandelier upon which cherubim become sportive under proper lighting effects.

One does not hear of the talented cherubim or of the scarabs until making a private exploration expedition. But the soda fountain! Its fame spread far and wide as one of the truly monumental spots in the Holy City.

At first one is only slightly stirred by the news that sodas and juices may be obtained in the YMCA, feeling a certain satisfaction in going native to the extent of reveling in gazoz [flavored soda water]. For a month—or perhaps two—the affinity survives and then, without preliminaries, something snaps within and it has gone. Alas, gazoz is no more than a ripple of a pebble in the sea. Now you too are yearning for the soda fountain.

The other day came the news that a fruit syrup manufacturing plant is to be established in Montefiore near Tel Aviv, operating according to "modern American methods."

This announcement, on the surface, means no more than further industrial development in Palestine. Yet, underneath, one senses an ominous rumbling. In the twinkling of an eye, the era of the chocolate soda, cherry sundae, banana split, orange frappe and coconut delight may be upon us. Palestine is liable to be submerged under a flood of marshmallowy, chocolate, whipped, creamy substances that are one of the backbones of life in America. The introduction of this era will bring considerations, philosophies, professions and institutions hitherto unknown in Palestine.

At the very outset it will give rise to a new school of literature. No self-respecting sundae is merely a sundae. It goes through life disguised as a "Manhattan Perfection," "Babe Ruth Balmy" or a "Roosevelt Rosy." Therefore, we may anticipate that some creative soul will go into exclusion to emerge with such touching catchwords as "Ein Harod Honey," "Rehovot Razzberry," "Levant Luscious," "Bethlehem Banana Dandy" and "Bialik Moonlight."

The advent of this era will bring into being a new race of men. After all, there is something frank, open and spontaneous about the personality of a gazoz vendor. He seems to feel a refreshingly abandoned joy both in himself and in his product. At times tenseness creeps into his voice as he hawks his wares. Yet one does not feel that he lies awake at nights brooding over the pros and cons of *gazeuse* [carbonation].

The soda water dispenser will be a more imposing, less lovable, and more awe-inspiring character. He will stand behind huge cans of cherries, chopped nuts and shredded coconuts with gravity at once overwhelming. True, he will make quips over the counter with a certain light dash. But as he places the crimson cherry in its nest of snowy marshmallows and adds one almond at a twenty-five degree angle, you realize that this is no mediocrity—but an artist in his own right.

And what of the pharmacies in Palestine, those miraculous drug stores that usually sell drugs? Will the soda water era mean that they are to be corrupted by selling light lunches and everything else, from fountain pens and alarm clocks to children's rompers? Alas, the American pharmacist cannot find a bottle of liniment without first moving an automobile tire, four Kodaks [cameras] and a pair of skates.

A visitor in Tel Aviv was heard to sigh while looking into a cake shop, "When I was in Palestine four years ago, the people didn't know what pastry was." The introduction of pastry made little change in the general tenor of life in Palestine. But will the invasion of the sundae, with all its ramifications, be so subdued?

THE PASSING SHOW

Zif Zif, pp. 45–46

Earlier version in *The Palestine Post*, "The Passing Show, Jerusalem's Outdoor Scene,"
July 30, 1934
Unpublished manuscript from Bar-Adon's personal archive

A humorous description of Zion Street in Jerusalem (1934) as a circus, demonstrating the cosmopolitan atmosphere of the city.

Forget your Piccadilly Circus—and Broadway and Forty Second Street— and Potsdam Platz—and come behind a large glass window fronting on Zion Circus in Jerusalem—your coffee will grow cold—and your cigarette go dead—while you watch the world and his wife pass by in four directions—the lazy gait of the East—the energetic stride of the West—all bound up in a symphony of movement—a sharp-eyed Arab vendor is displaying a grass rug to a British policeman—the rug is embellished with a lion—is the policeman bargaining for it?—We hope not—it would be terrible to wake up in the middle of the night to see the beast all of a sudden—but the policeman is apparently only asking for a license—wise policeman—we are relieved—a shiny car pulls up in front of the cinema house—an Arab woman in a glorious red embroidered dress emerges—looking as though she should be drawing water in some village—but she is passing by Zion Circus instead—everybody passes by Zion Circus—plenty of sun helmets always reminding you of big game hunting in Africa—plenty of white suits—two Eskimo pie boys in a scrap—you expect to see the street deluged with Eskimos any minute—someone intervenes—the day and the Eskimo pies [chocolate-covered vanilla ice cream bars] are saved—two old Jews looking like a vaudeville conception of what old Jews should look like—they're laughing terribly hard—you wish part of the story would penetrate your window—suddenly lots of donkeys—about twenty in one party and they are actually galloping and the donkeyteers are sprinting after them—where can they be rushing to—a bus swerves round the corner—did it strike the last lagging donkey—no—two Germans—newspapers under arms—so engrossed—maybe one of them is telling the other that the whole business began when Hitler spilled a cup of coffee on Goebbels in a Berlin café—and the other man maybe answering that it didn't matter much because Goebbels' shirt was brown anyway—or maybe they're not saying that at all but they're so engrossed—a little Oriental boy who would look nice selling mishmish (apricots) is vending children's dresses instead—pink ones—they look enchanting from here—even the Yemenite with a suggestion of underwear peeking from one trouser looks enchanting—your garbage man lolling on the sidewalk looks enchanting—everybody—and everybody—and everything—passes by Zion Circus—and when you see it from behind a plate glass window—it looks enchanting.

MEN WITHOUT WOMEN

1934
Zif Zif, pp. 11–13
Unpublished manuscript from Bar-Adon's personal archive

Reflecting on Election Day for the municipality in Jerusalem in 1934,
Bar-Adon concludes that in Jerusalem the vote is for men only.

One had to make herself immune to undisguised stares and titters if she was to invade the "no-woman's-land" of the polling districts when Jerusalem elected a mayor. Diogenes could not have found a true skirt no matter how bright his lamp, unless it was being worn by a fellah.

For a woman to invade the voting precincts was as deceitful as handing a boy an empty bag marked "licorice drops." Before the war had even stopped, the windows were bombarded with circulars of every color, extolling the sterling qualities of the respective candidates. Imagine the disappointment for the ward heelers when what emerged from the mass of paper was only a woman.

And a woman at a Jerusalem election is about as useful as ice skates at the Dead Sea. One boy in the Orthodox Jewish district of Mea She'arim, who had either a sense of humor, a sense of irony or was so excited that he had no sense at all, pulled my sleeve and implored that I "vote for Perlman."

It was amusing—after having felt like an important cog in the Ship of State when you cast your vote for President Roosevelt—to discover that in Jerusalem at election time you are as important as a crumb (and a crumb should be swept away, as soon as possible). Indeed the sight of one of the frailer sex walking into the midst of the voting arena caused as much ado as a man walking into a beauty parlor when the clientele is crowned with curlers. Any attempt to gain entry into the sanctum sanctorum where the votes were actually being cast was met with a near-panic or stern refusal.

At the Old City Station I did enter the polling room. But the wheels of progress immediately stopped; clerks were unable to continue with their work and inquiries of "What do you want?" came from all direction in the three official tongues. Alarm seemed to spread as though no one was quite sure whether this insidious female was going to try to slip a vote into the box for the most handsome candidate—or to appropriate the entire box—(which was decorated with ribbon) for her boudoir table. Or perhaps she was one of these tourists who were bent on capturing the whole room as a souvenir of election day in Jerusalem.

The police at St. George's School, the Arab district, presented this stir with a cold, "entry forbidden."
By peeping through the window, one could see finely attired sheikhs looking like a page from Arabian Nights. One might surmise they were discussing moonlight and white steeds—but of course the conversation centered on the two mayoral candidates Ragheb Bey Nashashili and Dr. Khalidi. In other sections of the city there were the pious Jews looking like a

vignette from the Old Bible. One might surmise they were discussing prophecy—but of course their conversation centered around Mr. Perlman and Mr. Ende [mayoral candidates].

The polling station at the railway station was least picturesque—but most reminiscent of election time in England or America. Young effendis in European clothes stood with their heads together making predictions as to the outcome and driving back and forth in open roadsters.

One felt, however, that more color could have been added to the scene if a woman ran out between washing the baby and cleaning up the lunch dishes to dry her hands on her apron and mark a cross after the name of her favorite. In any other civilized country the women are the part of the election—they challenge the challengers so well. The politicians even send automobiles to bring women from the cradle to the polls. But in Jerusalem, voting is a man's prerogative and he guards it jealously.

THREE GLASSES OF TEA [LOCAL COLOR]

Zif Zif, pp. 14–15

> *Moshe—the Moshe of the Café Vienna in Jerusalem—was busy as usual Monday morning dispensing magazines, drinks, and casual conversations. Between times he puzzled over a newspaper. He had already read the Hebrew accounts of Shmaryahu Levin's [1867–1935; Zionist leader and author] death the day before. But the English version was difficult. He picked his way through it word by word.*

Moshe is not sentimental. Like all waiters who remain in one place watching a parade of people drifting in and drifting out again, Moshe had absorbed the philosophy of the rightness of people drifting in and drifting out again, in the broader sense. And like so many of us, Moshe expressed his mystification over the slim thread between life and death with the phrase "And only the day before the Festival of the First Fruits, I brought Dr. Levin a set of chessmen."

It seems that Dr. Levin's never-failing greeting when he entered the café (which was a daily occurrence except when he was confined to his bed) was, "Shalom. Nu? Yesh mishahu?" (Hello. Well? Anyone here?). Then it was Moshe's special tafkid (duty) to unearth a chess opponent. Sometimes it was easy. Sometimes no one was available, in which case even

Dr. Levin would settle down to read a newspaper, after having given Moshe instructions to find a partner, "even if you have to get someone from the street."

Moshe took the matter of finding a chess partner most seriously. Sometimes he would be forced to take Dr. Levin's command almost literally and would bring him a stranger. Moshe would make the necessary introductions. So pleased was Dr. Levin with Moshe's success in securing a partner that he would pay scant attention to the introduction formalities so long as the partner knew the difference between a castle and a knight.

Of late Moshe had been concerned with Dr. Levin's failing health and felt it part of his tafkid to take precautions that the chess games were not too trying. He would take it on himself to ask the partner of the day to allow Dr. Levin to win a game or two, in case he was not up to his usual form.

Moshe remembers the Yiddish stories of Shmaryahu Levin, and he remembers too that all chess opponents who played a poor game brought down on their heads the taunt of *shuster* (shoemaker).

Moshe's other important tafkid concerned tea. He remembers that Dr. Levin seldom drank anything else but tea—Russian tea.

"He could drink much tea," Moshe will tell you, "As soon as he sat down, I brought him a glass of tea without waiting to be asked. Then, when his glass was empty, I brought him a second glass, without waiting to be asked. But for the third glass—here Moshe raises his had to emphasize the climax—ah, for the third glass, I always had to wait until he asked."

ARTICLE

Probably written 1936
An article from Bar-Adon's personal archive, without a title

On the basis of her experience as a journalist in Atlantic City, New Jersey, Kahn ironically interviews herself on differences between being a journalist in the United States and in Palestine.

From America to Jaffa Road is a long journey. How does being a journalist in Palestine compare to being a journalist in America?

How does it compare? Well, you lose any superiority complex that you might have had. Most Americans adore publicity. Perhaps this is because the country and the people are so delightfully young. They have no secrets—they enjoy telling all. So, of course, the newspaper reporter is a very popular fellow. He walks through open doors and everyone is glad to see him.

And here?

The country is older and perhaps the people are wiser. At all events, I've never had any flags unfurled when I came in quest of information. I interviewed a few presidents of the United States with no difficulties. But in Palestine I've waited around two days to talk to a farmer who was too busy repairing a chicken coop to receive me. You see, the people here aren't what Americans call "publicity conscious." If you tell a falafel vendor that you want to write about him, he grabs his falafel and runs for his life. In America you walk around with your press card pinned to your lapel. But here it's more comfortable to sneak around disguised as an olive tree.

That must be annoying.

It is, but you get used to it. In the beginning I longed more than once for America, where a murder story is sure to receive three or four columns of space. It seems strange to write a few lines to the effect that some fellah had murdered his wife, grandmother, two children and a camel. Surely, the public would want to know the life story of the fellah and his grandmother and his camel.

But you found that the public wasn't interested?

Not at all. The completion of a new road leading to somewhere or a political opinion of so-and-so is worth more space than the finest murder that was ever perpetrated.

So, the people here are political minded. And what are the other difficulties?

Language—language—and again language. You know that Americans are the most monolingual people in the world. For most of us, mastering another language is a life's work. Here it's difficult to get any information about the weather in the Old City unless you know a bit of Armenian, at least a few words of Amharic, and a smattering of Persian. I remember that when I arrived in Palestine, I was sent to get some information from an Arab butcher concerning a crisis in the meat market. I couldn't understand him so he drew a sketch which I took back to the office. But since nobody could tell if he had drawn a sheep or a cow, we didn't know whether the supply of beef or mutton would be stopped on the morrow.

Yes, I suppose language is a journalist's first tool.

More or less. But you learn to speak any language by proper motions and a smile. I remember that the late Mayor Dizengoff [first Mayor of Tel Aviv; died in 1936], who spoke many languages fluently, was amazed to find that I spoke only English and remarked with horror, "Did it ever occur to you that if you didn't know English, you'd be dumb?"

Yes, that's a very upsetting thought. But one can go far in Palestine with English.

You flatter me. Here in Palestine, I have learned that I don't even speak English. Just American. Many times people shake their heads ruefully and say, "I studies English, but I don't seem to understand American! By the way, do you understand me?"

Almost.

According to the popular song, you say tomato and I say tomato, so let's call the whole thing off.

Oh, not yet. You seem to enjoy being a journalist in Palestine. So tell me some of the things that compensate you for the falafel men who evade you?

Well, the size of the country. It's as small and convenient as a pocket comb. If you hear about a story on the farthest frontier, you can be on the scene within a few hours. You can get anywhere in the country and home again between breakfast and dinner—with your story safely up your sleeve or under your hat. Surely, this is a paradise for journalists who have a reputation for wanting to be everywhere.

Yes, it must be easy to keep in the swim of things when the sea is so tiny. But how can you find enough to write about in such a small country. Don't you feel sometimes that you've just about reached the end?

To the contrary. It always seems as though you haven't begun. There is such a diversified wealth of people, creeds, beliefs and experiments. Then too, the country is closer to the city than elsewhere. In America, the rural correspondents handle the cows and the chickens and the beehives. But here, Kiriat Anavim [first kibbutz established in the Judean Hills—1920] is just a step from Jerusalem, and the farms of Judea aren't very many steps from Kiriat Anavim, so you have to be a dilettante farmer.

Then there is no dearth of news?

Never. You just open your inkpot and the stories flow in. Or, to be more exact, you uncover your typewriter and the stories hop onto the keys. Of course, I'd rather—

Now, you say rather and I say rather—so we'd better call the whole thing off, especially as the time is up.

CHAPTER SIX

World War II—the Palestine Home Front

In autumn 1939 the Jewish population of Mandatory Palestine numbered some 431,000 Jews. Until the allied defeat of Axis forces in the Western Desert campaign in North Africa (1942), the danger to the Jewish population from a German conquest of Palestine was real and present. About 38,000 Jewish women and men from mandatory Palestine served in the British Army: 5,000 of them in the Jewish Brigade Group formed in 1944. Jews from Palestine took part in fighting in North Africa, Italy, and northern Europe.

This chapter contains two personal letters and one unpublished article; the latter contains Bar-Adon's personal impressions of her visit to detention camps in Cyprus, in which the British Mandatory authorities incarcerated so-called illegal Jewish immigrants to Palestine (refugees from Europe after the Holocaust).

LETTER

20 Abyssinian St.
December 1942

Dear Elene:

You can't imagine my excitement when I see an American stamp—as I did this morning. Nobody writes to me—as I deserve, since I decided to call a moratorium until after the war. After earning my living for twenty years by being a verbal exhibitionist—I find myself terrified of censors! Besides, I don't like to burden them with long effusions—and short letters are so inadequate when I long for hours of talk with you. I enjoyed the way you started right off by giving me hell about Ethel Harrold—sounded like old times—anyway, I'm writing to her in this very mail. I must explain to her that I don't write to anyone—not even Bea—except you—and what can you do with someone who pursues you with letters via Australia? Your letter was tantalizing—you unconsciously left everything indefinite. Who is Jimmy marrying? Yes, it does make me feel ancient. Does Ada's doing publicity for a singer mean that she's left A.C. [Atlantic City]? Does your Newark Ave. address mean that you have left Blatt's? Then, I racked my brain for hours about the red bucket—finally remembered that it was made of wood and deserves to have a romantic history—but I suppose it was just a pickle bucket or something. And with Syd away, what has happened to Es and how is their mother? And how does your Edward claim the honor of living in a place named Carmel, which I hope you know is our most beautiful mountain range and used frequently in the Bible as the symbol of beauty. So please say "a bit of Palestine" and not a bit of Switzerland. And you don't mention Virginia and Marie of whom I am so anxious to hear. And what of Lou Stern? I heard that he was in Turkey and touched our shores. Is it true? I was very excited for a few days and then he seemed to slip off again. A woman named Goldie Myerson leaves shortly for America—prominent in the labor movement—if she speaks in A.C. talk to her—she can give news of us. Also, please send future letters to The Palestine Post, Jerusalem. We are hoping to settle in some farm settlement—although our plans have been so delayed that it becomes sort of Mice and Men with me asking Azziz [nickname of Pessah Bar-Adon, Dorothy's husband] to tell me a story about when I'll be tending rabbits. Anyway, the Post is the best address because I am always in close touch with them no matter where I may be. I think you were showing off when you disposed of Skippy in two sentences—trying to prove that you're not the way I know you are. Well, I have no such pretensions. (If I don't talk about Doron Gur [Dorothy and Pessah's son], there isn't much to talk about—you know I never did anything halfway—so I'm that kind of a mother. He's two and a quarter now—at the jabbering stage. Luckily his words of wisdom lose their flavor in English—so you're spared. Owing to the scarcity and exorbitant cost of nursemaids—I put him in a sort of prekindergarten when he was two. A few weeks ago they had their Chanukah festival and he performed with the rest. And you would have laughed at me—the teachers make me conceal myself in some rafters to keep him from being self-conscious. From the moment he marched in, wearing a lopsided cardboard crown and carrying a candle I wept quietly standing on my head in the ceiling—and when they marched out, singing a rousing song about the Maccabees and carrying little Zionist flags—me and the rafters simply got hysterical. I take back anything I ever said about you. And when he sings complete Hebrew songs—my cup flows over and all that sort of thing. My Hebrew, as you know, is scandalous and my friends were skeptical about my experiment of raising him only in Hebrew. But I get along—except when I'm terribly angry and have to send an SOS to Azziz to "scold him for me." I am told by pedagogues that when he realizes that my accent is bad and my grammar frequently incorrect—he will lose respect for me. But I have no inferiority complex, and I maintain that I'll win his respect in other ways—even if I have to learn tightrope walking—or how to bake a jelly roll. And now that your getting bored with my son—we live a quieter life than you can imagine in a little Arab house of one room, comforts outside—and a lovely garden in which almond blossoms have already appeared. I freelance, which gives me time for my domestic duties. Azziz grinds out books—but publications are hampered owing to paper restrictions—however, a collection of short stories on horses is scheduled to appear soon—and, if all is well, a novel based on a fishing village, will appear after that. We are stay-at-homes, only going to the orchestra and theater occasionally—we discourage visitors except on Friday evening when we ooze the Sabbath spirit and welcome all and sundry. Doron Gur adores the Sabbath—puts the candles on the table and drinks milk when we drink wine. I don't think I've changed a bit—which you may take as a good or bad sign. I still enjoy everything with resounding enthusiasm—and best of all a good "schmooze" with a good friend and good cigarettes and coffee. I am an old-fashioned mother, which I always believed in theoretically, even when I thought you overdid it. When my work takes me out of town for a day and I miss putting my Gur (lion cub) to bed—I curse the universe and professions for women. Housekeeping is an art these days since we have the honor of having the highest food index in the world—a 250% increase in food costs. I can't say that I enjoy housekeeping or ever will—but I do it almost as well as the next fellow—learning such important things as the fact that beans and milk are almost a perfect protein food and a dozen olives are almost as nourish-ing as an egg, etc. We have been unbelievably fortunate—almost everything is available—it's only the cost that's the kink. Doron Gur even wallows in corn flakes—which he calls "Forn lakes." This is all that my conscience lets me clutter up the mail with. It will be Christmas in a few days—so give my love to all those who I should have sent cards to and didn't although I think of them—Christmas for me now means a card from Ada—she never forgets me, and I wait for it. Despite my having apparently broken a lot of connections—you'd be surprised how many times I say that people can't make new friends after a certain age—and most people here suffer from that. You are on your guard—you feel the necessity for explaining yourself—I suppose the main thing is that people consider you a sensible woman of thirty-five (last August), which people like Virginia and Marie or Elene wouldn't be. Just a few weeks ago I mentioned Virginia and Marie in this connection—they couldn't begin to understand the main currents of my life now—and yet I feel closer to them than most people who are in the same boat with me. The very fact that they knew my father means a great deal. And who here could possibly understand—like you understand without any explanation—what it means for me to have a son whose mother tongue is Hebrew—there were so many hurdles to be jumped until I got there. All of which doesn't mean that I haven't made close friends here—three women—Ida Davidowitz—and Harry, of course—the English woman, Hana, whom I met on my first day in Palestine ten years ago—and Lea, a grand old Russian woman, a member of the communal settlement where I formerly lived. Enough! You see what I'm like when I get started. My love to everyone—and Albert, Rhea, Edward, Skippy, the old oaken red bucket and the fish—

As always,

Dot

THE ISLAND SICKNESS, COMING HOME FROM CYPRUS

Probably written in 1947
An article from Bar-Adon's personal archive

The illegal emigrants to Palestine who were captured by the British were brought to Cyprus and put in displaced persons' camps. Bar-Adon describes the life in the camps.

There is the usual run of human ailments in the Cyprus concentration camps [camps run by the British government for internment of Jews who had immigrated or attempted to immigrate to Mandatory Palestine in violation of British policy; the camps operated from August 1946 to January 1949 and in total held about 51,000 people], ranging from migraine headaches to galloping consumption. But medical care is adequate, and the general health conditions are satisfactory. However, one ailment is infectious, rampant and beyond the power of doctors to cure. For want of a more scientific label, we may call it simply, "sailing fever." This is the frenzy that seizes the internees several weeks before a ship is scheduled to sail for Palestine.

According to the description of a Palestinian doctor who has just returned from Cyprus with a boatload of refugee patients, this frenzy comes out of the blue like a tropical storm. The diagnosis is easy— homesickness, freedom-sickness, and an overwhelming fear of being left behind.

Between sailings, says the doctor, there is comparative peace and calm in the camps. The refugees exist on the hope that soon they will be sailing. They devour the postcards and letters received from their more fortunate comrades who sailed last week or last month. They pore longingly over the postmarks—Tel Aviv, Haifa, or some obscure village that they never heard of. So Chaim has arrived! And meanwhile, as far as animal comforts go, they are well looked after now. Food is sufficient, if monotonous. Their self-service and self-organization works fairly smoothly. They have enjoyed an exceptionally mild winter. Above all, the British military and civil staffs have been understanding and helpful. With children under supervision and a number of adults absorbed by camp duties, day-to-day life proceeds in a quiet groove.

"Sailing Fever"

Then, two weeks or ten days before a ship is due to leave, the calm blows up. It is as though a typhoon suddenly swept over the camp. A ship is going to Palestine! Every man, woman and even the children are infected by this "sailing fever." If they had managed to stifle the ignominy of their confinement for a few weeks, now the barbed wire springs to life because freedom is in the offing. There is an absolute frenzy to be rid, once and for all, of this barbed wire that has been their constant companion for years on end.

Who will be the lucky ones? Who will win through on this last weary lap to home? Who will be left behind when the ship sails? Every other consideration fades into insignificance. What Mr. Bevin may have said to Mr. Ben Gurion, or what The Times thinks about what Mr. Bevin [Britain foreign secretary; refused to remove limits on Jewish immigration to Palestine in the aftermath of World War II] said, is of little interest. The broader issues don't count now. Who really cares what may happen next year or the year after? The big thing is to get out of the gate—to get on the ship—to get home. Will I make it? Will I be left behind?

Camp life begins to deteriorate from the moment that the "sailing fever" breaks out. Cooks become lax. Study groups are badly attended. There is a grim, tense, sullen atmosphere. They gather in knots to speculate and to chew over what has been chewed over before. Rumors about the sailing are rife. There are jealousies and the raw nerves of desperate people trying to get home. Somehow, the shadow of the ship hangs over the camp like an eerie ghost. Meager possessions are packed, unpacked and repacked, even by those who have no hope of sailing on this trip. They pack. Who knows? Perhaps a miracle.

No Faith Left

Still, in their hearts they don't believe in miracles. They don't believe in anything or anyone. They have no faith in human beings. How could faith be left to them when they've lost everything else? They don't even believe the Palestinans who have come to help them. That's why families refuse to be separated when one member could and should precede the others for reasons of health.

"How can I leave my husband and children behind?" asks a desperate woman on the preferential sick list. "How do I know they'll come on the next ship? You tell me. That's not enough. I don't believe you. I don't believe anybody. Why should I?" This is the kind of broken people the Palestinians meet in Cyprus. It's a malady that the doctors can't cure when the patients are behind barbed wire. And so, making the passenger list is a complicated business. Families won't be separated. They're terrified of being torn apart. Being together is the only thing left to them. You can't talk to them about other ships. They don't believe. They only believe in the ship that's sailing tomorrow, and they'll fight, lie, cheat to get on it. Palestinians are frightened and bewildered until they become adjusted to this new specimen of desperate man, fighting with his fingernails for the right to freedom.

A ship is sailing. Who is going? Who is staying behind? Who is going to make that short voyage between barbed wire and home? There will be other ships. I don't believe you. It's this one that counts. It's this one that's sure. There is no next week or next month for those of no faith. There's only this ship and the grim desperation to be on it.

The lucky ones go through the barbed wire with their knapsacks and turn their faces toward freedom. Those left behind settle down again to the barbed wire routine. Then weary eyes and hearts fasten on the next ship. And again "sailing fever" grips the camp.

LETTER TO MOTHER

Sunday, September 1, 1946

Dear Mom:

This is just a note to tell you that your grandson began school today (in honor of which I just put on a new typewriter ribbon). And what excitement—Azziz, who has gone to bed in a state of collapse, just said that thank heavens we will have no further upheavals until he's bar mitzvah in another seven years. It is, of course, all very hick—the little red schoolhouse sort of thing—the school is in the next village—Affulah—and that means a bus ride of a few miles, which adds greatly to his excitement and to our worry. The bus leaves around seven, which means rising at six— and soon it will still be dark when he goes off. And here's a picture of him this morning—hair plastered down with a quart of stinky brilliantine, which he adores—a very manly and sporty blue blouse labeled "Groneup" which Rachela sent him—short khaki trousers like his father's—a shiny new lunchbox—his leather briefcase—and two front teeth missing—altogether a handsome specimen. Of course, I was up at five—in fact, I didn't sleep at all, and we both escorted him to Affulah. The older children of the village, who are accustomed to grinding him in the dust, were very impressed when he entered the bus), his pants now held up by a belt instead of straps as hitherto) and greeted him with due respect. Whereupon tears began dripping from my brown eyes and continued to do so until we reached Affulah, for—from the moment the older children greeted him as "Doron" instead of the usual "Pishpesh" (bedbug)—I could see that we were entirely unnecessary—he felt like a million. I was anxious to see the teacher, as he had already told us that if she was ugly he intended to walk out and come home. She is no Garbo—but neither is she cross-eyed or bucktoothed, and it seems he's decided to make the best of it. We left him at the door—went to a café for black coffee and hung around till noon to take him home again since this was the first day. However, when school was out, he was very embarrassed to see us and sent us packing and came home in the bus by himself. At home, the large blackboard—which I told you in a previous letter I was having made—was waiting for him with the colored chalk you sent, and he thought you very clever to have gotten the chalk here just on the first day of his school. So now he's on the road to being educated. His father has been assuring me for two weeks that he has the head of a cabbage—no power of concentration—and will pass no grade at all—and that next year I will be among the line of parents we saw this morning waiting to talk to the principal about children who were left back. This week there was an article in the paper about children beginning school—that they are liable to be nervous at first, lose their appetites, have nightmares, etc. So far, says Azziz, I'm the only one affected—Doron Gur is eating as usual, but I've been bilious from excitement for a few days. He wanted to hear about me in the first grade—strangely enough (or logically, according to Mr. Freud), while I can't remember the names of people I met yesterday—I instantly recalled the name "Miss Sharpless," which I'm sure hasn't been in my mind for thirty years. Do you remember that broomstick? But he was suspicious of the name because here they call the teachers by first names—so I named her Fifi. Please let me know if you get this and previous letters. Whether there is censorship or not is vague—but I have an idea that a letter I wrote to Hillel and Rachela didn't reach them since I asked them for some information that they haven't sent. I had papers from America. today, and I can imagine that you are worried. I can't say that anything was incorrect—still the effect is exaggerated—I mean, when you read it, things sound worse than they are—you get the impression that the whole country is disturbed and everyone standing on their ears, which isn't true—places are disturbed in turn, and in the rest of the country, life goes its wonted way. For instance this week we attended a big wedding in this village and danced till morning—yesterday, Saturday, we went to bathe in a river some twenty miles away with the kids and had a swell time—next week we plan to go to a big four-day festival celebrating the twenty-fifth anniversary of a village—Nahalal—and so life goes on. I hope soon to have an account of our trip. Enough for tonight as it is very late, but I wanted to get this sent tomorrow. Love to you and Rus and the Bibles from all of us—

Dot

CHAPTER SEVEN

The Collective Village

INTRODUCTION

A kibbutz (from the Hebrew for "gathering") is a collective community. The first kibbutz—Degania—was established in 1910; as of 2010, there were some 270 kibbutzim in Israel. During the first years after its establishment, until it achieved economic viability, each kibbutz was usually supported financially by the Zionist movement. As a central part of the Zionist endeavor of settling the land, kibbutzim were at first based almost exclusively on agriculture. Currently their economic base includes industrial plants and high-tech businesses, as well as services such as those connected with tourism.

The kibbutzim were ideologically based on a combination of Zionism and socialism. Establishing a Jewish settlement in nineteenth- and early twentieth-century Palestine was almost impossible for an individual family; such pioneering demanded a high level of cooperation within a group.

Many of the settlers came from European youth movements and organizations that had socialist orientations. The internal organization of the community was based on the concept of "from each according to his ability, to each according to his need." (The latter slogan was coined by Louis Blanc in 1851 and was common to socialist movements in general; its first use was mistakenly attributed to Karl Marx.) All property was owned communally; all income was pooled and divided according to individual/family needs; the community provided many of the basic services traditionally provided by the individual family. Meals were prepared and eaten in a communal dining room; a communal clothing shop and laundry provided, mended, and laundered clothing; healthcare was provided for all; children were cared for in communal children's homes.

The decision in most kibbutzim to house and raise the children in communal children's homes was based on a number of considerations. Kibbutz members believed in gender equality and wished to enable women to have professions other than housekeeping, cooking, teaching, and childcare. The early kibbutzim were often very poor and aimed to provide their children with better living conditions than could be provided to adults; better security for the children was also a consideration. It should be noted that the communal children's homes were not meant to "replace" the family; indeed, every afternoon and evening the children spent three to four hours of quality time with their parents and siblings.

By the 1970s in many kibbutzim the children lived under the same roof as their parents; now all do. The children's homes still provide year-round quality childcare six days a week, usually from 7 a.m. to 4 p.m.; the children attend local schools.

Since the 1990s most kibbutzim have chosen to undergo a process of "privatization." Property, including means of production, is still owned communally; members' income is still pooled. There is a high level of mutual assistance in areas such as healthcare and children's education. There is a connection, however, between the individual income of the family unit and the financial "allowance" that each unit receives.

A moshav (Hebrew for "settlement") is a cooperative agricultural community composed of individual small farms. The first moshav—Nahalal—was founded in 1921. As of the 1990s there are some 450 moshavim. As was the case with the kibbutzim, the establishment of moshavim was central to the Zionist project of settling the land and, of course, enabling the Yishuv to feed itself. From the beginning each family farm was individually owned, although the farms were of an equal, fixed size. Each family produced crops such as vegetables, fruits, grains—and other agricultural goods such as dairy products, meat, etc.—via individual labor, although labor and other resources, such as heavy agricultural equipment, were often shared within the community, and agricultural produce was often marketed together. Each family was an individual economic unit, providing for its own needs via the profits of its farm, other small businesses belonging to family members, and work done outside the village.

The years when Kahn Bar-Adon was an active journalist saw great international interest in the Jewish cooperative and collective movements that flourished in the form of the kibbutz and moshav. To this day, these forms of community and the changes that they have undergone are widely studied. Kahn Bar-Adon wrote at length on both as a result of her extensive personal experience: prior to her marriage, she was a resident of Givat Brenner kibbutz and "covered" life in the cooperative and collective villages for *The Palestine Post*. After her marriage and the birth of her son, she and her family resided in the Merhavia moshav, and her son was cared for (during the day) in the children's homes of the Merhavia kibbutz (the two settlements of the same name are contiguous). Bar-Adon was thus uniquely qualified to discuss the advantages and disadvantages of these forms of settlement, both as to their contributions to the Zionist project of settling the land and from the point of view of a mother raising a child.

GOD COMES TO THE COMMUNE

No date; probably written when Bar-Adon lived in Kibbutz
Givat Brenner (1936–1939)
An article from Bar-Adon's personal archive
Earlier version in *Palestine Review*, "Town and Country" section

Most of the kibbutzim were established by non-religious young people. Many of these idealists had been raised in orthodox religious homes in Central and Eastern Europe, but before their immigration to Palestine, they had "lost their religion." The kibbutzim and moshavim were, however, committed to giving expression to their sense of belonging to the Jewish people via the creation of a secular expression of Jewish holidays, memorial days, and the Sabbath. In this article, Kahn describes the first communal Sabbath program in an unnamed kibbutz as well as the arguments among the kibbutz members that preceded the Sabbath celebration.

In one of the larger communal settlements of the country, the Sabbath queen is standing before the gates. But whether or not she will be invited to enter, and in what guise, is a question under heated dispute.

The subject was raised some weeks ago when the cultural committee introduced a Sabbath program on Friday evening. This action was revolutionary in a communal settlement belonging neither to the Mizrachi [Zionist religious political party] nor to Agudat Israel [orthodox religious political party]. True, the Sabbath spirit has always prevailed, expressed by rest from labor, white tablecloths and flowers on the table, special Friday night entertainment and a general atmosphere of relaxation. But this new program was a distinct departure. Among other innovations, there were Sabbath candles on the children's table and passages were read from the Bible, which contained the word God.

The members attended the initial Sabbath ceremony with mingled curiosity and astonishment. The children were delighted to be allowed to eat in the general dining room, to sing songs and to stay up late. The old parents were beside themselves with joy. They would not venture into the non-kosher dining hall, but the reflection of the Sabbath candles reached their little synagogue. They said to each other in Yiddish, "At last our children are beginning to be sensible."

But the communal settlements are democracies. Even in matters of culture, the cultural committee is not the final word. After the quiet of the Sabbath had passed and the tallow of the Sabbath candles had cooled, a storm broke loose among the members.

God, in the accepted, familiar form has thus far been eliminated from the communal settlements. The words "labor," "soil" and "equality for all men" have been substituted by these pioneers while treading new ways of life. With God, the traditional observances in their orthodox forms disappeared. Other forms were introduced, but only in a provisional, experimental spirit.

During these three weeks, the judgment of the cultural committee has been weighed, measured, and torn to shreds. There are those who are opposed to any formal Sabbath ceremony. There are those who favor the ceremony, minus God. And there are a few—a very few—who favor the ceremony plus God. Between these distinct camps are hundreds of varying shades of opinions and theories. During the recent troubled years, the major discussions have centered, perforce, around practical problems. How to make both ends meet when the orange crop brings a loss? How many parents will the budget allow us to accept from Germany, Poland, Austria? How dare we not accept all? How can we afford to build new living quarters—and how can we afford not to build them?

But since the Sabbath candles were lit, practical considerations and budget deficits have been relegated to the background. Everyone—including the harassed treasurer himself—has been discussing philosophy, ethics, theology, mythology and psychology. There was no corner of the settlement immune from these discussions. Philosophy and theology stalked into the vineyards, the tomato patch, the laundry, the barn, the sewing room and the orchard. Determined souls continued with their tea at 5:45 a.m. and with the argument that they had begrudgingly interrupted at 11:45 p.m. the night before.

The fullest debates occur during the evening meal. The dining room workers are annoyed when, long after 8:00, members still sit over plates of half-finished food while they expound to their neighbors, "If we teach our children about fairies and gnomes, why can't we teach them about God?"

The arguments rage in the shower baths. Someone turns off the tap long enough to question through the soapsuds, "Why are you all so afraid of the word 'God'? You remind me of the man who said, 'At last, blessed be the holy Name, we have finished with God.'" The shoemaker nails a heel where a toe ought to be while he points out, "I have devoted my whole life to this revolution. Now the cultural committee gives us a Sabbath program with passages about God. Before I know it, my son will be growing side-curls and wearing a skullcap!"

"I came from a religious Lithuanian home," comments a worker in the vineyard as he ties up a branch heavy with unripe fruit. "I never heard a lie in my home. Whether or not I agree with my father is beside the point. What he told me, he believed. With all his heart. We must do the same for our children. We cannot teach them things that we do not believe."

"You're right" comes from the other side of the vine. "If we are going to read on the Sabbath, let us read from Brenner or from Shakespeare or from anything that has a bearing on our life and our problems. But nothing in which we do not believe."

During these hectic three weeks, one learned that one hadn't really known one's own comrades. Rachel, the delicate little girl from the tree nursery who looks as though she had never quite stopped believing in elves, proves to be a fierce and uncompromising rationalist. Naphtali, the husky six-footer who rumbles through the orange grove on a tractor admits unblushingly that while he is reading the Bible, he believes every word of it. Rachel laughs condescendingly. Naphtali stands his ground. For an hour, while their tea and beans grow cold, they are at daggers' ends.

"You can't deprive children of God," argues Naphtali. "It's an instinctive hunger. Besides, if we eliminate the word God, then we must eliminate the Bible."

"Not at all," retorts Rachel. "The Bible can be taught scientifically. The children can be taught that once upon a time people believed in many gods. Later, they believed in one God. And now we have gone beyond this. It can be taught in the same way as Greek mythology."

"I am not prepared to rank the Bible with Greek mythology. You are too poor. You believe in nothing," flings back Naphtali and leaves the table.

"You are too rich. You believe in everything," Rachel calls after him.

This week a general meeting was held with the Sabbath as the sole subject for discussion. "On the first Sabbath there were no seats to be had in the dining room and many of us were standing. But in the third week there were plenty of empty places," states a member as conclusive proof that the present ceremony is not popular.

"That's because we added more tables and benches in the third week," interrupts a rabid "pro."

The chairman raps for order. Numerous pros and cons are heard. And then the discussion is ended in order to give the floor to Dr. Mordecai Kaplan [founder of the Reconstructionist movement in Judaism], now at the Hebrew University, who happened to be spending the weekend in the settlement. After his summary, the meeting is adjourned until next Wednesday. But after the formal adjournment, the meeting begins again. Excited groups gather in knots to declaim in Hyde Park fashion.

"Standing on a bench talking about 'science' and we can't tell the children that what they see in the …by the worker and the Histadrut!…that those who are most opposed to the singing on Friday nights are the very ones who sing Hasidic [Jewish religious] songs the loudest in the shower. I've even heard the Kol Nidre [declaration recited in the synagogue before the beginning the evening service of Yom Kippur, the day of atonement] around the New Year. It's simple psychology. When a man is divested of his clothes, he becomes his natural self."

MISHMAR HAEMEK

Zif Zif, pp. 177–182
Unpublished manuscript from Bar-Adon's personal archive
Earlier version in *A Journal of Jewish Life and Letters*, December 1935, pp. 18–19

Kibbutz Mishmar Haemek was established in 1926; it was the first kibbutz in the western part of the Jezreel Valley. Life was hard during the first years, both physically and emotionally; the assumption was that

the young members were motivated by their commitment to communal
living and devotion to the cause of settling the land. Bar-Adon's article,
written less than a decade later, celebrates the signs of individuality that
began to make themselves felt: the desire to dress festively after work and
to decorate one's personal living space.

The settlements in Palestine have come to be blanketed under the term kvutzoth. About this blanket term has sprung up a definite hypothesis. This hypothesis includes certain accepted equations: that the motivating idea and ideal behind all the settlements is communal living; that the struggle with the stony soil and the aridity is terrific whether they are cultivating citrus fruit, stone fruit, or wheat; that the children are beautiful and live on the fat of the land; that the adults live on the lean, and many of them suffer from ailments engendered by undernourishment; that their moral codes are confusing; that they dance the hora even after an excruciatingly hard day's work; that their religious beliefs are rather unorthodox and that they have transcended material needs.

These equations are dramatic and easy to grasp. Therefore they are apt to shut out from the casual observer the less dramatic but equally import-ant lights and shadows that distinguish one colony from the other. For the chalutzim have not been taken in by the blanket term. They are not content to be merely members of another kvutzah. Unlike experimental settlements in other countries, each group here fights an individual battle to achieve what it believes to be the "life abundant."

After the observer has become familiar with the accepted fundamental equations of kvutzah life, he is apt to turn to these lights and shadows to find that distinguishing spark that in the end is to spell out the immortality of the Palestine experiment.

This spark, this gesture in the direction of perfection, should, I sup-pose, be something imposing and high-sounding. I am therefore abashed to admit to having found what I believe to be of tremendous value lurking in a pair of polka-dotted curtains, a cracked vase of anemones and a rather poor watercolor of a tree. I remember that the first day I encountered these commonplace things in a hut in the colony of Mishmar Haemek [the first kibbutz established in the western part of the Jezreel Valley, in 1926]. I wanted to shout from the very summit of the hills, "Eureka." It seems that in this pair of curtains, the members of the Mishmar Haemek colony have linked the sacredness of privacy with the sacredness of communal living, and thereby have overcome that morbid "mass living" that, to many, would seem to preclude the possibility of a rich life in a kvutzah.

Not that you will not find curtains and a vase in other kvutzoth. You will. But they have happened in passing. In Mishmar Haemek they are not casual. They are part of a definite kvutzah philosophy of remembering where communal life ends and privacy begins.

Mishmar Haemek, located in the Haifa district, is not as widely known as other groups since it is comparatively young, little more than six years old.

Its history is a repetition of past experiences in the settling of Palestine. Six years ago, this spot that is now one of the healthiest in the country, was malaria infested. In the early days there were three shifts of workers; one was hired out to help in neighboring settlements, thus bringing income to the Mishmar Haemek budget; one worked in Mishmar Haemek; the other was in a hospital.

There is a fine school now. And cow sheds. And an incubating room in which four thousand chicks were to be hatched several days after I left. There is a forest in embryo which, although the trees will not be full-grown for twenty-five years, is already proudly referred to as "our forest." There is the machinery house in which are three giant tractors, a baler and a thrasher.

I remember one night being invited to see what they termed "the changing of the Buckingham Palace guards." Since the soil was still damp from the rains, it was necessary for the plowing to continue day and night. Therefore the chalutzim work in three shifts. Three laborers, who were to man the tractors at 10:00, piled into the truck with us and we started out to bring back those who had been in the fields since 5:00. Bumping over the narrow road with the moon casting eerie shadows, the plowed fields appeared like a "no-man's land." In the distance were the small lights of the tractors. After a half hour's ride, we reached the appointed spot and the tractors pushed through the soil like war tanks, in our direction. Tired workers emerged from the machine, exchanged greetings, and piled into our truck. The workers who had come with us slipped into their places on the machine, and again the tractors were off, plowing through the soil.

When we returned, I expected to find the laborers in bed, as they must rise at 5:30 in the morning. But through the doorway of the communal hall, serious faces were outlined in the flickering oil lamp. One of the meetings, which take place three times weekly, was still in progress. There is much to be discussed since everything from the purchase of a tractor to the minute detail of kitchen management concerns everyone.

It was at one such meeting, in the early beginnings of the colony, that the settlers decided to purchase barracks that had been used by some soldiers in Haifa. The budget was small. Every piaster counted. The purchase involved a momentous decision. It meant allocating money for which there were numerous other uses. Other colonies had constructed large dormitories, delaying the luxury of individual abodes for more prosperous days. But Mishmar Haemek decided that, regardless of the pinch in other directions, individual houses were not a luxury but a necessity. They had come here to share their food, their labor, their hopes, their dreams. But the indefinable "I" faced in an hour of meditation they will not share. And so they bought the barracks and have added other barracks to them as the colony grew. One person, or a couple, occupies each.

They have surrounded the "I" with a few things of stark simplicity and yet amazing charm. So the visitors cannot—as in some other colonies—visit one house and have seen all. If you would really know Mishmar Haemek, you must get a glimpse of the interior of each of these externally ugly shacks, for no two are alike. The furnishings have been made literally from scraps, as the budget does not provide for such luxury. There are desks, tables, and smoking stands of charming design, in the wood and iron combination that is the choice of the modernistic furniture maker. What is the secret? They were fashioned from discarded beds, the iron rods of which now form borders and knobs for these pieces that could stand without apology in any home.

The furniture had been made during rest hours and on the Sabbath. Sometimes exchanges had been effected: a man who knew carpentry working on the furniture when it was his turn to work in the fields on the Sabbath, while the prospective owner of the furniture did his stint in the fields.

Some of the houses have small flower gardens. Others have climbing vines. Another has a walk outlined with carefully chosen stones. Most of them have doorknockers. And they are used. For calling, in Mishmar Haemek, is a formal event. These people retreat into their modest "palaces" to read or to work, and their comrades are most careful not to overstep the bounds of intimacy. In other words, they have taken with them into this little outpost those social amenities that enrich but do not encumber civilization, but they are indeed rare specimens of youth in revolt because they show discrimination. They have had the wisdom not to revolt blindly against everything the outside world accepts.

Mishmar Haemek has a "music room." This too is a barrack and, I suspect, a luxury. They might, as in other colonies, have been content with a piano in the dining room. But somehow they have managed to scrape up an extra piano where the chalutz musician may be alone. The room is unfurnished except for the white bust of a chalutz who was drowned in the Jordan. At the base of the bust, the work of a comrade, is a medicine bottle filled with flowers.

The girls in Mishmar Haemek also have revolted wisely against society. They have slyly retained a bit of vanity for which they make no apology. The majority of them had a few clothes when they entered the colony. Others have relatives who send them things from time to time. So the majority of them "dress" for dinner. By "dressing" I mean a blouse with a frill or a perky red bow at the neck. So simple is the wardrobe that it in no way interferes with their communal creed. But somehow it adds a dignity—a variation to their evening meal of fruit, soup and thick bread. You are less aware—and I think they are too—of the backbreaking task to which they have dedicated themselves. There is something magnificent in this gesture to brush aside the morbidity of peasant life. A girl will plow the soil under a cruel sun all day; she will help to reforest the land; she will live on the simplest fare. But in the evening she wants to put a blue ribbon on her hair because it matches her eyes and nobody else's eyes. Then she becomes Rachel of the blue ribbon—a very different person from Ruth of the pink ribbon who is eating cucumbers at her elbow.

Such tiny things—a pair of polka-dotted curtains—a path outlined with stones—a blue ribbon. Mishmar Haemek achieved them by sacrifice in the beginning. But already she has reaped and reaped again the seeds she sowed in the name of the irrevocable "I" in all of us.

BUILT IN A DAY

Probably written in July 1937
An article from Bar-Adon's personal archive
Unclear where the article was published

The British Mandatory authorities severely monitored and restricted new Jewish settlement in Palestine. During the 1936–1939 Arab Revolt, however, the Mandatory authorities agreed tacitly to the establishment of fifty-seven Jewish settlements: fifty-two kibbutzim and five moshavim. These settlements were established on land that had officially been purchased by the Jewish National Fund. The legal basis for the authorities' turning a blind eye was a Turkish Ottoman law, still in effect under the Mandate, according to which a new building, even if illegal, cannot be demolished after its roof is completed. For this reason the new settlements were each set up in one day. Building materials were brought, as well as all necessary equipment for living on the site and beginning to work the land. This method of settlement was known as "tower and stockade." In this article Bar-Adon describes the first day—the actual establishment—of Kibbutz Kfar Menahem.

"Three o'clock. Three o'clock."

The darkness and deep morning silence is broken by the voice of the shomer [night guard]. He makes his rounds, calling the hour into the tents and shacks of the twenty men and two women who have been chosen to represent Givat Brenner [kibbutz founded in 1928; Kahn lived there for three years] today at the establishing of Kfar Menahem [originally founded in 1935; during the Arab Revolt in 1936, it was abandoned by Jews and destroyed by Arabs; a kibbutz was reestablished in the same location as part of the Tower and Stockade method in 1937], named for Menachem Ussishkin [Russian-born Zionist leader and head of the Jewish National Fund]. At the same time, a discordant chorus of alarm clocks issues from the dwellings of those who feared that the shomer might forget to awaken them. Almost all of the 450 workers would have liked to lend a hand in the founding of this new kibbutz. Like the recent settlements in the valley of Beit She'an, the walls, watchtower, and dining hall must be built in a day. There is, however, too much work now in the fields of Givat Brenner to permit a general exodus. The chosen few could not risk being left behind.

The shomer and the alarm clocks do their work and, in a few minutes, shadowy forms, some carrying lanterns, quietly make their way through the sleeping settlement to the dining room. It is an odd hour. There is little conversation. All partake of their bread, tea and tomatoes in silence.

Gathered around the table in the eerie light, it is a motley little crew. There are the *ghaffirim* [Jewish police unit that protected Jewish settlements] in their uniforms and tall brown hats, carrying rifles. The others, in all manner of working clothes, are carrying all manner of tools and implements: saws, spades and hammers.

At the appointed hour, four o'clock, we are all waiting on the main road for the contingents of workers from Rehovot, Na'an, and Kfar Bilu. It is not yet dawn. Workers, ghaffirim and tools are sprawled on the ground, taking queer shapes in the uncertain grayness. A few snatch catnaps, their heads nestled on the asphalt road. The majority listens anxiously for the sound of approaching wheels. They have a long day's work ahead of them and are eager to be well under way with it before the sun climbs too high.

Wheels, coming from the direction of Kfar Bilu. They speed along the empty road. Almost as soon as we hear the lorries, we see them. They draw up and are greeted with shouts and cheers. It is an exciting procession! Five lorries, led by a small car, the Pathfinder. The lorries are filled to overflowing with building materials, tools and workers. The wooden walls that are to encircle Kfar Menahem, as well as parts of the dining room, were constructed in Kfar Bilu. Now they are being transported to the site of the settlement. Arms and heads emerge from the closely packed segment of the wall. The workers of Givat Brenner pile into one of the lorries and the procession moves on.

At Gedera [one of the first Jewish colonies in Israel—founded 1884— today a city] our members are increased. Once again, the ribbon of vehicles moves on. Ahead of us and behind us are queer pyramids of building materials and workers. A few kilometers after Gedera we leave the asphalt highway and turn into a dirt road.

From now on, most of our energy is devoted to trying to maintain our balance. We are packed into the lorry like sardines. With every lurch (and there is lurching every foot of the way) we fall backward and forward like a pack of cards. Each one clutches the shoulder and belt of the man in from of him, as though for dear life. Now the lorries in front of us and behind us look like a caravan of camels, their passengers and loads swaying precariously.

We pass through Arab villages, which are still half asleep. The women, in their brightly colored dresses, have just come to the well for water, earthen jugs on their heads. The camels look lazier and sleepier and haughtier than usual. A villager peers out from under a black umbrella and rubs his eyes several times as though fearing that he were still asleep and dreaming. But the children, who are surprised at nothing and pleased by everything, wave their hands and shout "shalom." The drivers wedge the lorries like shoehorns through the narrow alleys.

But now we have even left the uncomfortable dirt road. There is no road at all. We go forward through untracked wilderness. The lorries navigate ruts and hills as though they were tanks. Yes, we are going forward to Kfar Menahem. But where is Kfar Menahem? We have lost the way.

For a while the lorries stand in the middle of nowhere while the small car endeavors to find our destination. Someone remarks, "No wonder it took us forty years to get to Palestine from Egypt." We cannot inquire of passing bedouins, "Where is Kfar Menahem?" because we are carrying Kfar Menahem on the lorries.

After some search, the settlers who are awaiting our arrival are found. The sun is just coming up over the horizon as our strange caravan approaches its destination. We know that we are twenty-eight kilometers from Rehovot and that the nearest Jewish settlements are Gedera on one hand and Be'er Tuvia on the other. But except for this knowledge, we might be on the edge of the moon. There is nothing as far as the eye can see but stubble and stone—stone and stubble.

Even before we reach the spot where the prospective Kfar Menahem settlers are gesticulating a welcome, work begins. There is a small impassable wadi that must be filled in before the lorries can cross. The workers alight, construct a temporary road, and we pass over.

The men are measuring off the ground with a tape. This is the only sign we have that we are standing near the site of Kfar Menahem. Within a few minutes other lorries arrive. Now the place is suddenly as alive as circus grounds. Vehicles are moving about. Workers are alighting. Building materials are being unloaded. The ghaffirim are lined up for inspection.

Then comes the shouted command, "Carpenters and iron workers, here!" Work has begun.

The women are given sacks and are directed to a nearby wadi to gather the stones needed to fill in the walls. The sun is still low. We work quickly. One sack is filled up after another sack. About every half hour a wagon comes to collect them. It is unfriendly country. The briars stick to your legs and your fingers. But one sack is quickly filled up after another sack.

Now the air is filled with the sounds of hammering. What seemed like a wasteland of the moon a half hour ago begins to simulate civilization. The sound of men hammering in the wilderness to make their abode— probably the first sound that ever burst on the ears of the world.

Squatting in the wadi, picking up stones, we can see nothing. But the sound of the hammering is like music, goading us on. We pick stones in time to the hammering. Another sack. Quickly, another sack. Soon the wagon will make its rounds again.

It is 8:30. The overseer of the work appears. "You must be hungry and thirsty. Come back to the settlement for breakfast." Settlement? Who said there was a settlement? We clamber up and look back to the spot where we left two men measuring the ground with a tape.

The long wooden walls stand in impertinent triumph. So we walk back to the settlement for breakfast.

We find the settlement convulsed with movement. A booth has already been constructed, and women sit on the mat floor dispensing food. A truck has arrived from Rehovot filled with purple grapes. The workers refresh themselves. The base of the water tower and a goodly part of the dining hall is already finished.

"Back to work!" comes the command. In a moment the air is filled again with the rat-tat-tat of the hammers. Workers fitting on the roof of the dining hall, constructing the walls, piecing together the water tower. Work goes on at high pressure. Not a minute to lose. Hammer. Hammer. Hammer. Lorries lumber in and out of the walls, replenishing the building materials. Hammer. Hammer. Hammer. Men building their abode. And the sounds of their building floats out over the wilderness like a symphony.

There are wagons of grapes and bread—and even bologna from Rehovot. But no water! There is no water in the vicinity of Kfar Menahem, and it must be hauled in trucks. The supply of water had been sent in a tank that formerly contained oil. It is undrinkable.

All morning and until early afternoon the workers suffer from thirst. The sun is scorching. The activity within the walls stirs the dry yellow sands until it seemed like the desert in a windstorm and chokes one worker. By the time the water supply arrives, the tongues of the workers are literally hanging out. No, life in Kfar Menahem will not be easy.

Toward noon, a triumphant shout goes up. Slowly, very slowly, the watchtower is raised from the ground to an upright position. Now the settlement is even more of a settlement.

After lunch comes the official inauguration. Everyone gathers within the four walls. A number of workers clamber up the watchtower, which is already strong enough to serve as a gallery. Others are perched on the skeleton of the dining room. One of the settlers of Kfar Menahem speaks. This is the second time that this group has tried to settle here. During the disturbances, their holdings had been destroyed. He was followed by a member of the BILU who had settled in Gedera fifty-five years ago, before Gedera was Gedera. He stands on the water tank, which serves as a platform, sturdy as an old olive tree, and punctuates his words of hope and encouragement with vigorous taps of his walking stick.

A rousing song, and then comes the command, "Back to the roof!" The workers go back to the roof of the dining hall. Hammer. Hammer. Hammer. Kfar Menahem has been inaugurated.

It is late afternoon. The dining room has been completed. Some of the workers are resting in one of the rooms. Others are eating in the other room. The wall is being completed. The stones must be filled in between the two layers of board to serve as a barricade against attack. The women stand in line and relay the baskets of stones from the lorry to the man who is lowering them into the wall.

Rows of hands reach out and rhythmically the baskets are passed from one hand to another hand. The overseer is without mercy. "Tempo! Tempo!" he shouts and the baskets pass along as though they were moving on an electric belt. Quickly. Quickly. The sun is setting. Tempo. Tempo. The baskets pass from hand to hand. There is no sound but the crunching of the stones as they are shoveled from the lorries to the baskets. Tempo! Tempo! Baskets passing from one hand to another hand. Your arms begin to ache. But no time to stop. Soon the wall will be filled up. Tempo! No sound but the crunch of the stones and the shout of the overseer. Tempo! Filled baskets. Empty baskets. Hands. Hands. Tempo!

It is time to return home. We clamber back into the lorry, except several of the ghaffirim who will remain for the night. Now we ride back in state over the wadi that we filled in the morning. Once again we are packed in like sardines and frantically grab hold of shoulders, belts, and even necks as the lorry careens over the pathless wilderness.

When we are a kilometer away, someone raises the cry, "Kfar Menahem." We look back. There it stands—four wooden walls and a watchtower. And inside the walls, the twenty men and three women who are determined to water this forbidding wilderness, after they have found water with which to water it.

Four wooden walls and a watchtower. Kfar Menahem fades out of sight.

FOREWORD

From the book *The Twin Villages of Merhavia*, 1948, pp. 5–7

Bar-Adon's explains the differences between the two different forms of collective settlements: kibbutz and moshav.

"Despite wide divergence in practice, they are twin branches growing out of a common trunk," wrote a settler of Nahalal regarding the kibbutz (collective settlement) and the moshav (cooperative settlement).

The collective twin, because it is more drastic and more dramatic (having eliminated the family as an economic unit and all private possessions), has been more talked about then the conservative cooperative twin. When you enter a kibbutz and see the communal dinning hall, the children's house, and the communal wardrobe, you realize that this is something new under the sun and warrants study. Many questions are aroused. What of spending money? What of the lazy member? What is the relation between husband and wife, between mother and child? This fascinating laboratory for human relations can hold your attention for years because it is never static. This collective movement to make new men as well as new farmers is one of the prime achievements of modern Palestine.

The cooperative twin is less spectacular. When you enter a moshav and see the individual houses and farm buildings, it reminds you of a village anywhere. You may admire the tree-lined streets and vine-covered cottages. Then you may dismiss the settlement with the vague knowledge that there's some sort of mutual assistance here. But there are fewer questions. The setup is more familiar, less provocative and less apt to inspire lyricism. The accepted romantic picture of the Palestinian chalutz (pioneer), plowing a furrow or dancing the hora, usually has a kibbutz background.

In this comparison between life in the kibbutz and the moshav, I wish to show the moshavnikim (moshav members) plowing their furrows and dancing the hora to the same rhythms as the kibbutznikim, although the arrangement is so different. I have made no effort to be objective or impartial because I believe the effort unnecessary. I have lived in a kibbutz and I have lived in a moshav. I see no question at all of which form of society is better. They are different. But both have raised a generation of sons and daughters rooted in the soil of the Homeland on the honorable basis of self-labor.

In comparing the two systems and the people, I have had to skip over many of the individual persons, and each is a story in himself. It was difficult to pass over the two streets of the moshav without stopping at the houses to tell the stories within.

And how can one write of the kibbutz without introducing T., the tractor driver who is generally inarticulate but talks poetry in prose when he describes his fields or the rounds of the seasons. And S., the baker with whom the children can arrange for pita (Arab flat bread) to be especially baked and be told with all ceremony when to call for it. And Z., the teacher who has taught a generation. And T., the driver of the lorry who can be gruff as a bear but is adored by the children, most of whom pass through the stage of wanting to be T. "when I grow up" Or C., the metapelet (nurse) [caregiver for kibbutz children] who swims through the currents of a collective kindergarten, talking psychology when necessary but remaining at core as warm and loveable as your old comfy slippers or a cinnamon bun, and washing fifteen sets of necks and behind-the-ears with as much deftness and heart as most mothers can wash one. Or Y., the carpenter who makes mandolins trimmed with butterflies and birds, as a hobby. And Y., the dentist who tends his lawn with the goldfish pond after working hours and still has time for art and dramatics; and his wife H., who combines being a children's doctor with being a member of the settlement. And S., the builder who dreams in stone and concrete and makes dovecotes as well. And Husha, master of Aza the dog, who loves the collective and the people in it so deeply that he can criticize them both, keep his sense of humor and perspective, and understand everything in spite of everything.

A word of safeguard. I have tried not to limit this comparison to Merhavia. But treating kibbutzim and moshavim in a general way has pitfalls. It would be easier, I imagine, to make a blanket statement about thousands of main streets in America than about a few moshavim in Palestine. Despite general similar lines, each moshav has its distinct personality depending upon the land of origin of the settlers, how long they've been here, whether the soil is rocky and whether water is scarce or plentiful. These differences are even more marked in the kibbutzim where political parties come into the picture. I happened to find myself next door to a kibbutz of the Hashomer Hatzair [Socialist–Zionist secular Jewish youth movement founded in 1913 in Galicia; was one of the four kibbutz movements in Israel]. This was by chance not by choice, for party differences are not of particular interest to me where the issue of collective living is concerned and I would have felt equally good had kibbutz Merhavia belonged to Hever Hakvutzot [one of the four kibbutz movements, founded in 1925; favored small kibbutzim], Hakibbutz Hameuhad [one of the four kibbutz movements, founded in 1927; favored large, unselective kibbutzim] or the orthodox Hapoel Hamizrachi Zionists [religious pioneers who founded collective settlements in Israel and were the smallest kibbutz and moshav movement; founded in 1935].

But it happened to be Hashomer Hatzair, and so it should be borne in mind that they are the most radical group and that this expresses itself, aside from political beliefs, in many small ways in day-to-day life. I have tried not to dwell on things specific to this group that would add nothing to the general comparison of kibbutz-moshav. But characteristics of Hashomer Hatzair were bound to creep in.

So this isn't a blanket main street of kibbutz and moshav. It is just one collective and one cooperative main street as I've seen them.

CHILDREN

From the book, *The Twin Villages of Merhavia*, 1948, pp. 57–70

As noted in the introduction to this chapter, in the kibbutzim, children were cared for in communal children's homes. Kibbutz members believed in gender equality and wished to enable women to have professions other than housekeeping, cooking, teaching, and childcare. The early kibbutzim were often very poor and wished to provide their children with better living conditions than could be provided to adults. It should be noted that the communal children's homes were not meant to "replace" the family; indeed, every afternoon and evening the children spent three to four hours of quality time with their parents and siblings.

The moshavim, on the other hand, were cooperative villages composed of individual family farms. As such, children were raised at home, attended local schools, and often took part in the work of the family farm.

In the booklet, The Twin Villages of Merchavia, Bar-Adon compares and contrasts the two forms of settlement. We have reprinted Bar-Adon's foreword, followed by her chapter devoted to raising children.

A group of children from the moshav and the kibbutz were traveling to a sports meet by train. At noon one of the kibbutznikim opened a neat cardboard container and distributed sandwiches and fruit, packed in waxed paper. Then the moshavnikim opened their individual lunches; some had more and some had less; some were well packed and some were in paper bags, damp from mayonnaise or mustard. The kibbutz lunches were well balanced and carefully thought out by the one woman who had the job to do. The moshav lunches depended upon the personality, mood and time at the disposal of each mother and on the individual likes of the child—pickles, hotdogs, a wing of chicken, even an indigestible piece of fried fish. One of the young moshavnikim eyed the opposite row and remarked deprecatingly, "Look, they're all eating the same thing! That's the kibbutz for you." The retorts pelted from the communal side of the coach included a resume of collectivism, brotherhood, sharing and equal sandwiches for all, ending with a triumphant, "Now that's the kibbutz for you."

The little scene stuck in my mind as a simple portrayal of two sets of children. The kibbutz child is reared intelligently, rationally, even luxuriously, although he may lack at times the personal touch implied in that fried fish. The moshav child is reared according to the intelligence and means of his parents for better or for worse. The kibbutz children, being reared in a group, have advantages and luxuries of which no moshav home can ever dream. On the other hand, the moshav child has free access to his parents.

When the kibbutz children go for walks with the metapelet, they are models of what the well-cared-for child should look like; and when they come from the children's house after their afternoon naps, they look as though each had stepped from a bandbox. Visitors to the kibbutzim are always impressed by these children, glowing with health and cleanliness, who are the supreme achievement of the kibbutz system.

When the moshav children come to play with my son, I am reminded of that juvenile film, *The Gang*, for they are a motley assortment of the well-cared-for and the neglected. Each child carries the imprint of his home environment. His manners or lack of them, his haircut or lack of one, his apple-red cheeks or his pallor despite the farm fare, tell us whether the mother has managed to keep her head above water in her sea of tasks. One child has a shiny new bicycle. His little pal, whose father doesn't believe in bought toys or can't afford them, is eaten by envy and must content himself with a discarded wagon wheel.

But when I remind them to go home for supper, they have a traditional breaking-up song that runs, "Habeitah b'simcha, simcha (going home with joy, with joy)." Despite their discordant voices, this is celestial music to my ears, for it means peace and quiet descends on my home and on my son. And as I watch them trailing down the road to their respective homes, this seems the greatest compensation for the moshav child—this "going home" after play to supper and bed in his parents' home. At sunset, the moshav child leaves "the gang" while the kibbutz child even goes to greet the sandman as one of a group. I should add that there is one little boy who is always loathe to go home because, "there won't be supper ready anyhow." His is a long story of a broken family—a stepmother—a home that isn't a home. He is neglected in a way that the cooperative system can't help. This wouldn't happen to a kibbutz child.

In many respects the moshav children can be compared to farm children anywhere. They live at home and attend the village school, which is supported by all moshav members whether or not they have children of school age. Starting in kindergarten, usually at the age of three, they complete high school when they are eighteen. During the last two years they study half a day and work on the farm half a day. There are clubs, choirs, drama circles and the village library. Still, the children are simpler and the cultural life less intensive than in the kibbutzim, for farming in an undiluted form is the dominant factor of their lives. They are closer to the traditional forms and holidays of Jewish life than the kibbutz child for whom there are now interpretations.

After graduation from high school, their education at the expense of the moshav ends. A large number continue their education, usually at agricultural schools, the girls going to Nahalal, and boys to Mikvey Israel or Kadoorie.

The moshav child's education is directed first and foremost to cultivation of the land, which he regards as the highest pursuit and the only sound foundation for the upbuilding of the Jewish Homeland. The farm tasks are not supplementary to schooling, as in the kibbutz, but are an integral part of the child's life. He doesn't give specified hours to a certain branch, as does the kibbutz child. But from a very early age—usually when he is ten—he has tasks on the farm that he already feels depend in part on him. At the age of fourteen or fifteen, he is an all-around farmer who can turn his hand to anything.

I recall when youth from the kibbutz and the moshav went to give a hand to a nearby settlement in need of help. Asked in which farm branch they were proficient, the moshav youth were vastly amused. They could work in any branch and handle any agricultural machine, providing it hadn't arrived from America just today. This opportunity to see them working together, showed that the moshav youth could work harder, quicker and with more initiative than the kibbutz youth. Later, the kibbutz youth overtakes him, but then usually as a specialist in his chosen branch.

The moshav child is less pampered than the kibbutz child—in fact, he's not pampered at all. True, in the moshav, as everywhere in Palestine, the child is regarded as the standard bearer of the Hebrew renaissance and no sacrifice on the part of the parents is considered too much for the child's welfare. Sending their children off to agricultural schools at the age of eighteen, when they could be most useful at home, is not easy for the farmers. But otherwise, the life of a moshav child is without the frills, comforts and luxuries enjoyed in the kibbutz. The moshav path is straight and one track—to produce farmers.

The moshav children share the accommodations and food of their parents, as compared to the kibbutz where the children's quarters some-times make the rest of the settlement look shabby in comparison. If the moshav children appear to work hard and at an early age, they are proud of their independence. One of them, a husky lad of thirteen told me, "When the kibbutz children are still being cared for by nurses, we're helping to run the farm." And another told me triumphantly that the kibbutz had telephoned that day to inquire if there was anyone who could operate a certain farming machine, because they were shorthanded. "Why, any boy on any moshav farm could run it," he exclaimed. The kibbutz child, on the other hand, is inclined to regard his moshav neighbor as a boor.

Naturally, the moshav girls help their mothers and are efficient "little women" in their early teens. These duties are spared the kibbutz child whose work in the branches is less drudgery. The other moshav children have a hand in caring for the younger ones; while in the kibbutz, each child of the family lives in the House of his age group. Frequently, the kibbutzim "retreat forward." I saw this in a young kibbutz that was experimenting with mixing the ages in a group, thereby approximating a family. In this way the older children help the nurse to take care of the younger ones and, I was told, they develop responsibility and a certain softness in their nature. This, of course, is achieved in the moshav by force of circumstances minus theory.

The life of the kibbutz child is always different from life "outside"—an oasis of sharing in a world of grabbing. From the time when he makes his first trip to town and wonders why shopkeepers sell their wares instead of giving them away, or is puzzled by a private kitchen in his aunt's house, he senses that he is "different." The moshav child is at home in the world since the fact that he is a "cooperative specimen" makes no perceptible dif-ference in his routine life. He learns early—and takes it for granted—that fellow members are helped in time of need and that often his father must wait impatiently for a needed machine until his slower neighbor finishes with it. Since there is no talk or possibility of accumulating riches, his mind simply doesn't work in that direction. So he becomes a "cooperative child" and grows into a cooperative man more naturally than the kibbutz child who has higher hurdles to jump.

In summing up the moshav child, it seems to me that the real peasant class—that is, a specific type of well-educated, aware peasant—will come from among their ranks. In fact when I watch them pass by our house on the way to the fields, it seems that the peasant has already been created in this generation.

The education of the kibbutz child—and the child himself—is far more complicated and provocative. He cannot be pigeonholed as a peasant; he cannot be pigeonholed at all. Since the kibbutzim have dared more with their children, they have accomplished more in some directions and laid themselves open to more mistakes in others. In the older settlements, the founders have the supreme satisfaction of seeing their children's children rooted in the collective systems.

However, the kibbutzim are showing themselves extremely wise in not considering the Children's House as a finished institution. There is constant revaluation. Whether or not you believe that communal rearing is a success in its present form, it is a vastly important experiment in which practically every accepted theory for child training was thrown overboard. Some theories have been permanently discarded and some retrieved on afterthought. To observe this child laboratory first hand (as I did when my child was there for a few years) is a stimulating experience. Certain phases will fill you with admiration and certain phases may make you say, "Perhaps I'm becoming stodgy—but I like the old-fashioned way better."

The life of the kibbutz child is passed in the House, which he is usually taught to call "home," although I believe he considers his parents' room where he has his private toy corner as his real home. He begins in the Baby House, then progresses to the Toddler House and the Children House, and then ends in the Mossad (dormitory high school). After graduation he became a full-fledged working member of his settlement with perhaps a year's interval in town or in another kibbutz.

The Houses are usually models of beauty and comfort, a real children's world in which even the washbasins are scaled down. In some, artists are commissioned to do the nursery murals. Here, with their plentiful toys, lawns, flowerbeds, shade trees, reed booths and seesaws, they grow up in a

little Garden of Eden, probably never before achieved anywhere by workers for their children. They live perfectly regulated lives with meals, naps
and sleep on schedule. They are tended by metapelets, except for during
the afternoon hours and the Sabbaths, which they spend with their parents.
It is estimated that there is one worker for every three children (including
the laundry, cooking, etc.). This makes the system very expensive when one
considers that many moshav women care for three children in addition to
all their other duties. Now that some kibbutz families are reaching four
children, it seems that a change will have to be made if the budget is to be
balanced, for at the present rate a woman would not be doing work equal
to the caring of her own brood. Of course, there is no individual account-
ing in the kibbutz, but the accepted "one worker to three children" figure
seems too high to survive an increasing birth rate.

The collective conditioning begins practically in the cradle when
another baby snatches a rattle and his nurse coos into uncomprehending
ears, "Let Jacob have the rattle for a while." This groundwork in rattle sharing doesn't help a few years later when Jacob also wants the building blocks
or the automobile just when little Isaac is engrossed in playing with it. It
is admitted that children are born with a deep-rooted ego and instinct for
self-preservation, even in a kibbutz. Therefore the first years are the hardest
because the child is constantly called upon to share and doesn't understand
why. The most numerous and elaborate toys don't seem to solve the problem because Isaac always wants a particular automobile just when Jacob has
it and no cavalcade of other automobiles will appease him.

In this respect, the child in a moshav, playing with a spool or an automobile made of matchboxes which he can call "mine," has the easier time
of it. These clashes could occur in any kindergarten or day nursery, but
there it is only for a few hours. Here he must fight for his rights from the
time he opens his eyes until he closes them. Sometimes it is a fight for an
automobile, sometimes for first place in the shower queue, sometimes just
for the nurse's attention or affection.

As time goes on, he learns to substitute *shelanu* (our) for *shli* (mine)
and knows why this means the creating of a better society. In fact, the very
idea of underprivileged children is vague, known to them mostly from
David Copperfield. It is taken for granted that the child of the widow or
broken family has the same advantages as everyone else. For some years
their attitude toward money and commerce is quite refreshing and utopian.
I remember with what charming naiveté my son, during his kibbutz days,

addressed an Arab in a train who had extracted some bread from folds of his cloak, "Comrade, give me some." And to this day he is puzzled and even hurt when I pay Esther for our month's food supply. "But she's a friend of ours—and she has more milk and eggs than she can use." Explaining the high cost of chicken feed doesn't combat the deep-rooted *kibbutz* idea that those who have should simply give to those who haven't. It's a splendid character basis. But unfortunately, the child must learn later that his is a private little paradise whose graciousness cannot extend beyond its own boundaries, and that he, too, as a kibbutz member, will be selling milk.

After his early lessons in sharing, the child learns the dignity of labor. Whether his mother works in the kitchen or in the secretariat, she has the same standing, and besides, her position may be changed next month. At an early age, he learns to revere productive labor, which will be one of the foundations of his future life.

The borderline between classroom and home life is rather hazy because the children are always under supervision. Book-learning and living-learning are wisely intermingled. They have a children's society conducted, insofar as possible, by themselves, along the lines of the larger society. The children mete out punishment to each other when required, and the desire for the good opinion of the society deters misbehavior.

School days are full and intensive. The children learn according to the "project system." All subjects (chemistry, physics, economics, geography, drawing, and history) are learned in relation to the project. Three months are devoted to each project, and there are three in the course of the year. Two sample projects used last year were "sheep" and "olives." They begin to study Bible at the age of nine. Outside of the curriculum, there is music, drama, swimming and other sports. There are numerous hikes, camping out and sometimes summer camps at the seashore. From an early age they cultivate school farms, and by the time they reach high school, they operate their school farm on a paying basis, selling their produce to the kibbutz.

The festivals play a large part in the life of the child, and most particularly the agricultural festivals. While the bar mitzvah is not observed in the traditional way, it is marked by a gift from the kibbutz, and in some settlements by special ceremonies of one kind or another.

Some of the settlements send their children to central high schools such as the Mishmar Haemek Mossad [a boarding school for Hashomer Hatzair kibbutzim teenagers], which is one of the showplaces. However, as the number of children increases, the kibbutzim are gradually acquiring their own high schools, such as the beautiful one opened last year in Merhavia and a few years ago in Beit Alpha. By this time, their days and evenings are so full that there seems, unfortunately, no time to "sit or stare" or for practically any free pursuit. At all events the life is highly stimulating, and it is plain that a new type will emerge, and obviously not the moshav peasant type.

What is the relation between the parents—the children—the House? In some kibbutzim, the House is regarded as an end in itself, creating a children's society that is the preparation for the larger collective society. In others, it is regarded as a means to an end, namely to give the woman an opportunity to work and to participate in the cultural life of the settlement unhindered. In the latter class, we may mention Degania (the oldest collective in the country), where children sleep in their parents' quarters, and Ein Harod, where they sleep with their parents from the age of six. In Degania the parents have a separate room for the children, while in Ein Harod, there is a sleeping porch. In my opinion, these two settlements have found the golden road: collective life during the day and quiet, security and parent's influence at night. Of course, the groups that look upon the House as an end in itself are against emphasizing parental influence since it might detract from group influence.

Ten years ago when I picked up courage to ask kibbutznikim, "What about Degania's system?" I was regarded at best as a heretic and at worst as a rank outsider who simply didn't understand. This group-sleeping was regarded as a pillar of the system. Today, there seems to be an increasing interest in the workings of Degania and Ein Harod. I believe that only two factors prevent some settlements from taking their lead. First, it would mean admitting an error in a very fundamental phase of the system. Secondly, the change would be technically difficult and expensive to the point of being almost impossible at the moment, involving the giving of another room to each member.

What are the failings of the House, which is so aesthetically attractive? Fifteen years ago, Joseph Baratz of Degania wrote, "To this very day, the attitude of a woman toward the common nursery is still the touchstone of her fitness for life in the settlement. She can be judged as soon as her first child is born, and not every mother measures up to the test. Age long habit holds the young mother in its clutches. She has all sorts of fears and suspicions that her child will not receive proper care. These bugbears can be dispelled only by a well-equipped and hygienic nursery in the charge of experienced nurses who are very patient and discreet in dealing with the mothers." This was written about Degania, where the children sleep with the parents. How much more pronounced are these "bugbears" when the children do not [sleep with their parents]? Then, too, the number of experienced children's nurses has lagged behind the growth of the child population, and it would be unreal to expect that every nurse in a large settlement today will be as "very patient and discreet" as in the little Degania family of fifteen years ago.

Generalization is dangerous, and it must be said plainly that the system is ideal for many kibbutz women who believe strongly in it, or are not the maternal type, or who are engaged in creative or public work. But the average woman—and I believe they form the majority—will go as far as you like in pioneering sacrifice and hard work, but regarding her child, she is as old-fashioned as lavender and old lace. Among the very young women who don't feel obliged to defend an ideology, you sometimes hear frank admissions like the following from a young mother in a new settlement, "No, I try not to be put on committees. Most of the women would rather leave these things to the men so that we can be fresh for our children." Another young kibbutz mother—age six to be exact—was heard to say to her friend while playing, "You can be the doll's mother. I'll be the nurse, so I can take care of her."

In actual time, the kibbutz parents are with their children a great deal more than the moshav parents, or perhaps than any parent anywhere. Where else do parents have hours on end to play games and read stories? So where is the hitch? Because children are human and not clocks, you can't measure the satisfaction they derive from their parents in hours. When they come from the House at four o'clock, there is a joyous reunion. But after half an hour they may be enticed by the 101 diversions that the farm offers—it is lambing time, or haying time, or older boys are playing basketball. Before they realize what has happened, the precious "family hours" have flown, and they go back to the House. When they grow older, say eleven or twelve, it is assumed that they are busy with "activities," and mothers will say with mixed pride and pang, "My son is so busy that I've not seen him for more than an hour all week." She says this with pride because, obviously, they are the most popular, vigorous and well-adjusted children who only have time to say hello and goodbye to their parents.

Assuming that the child does spend three or four hours with the parents, it doesn't seem to solve the problem. There is something primeval about the relationship between child and parent in that magic dusk hour before he drifts off to sleep. He is a combination of drowsiness and keen awareness. He is filled with impressions and confessions. He is simply a different being than he was at four o'clock in the afternoon when he wants to watch the silo working. I believe that this delicate detail is overlooked when we say glibly, "Kibbutz parents and children are together so-and-so many hours." Which hours? Can they be measured by mathematics or minutes? Can that first morning smile of the child happen at any other time of the day? By contrast, the moshav woman has no free "hours" for her children. But she has those moments here and there—the natural intercourse of a mother who, at her busiest, must feed her brood and put them to bed. And the children have that deep security, which seems to come from a mother's mere presence, even when she's too worn out to tell a story or play checkers.

The kibbutzim recognize this bedtime problem. There are two methods in use; advocates of either will usually say, "Ours has its faults—but it's the better of the two." In the Hakibbutz Hameuhad groups, the parents bathe and put their children to bed. This allows for a story or lullaby at the bedside. But with fifteen children and about thirty parents milling around, the ensuing bedlam can be imagined. And all this takes place just when the child should be relaxing. Then, too, the orphan is most keenly aware of his lack at this hour.

Hashomer Hatzair has done away with all this by having the children leave their parents at the door of the House, the nurse putting them to bed. This is more orderly and more cold. When you stand outside the House window to eavesdrop (which we did on many evenings, although no self-respecting kibbutznik would) you can hear the metapelet singing a wholesale lullaby for all, and for a long time afterward, you hear the children exchanging those precious "impressions and confessions" that might better fall on older, more appreciative ears. For instance, when one of them asked, "Who is stronger: Samson, Trumpledor, or Amanayahu (the oldest son of Merhavia)?" there is no one to give the proper answer.

Against this background, we need to consider only briefly the other "bugbears" of the average kibbutz parents, and especially of the mother. In many respects, the House remains an "unknown quantity" despite the closest contact between parents, metapelets, and teachers. I doubt if children anywhere are so much talked about or thought about. If they are too shy, or too aggressive, or too thin, or wet their beds, or have nightmares, or suck their fingers—it may become a problem. This is because of the Unknown Quantity. Perhaps there is some undiscovered cause for his behavior, reasons the worried mother can only conjecture or be told secondhand, concerning his life during twenty hours of the day. On the other hand, the metapelet may wonder about the influence of the parents, which is admittedly strong. Perhaps they are paying too much attention to a newborn baby and the older one takes revenge by wetting his bed? The approach to each problem is serious and intelligent, with due attention to Freud. One would not ask for a reversion to the simpler whipping method. Still, when everything from reflexes to lack of appetite is considered against the Freudian background (and not always by experts), many children become appallingly complicated. This, of course, is quite different from the oversimplification of the moshav where he may get a cookie when he's good and a heavy hand on his little backside when he's bad. There should be some middle path.

This little glimpse behind the exterior of the architecturally beautiful Houses should not blur the larger picture of thousands of splendid collective children growing into a society that will be one of the strongest sections of the future Palestine. I still carry with me the memory of Tel Yosef's twenty-fifth anniversary when we saw the youth three hundred strong gathered in the dining hall. One forgot to listen to the speeches, becoming engrossed in studying the faces of this fine youth, the fruit of complete equality and opportunity for all.

"Do the children ever leave their settlements?" This question is often asked. It is estimated that ninety percent of the moshav children remain in their home villages while a majority of the other ten percent remain in agriculture elsewhere. If a kibbutz child has ever left his home settlement (except when he marries into another kibbutz), I have never heard of it. The lodestar of their lives is to carry on the great work begun by their parents—and this they do. They are carrying on deep love for this collective country that they are building together and readiness for self-defense when necessary. Both in the kibbutz and the moshav, those of age were quick to join up during the war.

Visiting a new settlement, 1938

At the wedding of Trans Jordanian Prince Talal, 1934

On the ship Polonia on the way to Poland, 1937

Bar Adon pregnant with her son, 1940

Journalist's ID card from *The Palestine Post*, 1933

Building of *The Palestine Post*

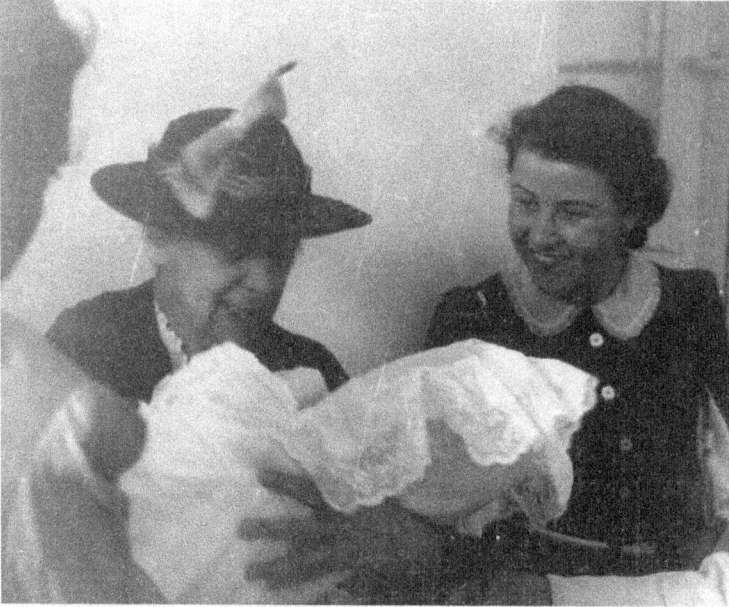

With her son Doron and his godmother, Henrietta Szold, 1940

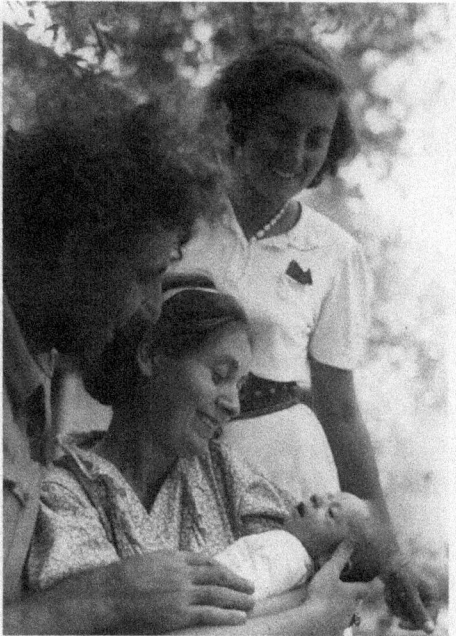

Dorothy with husband son and sister in law, 1940

The Bar Adon family in front of their home in Merhavia, 1947

CHAPTER EIGHT

Youth Aliyah

INTRODUCTION

Following the Nazi party's election to power in Germany in 1933, the Eighteenth Zionist Congress, meeting in Prague (August 21–September 3) decided to establish a bureau for the settlement of Jews from Germany in what was then Mandatory Palestine. Arthur Ruppin, head of the newly established bureau, and Chaim Weizmann, president of the Zionist Organization, worked to carry out this decision. The project of bringing teenagers to Palestine, funded and run by the international Zionist Organization, was named Youth Aliya.

Youth Aliya was headed by Henrietta Szold; the latter was among the founders and then the first president of Hadassah, the Women's Zionist Organization of America. Youth Aliya's mandate was to bring Jewish teenagers to Palestine (youngsters whose families remained in Europe) and establish educational and social frameworks for the young people during their first years in their new homeland. For the most part, these were teenagers who had been forced to leave school in Germany because they were Jews; they were settled in educational frameworks in kibbutzim, moshavim, and youth villages. The guiding educational principles were studies, work, and encouraging the youngsters to take an interest in building a new Jewish society in Palestine.

By the outbreak of World War II, some five thousand teenagers had been brought to Palestine under the aegis of Youth Aliya—ninety percent from Central Europe and the rest from Eastern Europe. After September 1939, at a time when many Jews were trying to reach Palestine from

Europe and other parts of the world, youngsters from Yemen, Turkey, and Iraq joined the educational frameworks of Youth Aliya. From 1941 on, Jewish teenagers from poverty-stricken neighborhoods in Palestine joined Youth Aliya educational frameworks, mainly in kibbutzim.

During the war, young people who had been rescued from Europe and other places (e.g., the "children of Tehran" in 1943) were brought to Palestine and educated in Youth Aliya frameworks; for the first time they included children of primary-school age. By the end of the war in 1945, some ten thousand children and teenagers had settled in Palestine under the aegis of Youth Aliya. From 1946 until the establishment of the state in 1948, another fifteen thousand children who survived the Holocaust came to Palestine via Youth Aliya, most from Germany and Poland, some from Bulgaria, Hungary, Czechoslovakia, Syria, and Lebanon.

Bar-Adon wrote much about Youth Aliya. After the war, when young people who had survived the worst horrors of the Holocaust arrived in Palestine/Israel, she interviewed many of them individually and brought their histories to public consciousness—and this at a time when the importance of documenting the genocide of Jewry on an individual level was not yet part of the national and international agenda.

AND THEY LIVED AND STOOD UP UPON THEIR FEET…

Dorothy Kahn Bar-Adon
July 1945
Merhavia
An article from Bar-Adon's personal archive

Bar-Adon interviewed refugees from Europe who arrived to Haifa in July 1945, among them 242 orphans who were released by American soldiers, as well as other legal immigrants. Most were Holocaust survivors from various death camps and concentration camps. Bar-Adon describes the first hours on the boat in the port of Haifa. She then accompanied the refugees to Atlit, their first stop in their new homeland. In this long article, Bar-Adon records testimonies of these refugees, focusing on the youngsters.

(The boat Mataroa arrived in Haifa in July 1945 with 242 orphans released by American soldiers in April 1945. They came with visas and with 1,164 new immigrants.)

"This flesh is not mine—it's American flesh," declared sixteen-year-old Zvi, proudly exhibiting an arm and flexing his muscle. The arm bore the blue tattooed number—177633. "The tattooed numbers seemed to be scratched on bare bones when the Americans arrived in April," says Zvi. "Then food began to arrive like magic—meat and chocolate and tinned food—we never dreamed that tanks could carry food instead of death." Zvi's weight increased from forty to sixty-nine kilos. Now he feels strong enough to undertake his share of work in the Palestinian agricultural settlement where he is being place by Youth Aliyah to start life anew.

Hundreds of refugees who arrived at Haifa aboard the SS *Mataroa* boasted of their "American flesh." Most of them had gained from twenty to thirty kilos. Their past and hopes for the future were summed up several days after their arrival at a get-together in the Atlit Detention Camp [detainee camp established by the British Mandatory authorities to prevent Jewish refugees from entering Palestine] by Aaron, a seventeen-year-old Polish youth who said, "We children of Buchenwald have experienced all the tragedies of the people of Israel. All the children here were dead. We were bones. When the Americans freed us, we were simply bones that muttered. Our skin was as yellow as wax, and we frightened people who saw us. I remember an old man, a man of truth, speaking to me, 'Can these bones live? O, Lord God, Thou knowest…and I will lay sinews upon you and cover you with skin and put breathe in you and ye shall live. And they lived and stood up upon their feet, an exceeding great army.' That old man, when already a candidate for the next world, predicted that these bones would live. I couldn't believe him. And now you see these bones—these beaming faces…. Many are bereaved of parents, brothers and sisters. Many do not remember how their mothers and fathers looked. Many have not studied for six years. Many things are lacking in their youth—but we have kept our souls. In spite of tempting promises in France, we all wanted to go home, and we felt that only Zion could be home. And so we said with once voice, 'Eretz Israel.' Somehow, we have held on to that thread. We saw many people in Europe who lost their balance. This youth didn't look at us. We will build, and we will be an example to the world—a lesson that they cannot destroy or break us. We will build the homeland. We hope that the Yishuv [the Jewish settlements in Palestine] will give these children an education and a chance to work. And then, in place of the sad Yiddish songs we sing now, we shall sing healthy, creative songs in Hebrew."

The scenes witnessed and the stories heard at the Haifa Harbor, and subsequently in the Atlit Detention Camp are difficult to put on paper because so much of it was beyond the range of human emotions as we know them. Practically every one of the 1,204 had been saved by some miracle or series of miraculous circumstances. The stories were difficult to believe even when you heard them from the lips of the survivors. And yet, you knew they must be true because only the miraculous could account for their ultimate arrival in Eretz Israel.

The refugees represented practically every country in Europe, a majority of the hellhole camps, and Jews of many types and character. As for the children and youth—the children and youth is a misnomer. During the past eleven years, youth of every description have found haven in Eretz Israel, starting with the Jewish children from Germany, fresh from comfortable homes, down to the Transdniestrian orphans. But youth like this we had never seen. Lads of fourteen and fifteen years boasted of murdering SS guards after the liberation, in revenge for their families. Like ancient superstitious warriors, they still wore the silk shirts (swastika-decorated) of the Nazi officers they had slain. Until now, the youth would tell you that their parents "went up in smoke in the crematorium." And if one of them used the phrase "unknown fate," his companions would break into laughter and comment sarcastically, "What 'unknown'? His mother went up the chimney, just like mine." A lad of fourteen related, "My brother died on his twenty-fifth birthday. He wanted to eat especially well on that day, so he stole a beet. The guard got him...."

The youth vividly illustrated their stories by the marks on their bodies. One fourteen-year-old showed us the mark of a whip across his face—that's a souvenir of the day when he couldn't ladle out his soup quickly enough to suit the SS guard, the ladling being done by his fingers since spoons were not supplied. Moshe, aged fifteen, exhibits grooves in his hands, gotten when he worked as a slave laborer in the coal pits, two years ago. Moshe, a Hungarian, age seventeen, is proud of a singed ear that, he says, is a memorial to the last shot fired by a German in Bergen-Belsen. An SS guard tried to murder him just as the Germans were fleeing from the Americans—he only singed the ear. A lad of fifteen explains that he doesn't want to go to a religious settlement because, "I was religious once. But I saw that the religious man was no better off at the crematorium."

All of them spoke with wonder of the coming of the Americans. One said, "It was the first time my little brother had ever seen smiles and real laughter." Another said, "You don't know what it meant to see good faces. In the camp, even families quarreled among themselves. None of us had good faces anymore. We didn't know there could be good faces still in the world until we saw the Americans. Their food was wonderful. But it was the good faces—that was something wonderful to see."

It was early morning when the SS *Mataroa*, which had docked the night before, began to unload. Formalities on board were brief. A tribute to Miss Szold and an explanation of Youth Aliyah were given by Mr. Hans Beyth, who greeted the leaders of the various youth groups from England, France, Italy, Bergen-Belsen and Buchenwald. What types were milling on the dock! There were the Mizrachi youth, eager to be off to the Beit She'an agricultural settlements. There were the Aguddat Israel with sidecurls and skullcaps, their eyes in the direction of Jerusalem yeshivot. There was the Habonim group [Socialist-Zionist youth movement] trained in England, who asked questions about the Huleh swamp—for they will join the Anglo-Baltic settlement, Kfar Blum, in Upper Galilee. There were women in their early twenties who looked middle-aged, after the experience of raping or forced prostitution. There were two old men— one a Hungarian rabbi who, despite the harrowing hunger of Buchenwald, had steadfastly refused trefa [non-kosher] meat and had come through, "with the help of God." There were the children who had been converted to Christianity, taken communion, and forgotten that they were Jews. There was the little waif, Beni, who did not remember his family and who was considered by the Bergen-Belsen inmates as their "good luck amulet." There was the eighteen-year-old girl who had saved her skin by working as a gentile nurse. There were those who owed their lives to the Jewish Brigade [military unit formed in late 1944 under the aegis of the British Army; fought the Germans in Italy; at the end of the war some of them assisted Holocaust survivors in immigrating illegally to Israel]. There were—and there were.

We heard a hundred stories, and there were a thousand to be heard.

Since the public could not enter the port area, the tension of waiting was more keenly felt at the railroad crossing in Atlit—what hopes and fears among those who strained their eyes along the tracks. Parents who had not seen their children for six or seven years exhibited frayed photographs of tots on hobbyhorses with the remark, "I am afraid I won't recognize him now." A number had come, although they knew of their family's death— perhaps, after all, some mistake. An eight-year-old child of Degania Bet had come with a few members of the settlement to meet her father. He was trapped in Holland some years ago, while carrying out a mission for the Histadrut, and was confined in a German camp.

The train arrives. For a few moments, the air is filled with the cries of those who—having been separated from their loved ones for years—cannot bear the split second more until they alight from the train.

Two youths, ages fourteen and eighteen years, coming from Bergen-Belsen, are reunited with their father. Today is Michael's eighteenth birthday, and he receives a precious gift—his father. It is six years since they parted, and—after Michael alights from the train—there are several moments of shyness on both sides—then reunion begins in earnest. Amid the joy of reunion are the hungry eyes of those who, although they have no relatives in Palestine to their knowledge, scan the crowd. Perhaps—after all?

The procession treks from the railroad crossing to the Atlit Detention Camp. A few are still wearing the zebra stripes of the concentration camps—as a gesture rather than from necessity. The majority have acquired clothes on the way. Only the numbers, burned into their skins, cannot be erased. Most of them appear to be in fairly good health—for only the hardier could make the trip, a number having died soon after the liberation from overeating! Although their luggage was sent in a separate train, we are not spared that haunting sight of the Jew with his *peckel* [little bundle], for a number have special treasures that they will not let out of sight, such as family relics or their prayer shawls. But many walk upright, unencumbered, drinking in the distant mountains. An ambulance bypasses the procession, taking several youngsters with measles to the Atlit hospital—the ambulance is marked, "The Greater Boston Jewish Community in Memory of Edlar R. Markson." The crowds are grateful to several British policemen who have entered into the spirit of the hour and lend helping hands to the old and the children.

The refugees are assigned to their barracks and settle down to the last few days of formalities that still stand between them and freedom. Some are glad to rest knowing that relatives are awaiting them. The youth eagerly seek scraps of information about the agricultural settlements to which they will be assigned. Some cannot rest because they do not know if a wife, mother or child is really in Palestine, and they chase after every wisp of possible information—a journalist, a nurse, a Youth Aliyah official; and—last but not least—they haunt the Information Bureau.

They inquire about old neighbors and friends. The search is complicated by the facts that many have adopted Hebrew names in Palestine. Someone looks for an old pal, Abraham, who "is expected to live in the country, but maybe he is living in town."

A portion of camp life centers around the barrack that serves as a synagogue. There is an amusing scene the first day when the East European Jews meet with a group of Yemenites. So these handsome, dusky little fellows, with their nasal chant, are also Jews? In less than half an hour they are comparing *tefillin* [a set of small black leather boxes, containing scrolls of parchment inscribed with verses from the Torah, that are worn by observant Jews during weekday morning prayers]. Sidecurls from Poland and sidecurls from Aden bend over books together, comparing notes and airing differences of opinion. A number of the concentration camp inmates have been without tefillin for a long time and to secure them is their prime desire. One old man anxiously inquires of a Palestinian if there is anyone in Palestine who could properly reblacken his tefillin and receives the answer, "If there were as many heads in Palestine to wear tefillin as there are hands to blacken them, we'd be all right."

In a corner of the synagogue barrack, we hear the drone of a *cheder* [traditional elementary school, in which boys are taught the basics of Judaism and the Hebrew language]. Some twenty youngsters of various ages are gathered around the rabbi who is discussing the *Shulchan Aruch* [code of Jewish law]. Who is this black-bearded rabbi who can hold their attention on this festive day when other youngsters are playing ball and generally enjoying life in the camp courtyard? He has little time for curious journalists and says, "I can't stop the lesson unless the matter is very urgent." Convinced of the urgency, he reveals that, under the imposing black beard, he is twenty-two years old.... The son of a Worms rabbi, Aaron became the director of a yeshiva and children's home at the age of nineteen. For two years, under unspeakable conditions, he held together his flock of sixty yeshiva *bahurim* [Talmud students]. He gave them Torah and bread when he could. And, with the world in fragments around him, Aaron's yeshiva went on. Some of his students came with him to Palestine. Studies continued uninterrupted on the ship, new pupils attaching themselves to his class. And here, in Atlit, they had found a corner in the synagogue barrack where Aaron was preparing them for *Tisha B'Av* [annual fast day commemorating the destruction of both the First and Second Temple in Jerusalem].

Tisha B'Av in the camp synagogue was stirring. The pupils filed into the dim, candlelit barrack, in stocking feet. Sitting on the floor they chanted the Lamentations. And it was as though Jeremiah had described their own past. "Mine enemies chased me. Sore, like a bird—they have cut off my life in a dungeon—the tongue of the sucking child cleaveth to the roof of his mouth for thirst—they that were brought up in scarlet embrace dunghills—we are orphans and fatherless. Lest our skin was black like an oven because of the terrible famine." That evening, in the Atlit barrack synagogue, we heard the Lamentations chanted with their deepest and most terrible implications.

Next evening, there was a party—a party where grimness and joyful thanksgiving made strange bedfellows. There were few in the camp that did not turn up, packing the barrack, with the overflow peering through windows. We were to see a program presented by the Buchenwald Jewish Entertainment Troupe, a valiant little "stock company." They had done much to hold people together in their darkest camp hours, if only by translating their grief into words and music and their dreams into concrete sentences. After the liberation, this troupe performed for the American soldiers and later in France. At Atlit, they apologize for the fact that their talent has thinned out, some of the troupe members remaining in France.

The master of ceremonies was Tuvia, a Romanian youth of seventeen who worked in the coal mines of Germany with two thousand slave laborers before he was taken to Buchenwald. Before the performance, he told us how he, his father, mother, and fifteen-year-old brother had been stood up in a line of five hundred people while an SS man indicated with a jerk of his thumb, "left" or "right," according to his whim. "Left" meant cremation. His mother, father and brother were marched off to the left. Fate willed him to the right. Tuvia opened the party with a little Yiddish song of his own composition, plaintive despite the valiant effort at gaiety, "I know very well what is in your hearts. But tonight we will laugh. We were all prisoners…but we shall not think forbidden thoughts…. Bury everything in the earth—the main thing is that we are together—and we are all healthy. Listen to our program with patience, and laugh, for this is a rehearsal for better times." Tuvia's call to laughter was sincere enough. Poor Tuvia—perhaps he had spent too much time in the German coalmines to remember what laughter is. The most amusing number of the evening was a dialogue between two inmates of Buchenwald who have gone mad and, in their madness, speak horrible truths.

The first number was the *Buchenwald Song* in German, sung by the Buchenwald Choir, "Buchenwald, I cannot forget you. When day breaks and the sun laughs and the lines of workers are driven to their day's toil. Amid the gray dawn and the black forest, the sky is red. And we go forward, our knapsacks on our backs; a piece of bread; and sorrow in our hearts." Then, the refrain, "O Buchenwald, I will not forget you. You were my fate. Only those who have left you can know how precious is liberty. O Buchenwald, we neither wail nor weep. Whatever our future may be, we will say 'yes' to life, because the day will come when we will be free." Second stanza, "The night is short and the day is long. But one song rings out—the song of the homeland. We will not lose our courage and faith. Strengthen your step, comrade. Guard your will to live." The next stanza, "The blood is hot—the girl is far away. The wind sings softly and I long for her. The stones are hard and our steps are firm. On our backs, the packs—and in our hearts—love."

The next was a Yiddish song written in Buchenwald, "Everyone calls me Zalmele. I had a little mamma. I haven't her anymore. I had a little papa. He watched over me, too. Now I am a little rag, because I am a Jew. I had a little sister. She is no more. Ach, where are you little Esther, in my hour of need. Somewhere, near a little tree, somewhere near a fence, is my brother, little Shlomo, murdered by a German. I had a little home. Now, things are bad. I am like a little animal that the butcher slaughters. God, look down from the heavens, on the earth below, look and see how the little flower is torn up by the scoundrels."

The next number on this "rehearsal for better times" was a charming duet between Abraham and Mottel. The singers were two sixteen-year-old orphans, Leib and Ephriam, of Poland, former internees of Oswiecim and Buchenwald. The words to the haunting melody were, in part:

> Mottel: You will laugh, you will laugh, little Abraham, you will laugh!
>   I have a plan, something wonderful,
>   I will mew like a cat and bark like a dog,
>   And that will be your first laugh.

> Abraham: The mother, who raised me, stands before my eyes
>   My brothers and sisters are scattered.
>   I am alone.
>   When I begin to remember sad things,
>   Tell me, how can I laugh?

Mottel: You will laugh, you will laugh, little Abraham, you will laugh!
What has been—don't give it a thought.
You will forget sorrow and suffering when happiness comes
Because to laugh today is the best thing, Abraham.

Abraham: When I remember my weak father,
My head begins to whirl,
Because I will never see him before my eyes, alive.
Now, tell me, how can I laugh?

Mottel: You will laugh, you will laugh, little Abraham, you will laugh!
You will laugh because the fates will it.
You will forget the suffering and sorrow in joy.
Because to laugh is more precious than gold.

Abraham: I will laugh, Mottel, I will laugh.
But this is not the time.
When the sun shines for us,
Then I will laugh and cry.

Mottel and Abraham together:
We will laugh, we will both laugh, we will laugh!
Because a new time is coming,
The sun already throws its rays.
Hark, the signal!
Come, and we will sing, full of joy.

These folk songs, most of which had been composed in the Buchenwald Camp, were Tuvia's "variety." And, at the conclusion of the performance, there was a pathetic attempt to sing the new Hebrew pioneer songs. A few knew the words, and the rest followed after like lame ducks. So that was the Buchenwald Party in Atlit.

"There are good times and bad times in Palestine—but it is home," said Ada Fishmann [feminist leader, founder of the Women Workers Movement, and its first secretary; served as head of the Histadrut's aliyah department], speaking the next day when the newcomers were welcomed on behalf of the Yishuv [Jewish settlements in Palestine] at a general meeting.

"We know that you are prepared to help us broaden our boundaries and welcome those refugees who may still come. When we came to Palestine thirty years ago, we came to bare rocks. There was no one here to greet us. Today, there are fertile fields and many Jews to greet you. Hitler did not send us, but we realized then that all this could happen and we yearned for soil under our feet. We have begun. Now it is up to you to carry on. There are many difficulties in Palestine. Now we and you must prepare for the remnants of Israel, yet to come. No people rise to life without land under its feet. We call upon you to turn to agriculture."

"You have come on the last certificates [visas to immigrate to Palestine] left to us under the White Paper," [policy paper issued by the British government in 1939 to limit Jewish immigration to Palestine] declared a representative of the Histadrut, welcoming the refugees in the name of 140,000 workers in trade, agriculture and industry. "We are engaged in a battle to open the gates. We must succeed, for there is no other road. During your trials, the Yishuv did not forget you. We call upon you now to remember your duty to the homeland."

A Polish refugee, in answering, declared, "During all our suffering, Eretz Israel was the only ray of life. We know what the Yishuv did to help rescue the children. We heard of the Jewish parachutists behind the lines. We know what the Jewish Brigade has done and is still doing at this very hour for the remnants. We will render back this debt." When he finished, there was a spontaneous singing of the *Hatikvah*.

While the general stories of Buchenwald and Bergen-Belsen are now well known to all the world, each of the refugees had his own story to tell. While a few resented publicity and probing, the majority seemed to get things off their chest. From early morning until late at night, one could circulate among the new arrivals, filling notebooks with horrors, already known but piling up, like a top-heavy structure.

One of the outstanding personalities among the refugees is Edie, better known by his Hebrew name, Beni (my son), age four, who has spent more than half of his life in the Bergen-Belsen Camp. Incredible as it may sound, this child, who has known nothing but horrors, is like a ray of sunshine. With his independent air, happy smile and friendly disposition, he captivates everyone. An orphan, numerous people wanted to adopt him, including a group of American soldiers who wanted to send him back to the States.

Besides, Beni already has a fosterfather, Shmuel, age seventeen, from Host, Czechoslovakia. When we opened conversation with Beni, Shmuel appeared and asked with a proprietary air, "What do you want of him?" Since the Americans tried to lure Beni to the States, Shmuel is on the watch. And this was the story we heard.

Prior to the war, Shmuel studied in a Hebrew school in Czechoslovakia. Ultimately, his parents, together with five brothers and two sisters, were sent to the Oswiecim camp. No word has been received from them. He was studying weaving in Budapest when, in December 1944, he was interned in Bergen–Belsen, where he was sent to work as a woodcutter.

"One day I saw a little boy, three years old, lying on a cot, half dead. All day he lay there, gasping for breath, and his eyelids were fluttering like a little bird's." Shmuel imitated the fluttering eyelids. "Nobody knew anything about him except that he had no father in the camp and his mother had died a few months before. A woman was tending him but she had already abandoned hope. And really, there seemed nothing to do. I don't know why—but I decided to take him and made a vow, 'if I live, he will also live' and I promised myself that with God's help, I would get him to Palestine."

The next chapter was supplied by fellow refugees from Bergen–Belsen. Shmuel, who was then sixteen years old, "gave him all the care of a mother and father rolled into one." He gave him most of his portion of food and he even begged crumbs among the internees for his ward. He gave him most of his own few drops of drinking water. And somehow—nobody can quite explain it—Beni was kept reasonably clean when everyone else was crawling with lice. To keep Beni clean and his stomach fairly full became an obsession with Shmuel. How infectious this obsession was can be judged by the fact that even several SS guards were know to throw a crust of bread secretly to Shmuel, pointing to Beni.

When the child began to call him "father," Shmuel gave him his first Hebrew lesson: the little boy began calling Shmuel "Aba" and was given the name "Beni."

The entire camp was deeply touched by Shmuel's tireless devotion. Often, when nostrils were filled with the stench of human bodies burning in the crematorium, Shmuel could be seen in a corner, quietly telling Beni a bedtime story about Palestine, which he was sure they would both reach some day. And, because superstitions thrive when hopeless people are looking for a straw to cling to, it is no wonder that Beni became not only a mascot but also a symbol. "We all felt that if anything happened to Beni, the fate of all of us would be sealed," said a former Bergen-Belsen inmate. And during the terrible days, just before the Americans arrived, they took hope from the fact that the youngster was as cheerful and carefully tended as usual.

When the Americans did arrive to liberate them, Beni was among the first to greet them and to eat the first bar of chocolate and orange that he remembered in his life. But this did not mean the end of his troubles. When Shmuel and Beni arrived in France with the other children, there was danger of Beni returning to his status of orphan and being separated from Shmuel. The authorities refused to recognize Shmuel's fosterfatherhood, an official charging that "you are only a child yourself." This meant the danger of Beni being detained in France since Shmuel could not answer for him. Shmuel worked hard, teaching the child to say "Eretz Israel." He was afraid to tax his memory with more than these two words. Whatever the authorities asked him, he must answer with these two words. Shmuel's pride knew no bounds when the child under examination, expanded his two word lesson to two sentences, "I am a Jew. I want to go only to Eretz Israel." And when they tried to bribe him with chocolates to remain in France, he staunchly repeated his theme, "I am a Jew. I only want to go to Eretz Israel."

So, he was slated for Palestine. But one more adventure was in store for him. A seventeen-year-old youth from Bergen-Belsen decided to remain in France. Needing funds to settle himself, he kidnapped Beni and sold him for eight thousand francs to a Hungarian family in Paris. When he disappeared, Shmuel was distracted. Ads were placed in the lost and found columns of Parisian newspapers. To no avail. On the third day, thirty-five comrades of Shmuel went off on a "needle-in-the-haystack" search. They divided Paris into districts, promising each other not to give up until Beni was found. After a long search, one of the youth heard the word "Aba" being shouted from the fifth floor of a dwelling. Beni was found. "I shall never forget the meeting between Shmuel and the boy," said a witness. After that, Shmuel watched his ward like a hawk until he had fulfilled his pledge to bring him safely to Palestine.

The story of the Jewish youth in Buchenwald is best told by David Landau, medical student, age twenty-six, who was their leader. After finishing high school in Lodz, David went to Lwow to study medicine. In 1941, his studies were stopped and he was placed in the ghetto. Then he worked in a Jewish hospital in Kielce until he was sent to Treblinka, destined for the gas chamber. He was saved from death by a German officer whose wounded leg he tended. However, he was afraid to remain a privileged character, dependent on the good will of a single officer who might be transferred. So he asked to be put in an ammunition factory among the "necessary Jews" where life was hard but more certain. Here he worked from twelve to sixteen hours a day on rations of 180 grams of bread and a portion of watery soup.

With the advance of the Russians, the factory was moved and David was interned in Buchenwald in 1943. "I came at a fortunate time," said David. Himmler had recently given an order to industrialize the camp. Therefore the better element, rather than the criminal element as formerly, were spokesmen for the prisoners. David gave a vivid picture of the 180,000 prisoners in the camp and its "suburbs" (smaller camps) all dressed in zebra stripes and wooden shoes. For a while he worked in the underground ammunition factory, "Dora," in which 5,000 prisoners were employed. "Very few came out of that alive," he said. "Every two weeks, about 1,500 new workers had to be sent to fill the places of the dead."

David was chosen by the Political Committee of the prisoners (comprised of both Jews and gentiles) along with eleven others to be active in organizational work. In Buchenwald, the word "organization" had a variety of meanings—anything that was for the good of the prisoners. One of the organizational jobs was the stealing of parts of ammunition in the factory. When the parts were reconstructed, each national group of prisoners had about eighteen guns in their possession. David stressed the friendliness on the part of the gentiles, many of whom shared their cigarettes and gift packages with the Jews who were forbidden to receive them.

When the Russian offensive began in 1944, Jews were sent in from all directions, all half or more than half dead. "Almost a hundred operations were performed every day—just hacking off arms and legs." Five thousand died in January and more in February. "As the bombings increased, there was less food, and hundreds of people died daily from starvation." When more German camp personnel were moved to the front, David was finally posted as a doctor in the camp hospital, although it was against the rules for Jews to serve. "We had no equipment and no medicines. There was nothing to do but cut.... Compared to conditions outside, being in the hospital was a paradise—we had better food."

A group of seventy youth were living in a small camp adjacent to Buchenwald. They speak with great affection of their leader, Mottel Stigler, formerly of the staff of the Warsaw *Der Moment* [one of the two most important Yiddish daily newspapers; published in Warsaw 1910–39], who maintained courses in literature and history during the darkest hours. He also wrote, and inspired them to write, many of the songs that came from the Buchenwald camp and that gave dignity and reason—were such a thing possible—to their sufferings. Stigler is still in France.

After a while, the number of youth in Buchenwald increased to a thousand, the larger group being inside the Buchenwald camp. Their leaders were Gustav Schiller, a Polish Jew, and Tony, a Czech non-Jewish political prisoner. When questioned about Tony, the youth in Atlit could speak only in superlatives and sounded like the disciples of a Hasid. In fact, were it not for their longing to come to Palestine, many declared that they would have followed him to Czechoslovakia, only to remain at his side. The youth claim that many of them owe their lives to Tony. "He was the soul of understanding, kindness and courage," said one youth. Another declared that he was "both father and mother to us. No one can reckon how many times he risked his life for us." When typhus, dysentery and tuberculosis were rampant in the camp, most of the one thousand youth under Tony's care were unaffected because of his diligence in maintaining some pretense of sanitation and his skill at securing extra scraps of food. He made forged papers for all of them. And none of them will forget the dramatic moment of the day, just before the coming of the Americans, when the Jews were summoned to the crematorium. SS guards came to the barracks and asked Tony, "Have you any Jewish children here?" Tony replied, "No, I have only children," and steadfastly defended his contention. From what we gleaned from the children, Tony emerged from the darkness of Buchenwald a great soul who, wherever he may be now, will always live in the memory of these Jewish youth for whom he risked his life on so many occasions with such grace.

Early in 1945, the guards were relaxed and the prisoners' internal organization strengthened. David pointed out that the prisoners maintained a radio to Moscow and to General Patton. On the morning of April 6, 1945, all Jews were ordered to come to the "sports ground," from where they were taken to the crematorium. A wild panic ensued. The gentile prisoners hid as many Jews as possible. Only two thousand Jews were taken that day. Then, for a few days, five thousand were taken daily.

The news of redemption came at three o'clock on April 11, when they were told that the Americans were approaching. Determined to seize the camp themselves, the prisoners put into action their carefully laid plans. Things went like clockwork. Armed prisoners put the electricity out of order. Yugoslavian and Spanish partisans cut the barbed wire. There was no opposition from the SS who began to flee. The prisoners murdered three hundred SS men before the American order to turn them over alive became known. At seven o'clock, came the stirring announcement over the loudspeaker, "Comrades, we are free!" The Americans were at Weimar, six kilometers away.

After the Americans arrived at eleven o'clock, the prisoners knew what a narrow escape they had had. There was a strange telephone call from Director Schmidt, who doubtless was a bit behind the times. Speaking to a Jew, he asked if orders had been carried out and "the work finished." It developed in the course of conversation that the "work" that he had ordered was the gas bombing of every Buchenwald inmate prior to the arrival of the Americans.

"I don't know where the flags came from—but every national group came to meet the Americans with their own flag," says David. Asked to surrender their weapons two days later, the prisoners coupled the ceremony with a memorial service for President Roosevelt.

After liberation and before leaving for France, the youth had ten days "holiday" when they visited Weimar and, we were told, settled some debts with former German persecutors. A group of a hundred was given a nearby farmstead by the Americans for agricultural training.

Sidelights on the Bergen-Belsen camp were given by two Hungarian lads, Isaiah, age nineteen, and Jacob, age ten. After the death of Jacob's mother, Isaiah had taken the younger child under his wing on the journey to Palestine. Jacob's father was deported to the Ukraine in 1941. He was sent to a camp in Austria with his mother. In December 1944, they were transferred to Bergen-Belsen. "I didn't work," says little Jacob, "I only hungered." Soon, he was down with typhus and confined to hospital. His mother sat by his bed night and day. Few people came out of that hospital alive, and it was only due to his mother's tender care that Jacob survived. While Jacob was still in the hospital, news came that the Americans were approaching. At the same time, the Germans ordered part of the camp inmates to Magdeburg. This order set loose a wave of rumors. Some said that those going to Magdeburg would be killed. Others said that it was fortunate to leave the camp, as the Germans intended to blow it up. The first building to be blown, rumor had it, was the hospital. Therefore, Jacob's mother stole from the hospital with the child, stills suffering from typhus, and joined the train going to Magdeburg.

The German guards had not taken their prisoners very far when they discovered that they were trapped. The English were behind them and the Americans had already reached Magdeburg. The prisoners spent one terrible night, literally at the front. In the excitement, the SS men began to flee for their lives. However, a dozen SS men volunteered to remain behind in order to finish off the prisoners. The plan was to mow them down with machine guns and throw the bodies into the Elbe.

The prisoners were lined up. The SS guards shot into the air, in order that the remainder of the prisoners would alight from the train quickly. The machine guns were ready to be manned by the dozen German butchers. At that very moment, the guns of the Americans were heard in the distance and the first tanks approached. The twelve SS guards surrendered.

The released prisoners will never forget the thrill of the moment when the first American stepped from his tank and said, "I am a Jew, Abraham Cohen." This was at four o'clock on Friday, April 13. "We fell on the ground and wept," says Isaiah. "We didn't have the strength to talk. We didn't look like people."

The Americans took them to a nearby village, installed them comfortably in German homes and began to distribute food. "Some people couldn't stand the shock of eating and died from the food." Here, too, in a German house, the mother of Jacob died, a few hours after release. This meant that the ten-year-old child was left alone. Isaiah took care of him for the rest of the journey.

One of those closest to the Bergen-Belsen children was a Polish woman, Hilda Hupart, who was in the camp since April 1943. She was in charge of twenty-six children from four to sixteen years old and was in close touch with the other sixty-three youths from sixteen to twenty years old. "Birthday parties in camp were great events," says Hilda. Friends of the child would save crumbs and crusts of bread for several weeks before the occasion. Then, on the birthday, the child could eat his fill of bread. She recalls a mother asking her child if he was hungry and receiving the reply, "Never ask if I am hungry. I might say 'yes'. Then you would give me your portions. Then soon I wouldn't have a mother."

One Bergen-Belsen child had a happy reunion with her brother under strange circumstances. The name of the brother, who was in Buchenwald, was omitted from the list of Buchenwald prisoners circulated in Bergen-Belsen after the liberation. However, someone brought the news that he had seen a child in Buchenwald who resembled her. The girl was determined to trace the possibility. She linked up with a family who had permission to travel to Buchenwald, taking the place of one of their children who had died. She was rewarded for her arduous journey by finding her long-lost brother. The reunion was delayed for several hours, the brother being in Weimar "on business" when she arrived. This "business," as described to us by the fifteen-year-old brother, was as follows. One day he had passed through Weimar with a work gang. He was terribly hungry. Smelling fresh bread, he couldn't resist creeping into the bakery—at great risk if he were discovered by the guard—and begging for a crust. The German baker threw him out and reported him to the guard who thrashed him soundly. For months the child dreamed only of this baker—some day he would have revenge. The day came. He went to Weimar, found the baker, and killed him. This was the "business" in which the boy was engaged when his sister arrived.

Another family from the Bergen-Belsen camp consists of eight children, ranging in age from ten to twenty-three years, of whom Youth Aliyah will receive six. The eldest sister, Miriam, an attractive blonde of eighteen years, tells the story. The family consisted of fifteen children (from several mothers). The father had a bakery in a small Hungarian town. After being placed in the ghetto for a month, they were deported to several destinations. One daughter, with her four small children, was gassed at Oswiecim. The mother and three other children were sent to Germany. Miriam, together with her father and seven children, was sent in a cattle car to Austria. In 1944, they were interned in the Strasshof camp. They were then selected as workers in a cement factory. Here the father died. At the end of November 1944, the eight orphans were sent to Bergen-Belsen where they joined the group of a thousand children.

Shulamith is one of the youngest refugees in camp. She was born six months ago in Switzerland. Her mother, Hanna Lobert, is a highly intelligent Polish woman, who showed great fortitude as a member of the Maquis [rural guerrilla bands of French Resistance fighters during the occupation of France in World War II]. Although she is a hunchback and badly crippled, one forgets these deformities when, in a restrained manner, she relates her story. In France, she received degrees in Greek and Latin. Soon afterwards, she married a German Jew, Shimon. Faced with the danger of being sent to a concentration camp, the couple joined the Maquis. Her husband was soon given the rank of lieutenant, and together they worked from the Toulouse headquarters. She carried on with the men, smuggling ammunition, forging passports, helping Jews to escape. In June 1944, the couple was arrested near a railroad station. Her husband was killed before her eyes, together with thirty other members of the Maquis; she has a photograph of this mass murder. She was pregnant. After being imprisoned for some months, she was freed and went to Switzerland where the baby was born.

Another Polish woman, active in the Underground Movement, is Ethel Reichmann. Age twenty, she acted as fostermother to twenty-two orphans, bringing them from France to Palestine. Ethel came to France from Poland before the war and managed to remain in hiding until 1942 when she joined the partisans. Still in her teens she joined in the hazardous activities now well known—traffic in arms, passport forging and sending children to Palestine. Ethel had a hand in arranging the transport of children who came to Palestine last year from France via the Pyrenees. Although she might have come to Palestine sooner, she bravely remained on duty in France until after the liberation. When she finally came, she brought twenty-two orphans from children homes. She says that a number of her flock were converted to Christianity. On their first evening with her, they knelt to say grace before the meal. Even on the journey to Palestine, she had difficulty in convincing some of the younger ones, raised in convents, that they are Jews.

On the one hand, the refugees in Atlit had a desire to talk—to get things off their chests—to enjoy their new freedom in the light of reminiscences. On the other hand, there seemed to be a feeling that everything had been said and nothing could be added. Some answered in "case history" language. For instance:

Jacob Zvi, age sixteen

"I came from Lodz. My father had a *tricot* [a type of fabric] factory. My mother, sister—aged seventeen years, and brother—aged twelve, were burned to death in Oswiecim. My father died of starvation in Dachau. I am the only one left."

Menahem, age seventeen

"We were in Mauthausen from January 1944. My mother, father and brother—aged fourteen—were hung. My brother, Asher, aged twenty-one, was shot. I was left alone and came here."

Miriam, age twenty, was in Lwow until 1942. Her mother and father, both doctors, were murdered. Then, posing as a gentile, she came to Warsaw and obtained employment as an anti-Soviet, Russian nurse. She is tall, good-looking and has a head of closely cropped blonde ringlets. Then in her teens, she endured a perilous period serving in enemy hospitals in Austria and Italy. When the English took Udine on April 25, 1945, she fled from the hospital in order to avoid surrendering to them together with the enemy. After clearing up her position, she was allowed to proceed to Milan and to enter a Hachsharah [pioneer training] center to prepare for Palestine.

Rachel and Lotta, both age nineteen, are the remnants of the fifty children who were brought from Berlin to Holland after the pogroms. The children were trained in a Hachsharah center of the Youth Aliyah until they were forced underground. The fate of twenty-five is unknown. Fifteen came to Palestine in 1943 and 1944 via Spain. After the liberation, eight were left in Holland. Lotta has a brother in the Jewish Brigade. Rachel has a sister, alive in Holland, the remainder of her family having been deported.

The two girls will be sent to a new settlement in the Mount Ephraim district, not far from Ein-Hashofet. They both asked eager questions about their future home (still unnamed) and were delighted to learn that it is only a few months old, that rocks are still being removed to make the soil cultivable, and that they are facing a real pioneering job.

Erna Gottlieber proudly shows her most prized possession—a certificate from the Maquis to the effect that her husband, who was killed with eighty other men, died the death of a hero. After his death, she carried on in his place with the Maquis for three years. She came to Palestine with their three children, Sabina, Abraham and Claude, ages five, ten and fifteen.

In Italy, 149 boarded the vessel including twelve orphans and thirteen youth, up to the age of sixteen, who were accompanied by their parents. They had come originally from Poland, Czechoslovakia, Lithuania and Italy. One of the youth told us that a group of about thirty pioneer youth who had been in Hachsharah centers in Bari accompanied them to the ship but couldn't embark. "Their grief at not being allowed to enter Palestine cannot be imagined," he added.

Germans, Austrians, Czechs and Poles were among the group of sixty-five Habonim who had been engaged in recent years in war industry and agriculture in England. Some of these will join the Anglo-Baltic settlement of Kfar Blum in the Huleh, and the rest will be dispersed in various settlements. Approximately thirty-five chalutzim (from twenty to twenty-five years old), trained by the Bahad (Brith Chalutzim Datim), will go to the Mizrachi settlement of Tirat Zvi in Beit She'an.

A "Certificato Patrioto" signed by Field Marshal Alexander is prized by a Polish technician, Herman, who under the name of "Henrique" had an exciting career. Posing as a gentile, he was sent from Warsaw to Berlin in 1943 by a business firm. Having finished his commission, he succeeded in getting a job with Todt (government suppliers). When, in November 1943, Berlin was heavily bombed, "Henrique" was placed in charge of the gangs cleaning up the warehouses. Among the debris, he found two blank travel documents. Taking a friend from Vilna with him, he escaped to Italy. Here, on the strength of his past experience with Todt, he was placed in charge of a gang of 1,040 Italians engaged in building fortifications. The first few weeks were difficult, but he quickly picked up a working knowledge of Italian.

Later, hearing that the English had reached Corsica, ninety sea miles away, he decided to reach them by motorboat. However, before he could embark, he was arrested by the gestapo. The gestapo disarmed him, relieving him of a gun. However, they overlooked two other guns on his person. This later enabled him to hold up a guard, take his keys, and make a break. He was in hiding for some time, after which he joined the partisans to whom he was useful because of his fund of inside information. In May 1944, he was appointed leader of a group of 1,600 partisans by the Italian Liberation Committee. When he heard in January that the Jewish Brigade was in Genoa, he went to see them. Stirred by what he saw, he decided to come to Palestine and was fortunate in obtaining a certificate at Rome.

Moses Wolf claims to be fifteen years old, but he looks several years younger. His underdevelopment is due to a long period of work with the slave laborers in German coalmines. Moses came from a small Romanian village. His parents and seven brothers and sisters were deported and, he is almost sure, cremated. He was sent to the coalmines. There he worked from twelve to fourteen hours a day, two hundred meters underground.

His job was filling the coal wagons. The daily ration was two hundred grams of bread and a liter of watery soup. "Most people died in the mines," says Moses. "I worked there nine months, and I don't understand why I live. Those who even coughed were sent to the crematorium. The Jews were sent to the most dangerous places, as there were often collapses of land in the mine." Moses lived through several such collapses and he still bears the signs on his hands of the shovel with which he filled the wagons with coal. At the end of nine months, he was sent to the Buchenwald camp. Moses sang us this song; the song of the Jews in the coal mine:

> The day dies out; night comes.
> On the city roofs, the sun rolls like a red wheel.
> Over the gates of the camp, evening is red and gray
> And the night watch stands ready.
> Here, the eight o'clock chime—tram-tra-ta....
>
> Hour after hour, the night fades.
> Over tired and aching hands,
> Over backs and over machines,
> The shadows dance on the wall,
> The shadows caress me
> And whisper a secret in my ear.
> "Outside shine the rays of summer."
> Our days pass in suffering...tram-tra-ta....
>
> I work the machines more quickly,
> The wheels go round, grinding teeth.
> More quickly, cursed Jews,
> And break ribs and bones.
> Among the red wheels, hangs your life—smoke and ashes.
> Toil day—toil night.
> And they have taken our freedom...tram-tra-ta....
>
> Carefully, come up to the air.
> Woe to him who pulls the rope.
> The dream of freedom leaps on the wall.
> And, in front, the outspread hands of the prisoners.
> Tram-tra-ta....

From Dachau—from Majdanek—from Treblinka—from large camps and from small ones. All the stench of Nazi Europe seemed to come up in waves as these refugees told their tales. The pith of the expressible part of their past was contained in these songs. The future lay beyond the gates of Atlit to which eyes and hearts were now turned—the hills of Ephraim—the Valley of Beit She'an—the Huleh swampland. And yet, even this hour of fulfillment was darkly clouded. For who could forget those left behind? Would the gates to Palestine be opened? A song, sung to us by a child of eight and composed by a youth who has since died in a concentration camp in Germany, is still as poignantly actual as when he composed it:

When will come the Day of Judgment?
Who hears our grief?
Will it not be too late?
Who hears our cries?

DOWN BURMA ROAD TO GILBOA: ORIENTAL NACHSHONIM

Dorothy Bar-Adon
November 1, 1948
Merhavia
An article from Bar-Adon's personal archive

In this article Bar-Adon describes the history of the first Youth Aliya group from Muslim countries; the group called itself "Nachshonim." (According to tradition, Nachshon was the first of the Israelites to cross the Red Sea after the exodus from Egypt.) The group took part in constructing the "Burma Road" to Jerusalem during the War of Independence and then lived in the Beit Alpha kibbutz.

After the first truce in the month of May, the Burma Road [a makeshift bypass road between the general vicinity of Kibbutz Hulda and Jerusalem, built during the 1948 siege of Jerusalem] was being built. It was an anonymous wartime job. Few knew—nor did it matter much at the time—who exactly was participating in the perilous feat. Now it can be told that, for a few days, there was a group of Youth Aliyah among the black laborers. It was a way of working their way down from Jerusalem, still besieged at that time, and up to the Emek where they were scheduled to begin their two-year training course. It meant risking their necks, and they were probably among the youngest Burma Road workers. But they got where they were bound for.

They are all Orientals. They call themselves "Nachshon" because they are pioneers in crossing the Red Sea of poverty, prejudice and the general underprivilege that engulfs a large part of the Oriental population. They come from the poorer, overcrowded quarters of Jerusalem. Most of them have contributed to the family budget from an early age. Some never got further than the fifth grade in school. A few were active in terrorist organizations. Most participated in the battle for Jerusalem.

You can easily pick them out when they wait on tables in the dining hall of Beit Alpha, at the foot of Gilboa where they are now in training, or when they work in the vegetable garden, barn, sheep pen, etc. They are distinguished by their dusky skins and bright black eyes—except for a few blondes and a redhead known as "Gingy." They are thirty-five in number of which eleven are girls. They are different from most other Youth Aliyah groups because they have a double program. Not only do they plan to eventually establish their own settlement—but prior to that, they intend to go back to Jerusalem and other centers of Oriental settlement to act as *schlihim* [emissaries] for their underprivileged Oriental brothers and sisters. So, although these Nachshonim are the usual Youth Aliyah age, they seem gravely mature when discussing their past and future. This is not the same tragic gravity of the youth who have come through the European hells bereft of everything. But it is the gravity of amazingly wise youth who are fully aware of the problems of the Oriental Jew even after he reaches Palestine, who are extremely "community conscious"—that is, conscious of being Orientals and proud of it, who realize that the Oriental juveniles who now form a majority of Israel juveniles are ill-equipped to face the responsibilities awaiting them, and who correctly evaluate the great potentialities of this hitherto neglected youth.

I made the acquaintance of the Nachshonim during the New Year holiday period when they presented an evening's entertainment in Beit Alpha. In addition to several talks by the youth summing up their half year in agriculture and reiterating their aims, there were songs, dances, skits and parodies, all of which were composed and staged by the youth. Afterward the Beit Alpha members purred like doting parents—for it had been a lively and satisfying evening, showing that their young charges are in stride.

Then, for several days, I picked up informal talks with the Nachshonim. On one moonlight night, I sat for three hours on the lawn with Schiffra and Abraham who, during the entertainment had revealed themselves as leading spirits, Schiffra delivering the address of the evening and Abraham having written most of the skits and words for the music. "Were any of your members in the terrorist groups?" I inquired. "I was in Etzel," [National Military Organization, a Zionist paramilitary group that operated in Mandate Palestine between 1931 and 1948] replied Abraham. "And before that I was in Betar [Revisionist Zionist youth movement]. It was then that I was arrested for blowing the shofar at the Wailing Wall."

These conversations could go on for hours because this wasn't merely the history and adjustment problems of another Youth Aliyah group. It involved the past and future of a large portion of Israel's population, a portion that will soon be considerably increased by Middle East immigration. And it was seen through the young eyes of those who believe that they see the way into the future more clearly than their parents. "We are Sabras," they tell you with pride [Israeli Jews born in the region]. "Most of us were born here. Our parents came from Syria or Yemen or Iraq. They came straight from the courtyards of Baghdad or Damascus to the courtyards of Jerusalem. They have been unable to help themselves adjust to the new life in Palestine, and too little effort has been made to help them. The Oriental will soon form the majority in Israel. We have much to give to the State. But we must pull ourselves out of the *butz* (mud). We are good workers, you know, and many of us are talented. We are poor, and we have large families. But we have as much to give as anyone else."

The importance of this straightforward, determined talk of Abraham can only be evaluated against the general Oriental background—and that is too long a story for an article. Still, the picture follows the general lines of underprivileged people. Most of the youth suffer from an inferiority complex that is often expressed in aggressiveness. In younger kibbutzim you will see them in large numbers and making good. In older kibbutzim you will see them in ones or twos, known as "our Yemenite," and usually outstanding as workers, singers and artists. The inferiority complex expresses itself in devious ways. For instance, Arabic teachers are at a premium. But it is usually difficult to find an Oriental in a kibbutz who will teach his mother tongue—he doesn't want to reemphasize his background. A kibbutz metapelet told me this little story. The mother was a beautiful, dusky, Yemenite—the father, a German—the baby, an attractive mixture.

Often when she put baby Ada with the rest of the group to sun, she would be surprised to find her moved by the mother into the Baby House. The reason? The Yemenite mother wanted her offspring to be "white"— not "sunburned."

Therefore it was good to hear Schiffra, Abraham and other Nachshonim speak with community pride and plan their all-Oriental kibbutz of the future where babies will flaunt their lovely, dark complexions and nobody will want them to look like "Ashkenazim," where there won't be inhibitions about knowing Arabic and where "We'll have spicy, Oriental food and not that Polish fish cooked with sugar!"

Abraham is a handsome Yemenite. His father, a rabbi, is a *melamed* [teacher] in a Talmud Torah [Jewish public primary school for boys of modest backgrounds]. Abraham has crammed much into his youth. Aside from his activities with the Betar, he studied handicrafts at Bezalel [Israel's national school of art, founded in 1906] and then entered the Brandeis School. But both attempts at self-education had to be abandoned owing to the lack of funds. These two dead ends were doubtless partly responsible for driving him into the lap of the terrorist group. But not wholly. Although he is now a loyal Hashomer Hatzair member, he reviews his past with a cool, analytic approach. He believes that much of what was done by the terrorists had to be done, and he is not ashamed of his part in it. The need having passed, he now wishes to devote himself to saving the susceptible Oriental youth from falling prey to other revolutionary winds that may blow.

Schiffra is of Syrian extraction—short and inclined to be roly-poly, with a quiet manner and much self-assurance. She is a member of the Mizrachi family. Now this particular Mizrachi family may not mean anything to you or me. But among Orientals, it's a name. The pioneer Mizrachis came twenty-five years ago and they've been coming ever since, Schiffra's family being among the latecomers. They now number three hundred souls, of which some two hundred occupy a single courtyard in a Jerusalem quarter. Her father was a porter. While conveying ammunition into the hills around Jerusalem, his horse was killed and his wagon splintered. With the compensation money, he opened a grocery shop. "Our Mizrachi courtyard lives almost like a kibbutz," explained Schiffra. "There isn't a common purse, but no one wants for anything as long as another Mizrachi can help. During the siege we all shared our bread—when we had it." There are eleven of these Mizrachis among Beit Alpha's Nachshonim.

The history of the group goes back several years to a Hadassah club where, under the influence of a leader highly respected and beloved by them, they became welded into a group that has found a common path and has stuck together through thick and thin. After deciding upon hachsharah, they went to work for several months in the Galilee Kibbutz of Dan. They did well, and now their minds were made up. They returned to Jerusalem to await their chance for training. Their group life during that period was dramatic, and they speak of the formation of Nachshon with the zeal of visionaries.

They continued to meet, in the face of stubborn family opposition—the necessity to contribute to the family budget and, later, the battle for Jerusalem. They secured an abandoned barn as a meeting place. They lived in scattered quarters, a few in Sheikh Jarrah [neighborhood in East Jerusalem on the road to Mount Scopus]. All were absorbed into defense work. Most came to the barn under fire. But they came. Those were dark days when the large Oriental families especially suffered from the lack of food and water. They lost brothers and fathers in action. And their private "war" at home was bitter, especially for the girls. Most of the parents resented being "robbed" of their children who had reached a useful age. And practically all of them consider "kibbutz" as synonymous with "witchcraft." A few of the younger parents understood and have even come to Beit Alpha to bask in their children's achievements.

Eventually, they made their Burma Road trip [a very difficult trip] to the Emek, working in Mizra [kibbutz in the Jezreel Valley] for a few months before settling for their course in Beit Alpha [kibbutz in the Jezreel Valley]. As for their adjustment—they do well in all branches during their four hours of physical work. For instance, Abraham is a shepherd and Schiffra is in the children's house. "Work is easy," they affirm. "We have all worked before—and longer hours." They are still living in tents and eagerly awaiting a barrack of some kind that they can fix up as a club. They suffered a period of depression when their group leader returned to Jerusalem and was replaced by a member of Beit Alpha. "We feel that only an Oriental can really understand us." But they are becoming reconciled and glad that their former leader will continue the work in Jerusalem.

The young Nachshonim can look back with pride on their Jerusalem chapter. The Beit Alpha chapter is just beginning. Whatever may come of it, this group of teenagers have grasped the essence of a problem that Israel will soon be called upon to face more squarely than in the past. In the words of Abraham, "We Orientals have great potentialities, you know."

INTERVIEW WITH ISRAEL MEIR LAU

Probably written in July 1945 when she visited Atlit and interviewed the refugees there
An article from Bar-Adon's personal archive

In this article Bar-Adon interviews eight-year-old Israel Meir Lau who was the youngest prisoner to survive Buchenwald concentration camp. Lau was saved by his brother Naphtali who is also interviewed in this article. Both brothers came to Palestine with other orphans and refugees; Bar-Adon interviewed him in the Atlit detainee camp. Israel Meir Lau served as the Chief Rabbi of Israel from 1993 to 2003.

Israel Lau, age eight, son of the former Chief Rabbi of Petrikov, Poland, had the distinction of being the youngest inmate of Buchenwald, where he was cared for by Russian officers. Chucked full of personality, Israel was a center of attraction in Atlit. He speaks Polish, Yiddish, German, and Russian, and had picked up "Shalom. L'hitriot." He was never seen without the toy gun that he received in France. However, he is proud of the memorable hour when, after the liberation, American soldiers gave him a real gun, and allowed him to stand with the Jewish guards in charge of the S.S. prisoners. Little Israel owes his life to the fortitude of his brother Naphtali, age 17, and to an almost incredible series of lucky breaks. He has an older brother in the Mizrachi kibbutz of Kfar Etzion (near Hebron) whom he has never seen.

Here is the story, as told by Naphtali. The ghetto in Petrikov [Czechoslovakia] was formed in the winter of 1939 when the Jews received yellow badges and were deprived of their rights. Until October 1942, there were pogroms, starvation and epidemics. However, in view of the concentration camp horrors that followed, the ghettos are now considered a "Gan Eden." "The ghetto was nothing," said Naphtali.

In 1941, the father, age 51 was take to prison as a hostage, together with doctors, lawyers and other professional men of the town. Forty were deported to Auschwitz and three were ransomed at a cost, including the chief rabbi, their father, who returned home.

In April 1942, large-scale killings and deportation began. Two youths, friends of the family, were employed in a nearby forest burying the victims of gas. Knowing that their turn to be killed would come after they had finished the job, they fled and took refuge in the chief rabbi's house. However, the rabbi had managed to obtain false passports and sent them on their way to join the partisans just several hours before the search was made.

"That was on Sukkoth, 1942," said Naphtali. "The youths were not in our house. But the gestapo were sure of their facts and furious at not finding them. So they took my father and deported him to Treblinka." No more has been heard of him, but it seems certain that he was cremated, as his cloths were identified.

By this time, only two thousand out of the twenty-two thousand Jewish population were left. These two thousand were employed in camp labor and factories. What were they to do with Israel, then age five? All children who couldn't work were deported. They had a rare stroke of fortune. A townsman, now a highly placed Nazi, who remembered the father kindly, placed Israel and his mother in the work camp. "There were only two other children in the camp, ages 11 and 12 years. But they worked." Israel was the only "unemployed." Until November 26, 1944, they remained in the camp. "We were beaten. We were hungry. But that's not worth writing about."

When the Russians began to approach, they were sent forward. His mother was sent to a women's labor camp near Berlin, and the two children were sent to a men's camp, Czestochowa in Poland. Here they remained until January 16, 1945. On that day, they missed liberation by twelve hours. "We were sent from Czestochowa to Buchenwald at noon. The Russians arrived at midnight."

It was a terrible crisis for the two children when the cattle cars came to take them to Buchenwald. Children were not allowed—and those left behind were instantly killed in order not to clutter up the place. Frantic with fear, Naphtali "packed" his little brother in his knapsack. "Oh-ho—how we fixed him," commented a pal of Naphtali who helped him. They covered him over with blankets, leaving air holes as best they could. "We had to cover him very well because the SS had a habit of cracking our knapsacks with cudgels as we marched along."

During the four day trip to Buchenwald, Israel "lived" in the knapsack, almost without food and water. He carried out the instructions not to whimper.

"We arrived at Buchenwald on a Shabbat, January 20, 1945," says Naphtali.

Now they were faced with another problem—how to smuggle him into the camp. Naphtali considered sending him with the women going to Bergen-Belsen. But he preferred keeping him with him if there was any chance. And again, fortune smiled. Having nothing to lose, as they were already at the gates, Naphtali frankly told his plight to a Polish, non-Jewish guard. Won over by Israel, the guard recorded him as being thirteen years of age, and he was smuggled in. "I gave that Polish guard my last possession—my father's gold watch—he really saved Israel."

Now, they were inside the camp. What to do next? The child could not be at large. Naphtali smuggled his knapsack to a barrack where, he had heard, there were kindly Russian officers. His instinct proved good. The officers cared for him tenderly for four months. "He was like a toy to them," says Naphtali. "They all cared for him, fed him and taught him to speak Russian." During that period, Naphtali was working and almost didn't see the child. "It was too dangerous to see him and the Russians told me, 'Everything is on us—he is our responsibility.'"

Then came a dark day. The allies were approaching. The Germans were making haste to do away with the prisoners. Russians as well as Jews were summoned for deportation. What to do with Israel? The Russians turned him over to a German social democrat who vowed to care for him. On April 6, Naphtali was taken from the camp with a procession of several thousand Jews to the crematorium.

"It was terrible leaving Israel behind, alone. When we passed a forest, I suddenly decided that I had nothing to lose by trying to escape. To go forward meant certain death." So he broke the line, hid in the forest, and awaited the liberators. Five days later—on April 11—they came. Naphtali returned to Buchenwald and found Israel, who had meanwhile become close friends with the social democrat and greatly improved his German.

After liberation, the children learned that their mother had been murdered in Bergen-Belsen.

Israel soon became the pet of the Americans, not a few of whom wanted to take him back to the States. He recalls the train ride from Buchenwald to France when the youth were allowed to stop the train on several occasions to "settle matters" with former Buchenwald guards whom they passed on the way.

Israel warms up to strangers very quickly, and when Naphtali had finished his story, the child asked if "you would like to hear me sing." After singing several Russian songs learned from the officers, he sang the following Yiddish song that he still remembers from the ghetto days.

> And at night, and when the storm raged,
> Tired and broken, I left my house.
> And the ghetto was surrounded by guards
> Of the barbarian regime.
> All that was is uprooted and will not return
> I cannot build another nest, under the blue sky
> No, no one can give me what was taken from our lives
> Because to me, come the cries
> Of the murdered millions.

Little Israel sings several verses of this ghetto folk song, with a pathos strange in an eight-year-old. But already he is keenly interested in the world outside the gates of Atlit, where he has been told there are no concentration camps. And meantime, he circulates around the camp, the toy gun over his shoulder.

Afterword

In her professional life, Dorothy Kahn Bar-Adon was first and foremost a correspondent for daily newspapers. Although she did not usually run after ambulances and fire engines, or camp out on the lawn of the recent widow, as might have been expected of what was then known as a "sob sister," her writing is time-specific in that she covered events as they happened. And what events they were! She lived in Mandatory Palestine during the period of mass immigration in the 1930s, the terrorist attacks on the Jewish *Yishuv* in the late 1930s, World War II, the end of the Mandate, the War of Independence, and the first two years of the State, with its massive immigration of survivors of the Holocaust in Europe and Jews expelled from Arab countries. For this reason, we have seen fit to bring to publication a collection of her work; we are sure that the twenty-first century reader has found these articles as balanced and meaningful as they were over half a century ago.

We should like to conclude this volume with the words of Steve Linde, editor in chief of *The Jerusalem Post*:

> For 17 years—from her arrival at the age of 26 in Palestine in 1933 from New Jersey until her sudden death in 1950—Philadelphia-born Dorothy Kahn Bar-Adon served as a correspondent for *The Palestine Post*, that was renamed *The Jerusalem Post* in 1950. She wrote about the growing cities of Tel Aviv and Jerusalem, the Jewish pioneering agricultural settlements, and of the Arab communities.
>
> Bar-Adon was committed to the Zionist endeavor of establishing a Jewish homeland in what was then Mandatory Palestine. At the same time, having cut her journalistic teeth in the United States, she brought with her a commitment to what might be called Western-style journalism, in that the reporter aspires to take a nonpartisan,

objective view of the events on that he or she reports. Such honest reportage is as urgently needed now as it was then.

Bar-Adon is part of the history of *The Jerusalem Post*. Her death from kidney disease at the age of 43 deprived the paper's readers of many more years of excellent reporting. She did, however, leave important published and unpublished work, much of that appears in this volume. These superbly written articles are as relevant as ever. We at the Post are pleased that they are finally available to a wide readership (August 23, 2014).

Esther Carmel-Hakim
Nancy Rosenfeld

Suggested Reading

DOROTHY KAHN BAR-ADON

Kahn, Dorothy Ruth. *Spring Up, O Well*. New York, London: 1936.
Kahn Bar-Adon, Dorothy. *New Life in Galilee*, Palestine. New York: 1940.
Kahn Bar-Adon, Dorothy. *A Trip Through Upper Galilee*. Tel Aviv: 1947.
Bar-Adon, Dorothy and Pesach. *Seven Who Fell*. Tel Aviv: 1947.
Bar-Adon, Dorothy. *The Twin Villages of Merhavia*. Tel Aviv: 1948.
Bar Adon's writings for *The Palestine Post/The Jerusalem Post* are easily available in the newspaper's online archives: http://www.jpress.nli.org.il/Olive/APA/NLI/?action=tab&tab=browse&pub=pls
(Her byline varied: Dorothy Kahn, Dorothy Kahn Bar-Adon, etc.)

History

Avineri, Shlomo. *The Making of Modern Zionism: The Intellectual Origins of the Jewish State*. New York: 1981.

Bauer, Yehuda. *Rethinking the Holocaust*. New Haven, CT: 2001.

Beasley, Maurine. *Taking Their Place: A Documentary History of Women and Journalism*. Washington, DC: 2003.

Boars, Barbara. *Reporting from Palestine. 1943–1944*. Nottingham, UK: 2008.

Chambers, Deborah, Linda Steiner and Carole Fleming. *Women and Journalism*. New York: 2004.

Gorny, Yosef. *Zionism and the Arabs*. Oxford: 1987.

Laqueur, Walter Z. *A History of Zionism*. New York: 2003.

Penslar, Derek. *Israel in History: The Jewish State in Comparative Perspective*. London, New York: 2007.

Penslar, Derek and Eran Kaplan. *The Origins of Israel, 1882–1948: A Documentary History*. Madison, WI: 2011.

Rabinovich, Itamar and Jehuda Reinharz, eds. *Israel in the Middle East: Documents and Readings on Society, Politics, and Foreign Relations, Pre-1948 to the Present.* Waltham, MA: 2007.

Reinharz, Jehuda and Anita Shapira, eds. *Essential Papers on Zionism.* New York: 1996.

Rubinstein, Amnon. *From Herzl to Rabin: The Changing Image of Zionism.* New York: 2000.

Shimoni, Gideon. *The Zionist Ideology.* Hanover, NH: 1995

Troen, Ilan. *Imagining Zion: Dreams, Designs, and Realities in a Century of Jewish Settlement.* New Haven, CT: 2003.

Sachar, Howard Morley. *A History of Israel: From the Rise of Zionism to Our Time.* New York: 2007.

Shapira, Anita. *Israel: A History.* Waltham, MA: 2012.

Shimoni, Gideon. *The Zionist Ideology.* Hanover, NH: 1995.

Sternhell, Zeev. *The Founding Myths of Israel: Nationalism, Socialism, and the Making of the Jewish State.* Princeton, NJ: 1998.

Tessler, Mark. *A History of the Israeli-Palestinian Conflict.* Bloomington, IN: 2009.

Women

Bernstein, Deborah. *Pioneers and Homemakers: Jewish Women in Pre-State Israel.* Albany, NY: 1992

Fuchs, Esther, ed. *Israeli Women's Studies.* Piscataway, NJ: 2005.

Kark, Ruth, Margalit Shilo, and Galit Hazan-Rokem, eds. *Jewish Women in Pre-State Israel: Life History, Politics and Culture.* Waltham, MA: 2008.

Tiger, Lionel and Joseph Shepher. *Women in the Kibbutz.* New York: 1976.

Glossary

aliyah ("ascent"), immigration to Eretz Israel. An immigrant is an *oleh/olah* (*olim*, pl.).

aliyah, waves of immigration to Palestine/Eretz Israel.

Davar, Hebrew-language newspaper of the Israel Labor Movement, founded 1925.

debka, a traditional folk dance of the Middle East.

dunam, an area of one thousand square meters (approximately one-quarter of an acre).

Eretz Israel, Hebrew for Land of Israel; the official Hebrew term for the area governed by British Mandate (1922–48).

gar'in, gar'inim (pl.), "nucleus"; a group of people who plan to settle together as a community in Eretz Israel, either forming a new settlement or reinforcing an existing one.

golah, dispersion of Jews outside of Israel.

Haganah, underground Jewish organization in Eretz Israel for armed self defense under the British Mandate; eventually became the basis for the Israel Defense Forces.

halakhah, the body of rabbinic law.

halutz (m.), *halutzah* (f.), *halutzim* (pl. m.), *halutzot* (pl. f.), pioneers in Eretz Israel, especially in agriculture

halutziyyut, pioneering.

halutziyyut, "pioneering," associated with pre-State Zionism and labor movements in Ottoman and Mandatory Palestine.

Hebrew, used to describe Zionist-Jewish endeavors in representing the attempt to establish a "new Jew" in Palestine as oppose an "old Jew" in Europe.

Histadrut (full Hebrew name, *Ha-Histradrut ha-Kelalit shel ha-Ovedim ha-Ivriyyim be-Eretz Israel*), Jewish Labor Federation in Palestine, founded in 1920.

Hovevei Zion, an early Zionist movement in Russia, predating Herzl, that established settlements in Ottoman Palestine.

Jewish Colonization Association (JCA), founded in 1891 by Baron Maurice de Hirsh, philanthropic association to aid needy or persecuted Jews to emigrate and settle where they would be productively employed (not necessarily in Eretz Israel); among locations for settlement was Argentina.

kevutzah, kevutzot (pl.), voluntary collective community constituting an agricultural settlement in Eretz Israel; eventually the term became synonymous with *kibbutz*.

kibbutz, kibbutzim (pl.), voluntary collective community constituting a settlement in Eretz
   Israel, originally based mainly on agricultural; today also engaged in various industries.

Kashrut, Jewish dietary laws; food prepared in accordance with these laws is called kosher.

Mapai (Mifleget Po'alei Eretz Israel, the Israel [previously Palestine] Labor Party), a Zionist-Socialist
   party founded in 1930; Mapai was the leading party from pre-State years until the 1970s.

moshav, smallholders' cooperative agricultural settlement/village.

moshav ovdim ("workers' moshav"), smallholders' cooperative agricultural settlement in
   Palestine and in Israel established on national land. It is based on family farms and individual working of the land, together with mutual liability and aid.

moshavah, moshavot (pl.), Jewish independent smallholders' agricultural settlement in
   Palestine. The earliest type of Jewish agricultural village in modern Eretz Israel; farming
   was carried out on individual farms, generally on privately owned land and using hired
   labor.

Nahalal, the first moshav founded in the Jezreel Valley, 1921.

oleh (m.), *olah* (f.), *olim* (pl. m), *olot* (pl. f.), immigrant(s) to Eretz Israel.

Sabbath, Saturday, the Jewish day of rest.

UNSCOP, United Nations Special Committee on Palestine, established in 1947 to formulate a recommendation to the United Nations about what to do with Palestine; it
   proposed partition of the country.

Va'ad Leumi, the national council of the Yishuv during the British Mandate period.

WIZO, Women's International Zionist Organization, women's Zionist organization founded
   in London in July, 1920.

Yishuv, the Jewish community ("settlement") in Palestine before 1948.

Old Yishuv, the traditional, religious Jewish community in Palestine; some had resided
   in Palestine continuously, despite the exile of most Jews at the beginning of the first
   millennium.

New Yishuv, the modern Zionist Jewish community in Palestine (1882–1948).

Index

www.ingramcontent.com/pod-product-compliance
Lightning Source LLC
Chambersburg PA
CBHW050339270326
41926CB00016B/3529